T0396205

GRAVEYARDS

*This book contains images of human remains in situ, in public
grave sites, memorials and some cultural institutions. We recognize
the ethical obligation to treat human remains with dignity and
respect, as individuals once living, and acknowledge the profound
connections between living people and their ancestors.*

†

GRAVE

YARDS

– A –

HISTORY

– of –

LIVING

with the

DEAD

– by –

ROGER

LUCKHURST

PRINCETON UNIVERSITY PRESS
Princeton and Oxford

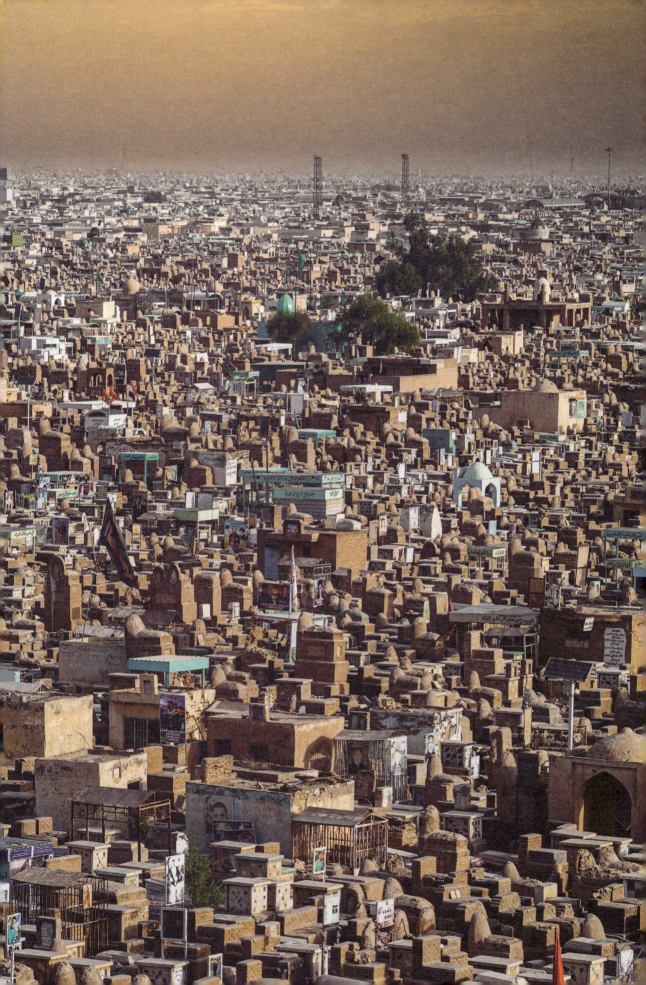

INTRODUCTION

'We mercifully preserve their bones, and pisse not upon their ashes'
THOMAS BROWNE, *URNE-BURIALL*

MEET YOU AT THE CEMETERY GATES

I am writing this book in an apartment block that sits right on the boundary line that marks out the limits of the ancient City of London. The windows look towards St Paul's Cathedral and its much-diminished, once famous churchyard on one side; on the other, onto the borough of Islington, where the spire of St Luke's Church sits in a green space largely cleared of headstones, except for a handful of elegantly weathered chest tombs. In every direction this is a city of the dead. Roman law required that burial be extramural – outside the city walls. Consequently, every gate into the old city of London is shadowed by cemeteries at least two millennia old. The ground at Smithfield beyond New Gate and Moorfields beyond Moorgate has long yielded up Roman remains: coffins, cinerary urns, bones and occasionally grave goods. In the medieval period, the Christian church invited the dead back inside the city walls, crammed into the consecrated ground under and around churches. Pocket parks remade from deconsecrated burial grounds now sit amid the gleaming financial towers of the City, the old gravestones pushed to the edges, uneasily repurposed as boundary markers.

Every compass point is covered. To the west lies Carthusian Street, which leads to Charterhouse, the site of a vast burial pit for those who died in their thousands from the Black Death in 1348 and the monastery set up there to pray for the souls of the otherwise unremembered dead. To the east, outside the line of the old walls, lies Bunhill Fields, its name a likely corruption of 'bone hill'. The Saxons buried their dead there; the thousands of bones from St Paul's charnel house were reburied there from 1549. Between 1665 and 1854, over 120,000 dissident Christians, the Methodists, Quakers and Unitarians who were barred from burial in consecrated ground, were also interred there. If I extend my walks just a little further, I pass over several plague pits and specialist graveyards: the pit under the Mount Mill cul-de-sac that received bodies from another outbreak of plague in 1665, and which Daniel Defoe visited for his *Journal of the Plague Year* (1722); the

above: Invitation to the opening of Bunhill Fields, London, as a public amenity, 14 October 1869.

opposite: Richard Gough, 'A body found in the S. aisle of Lincoln minster ... 1781', *Sepulchral Monuments in Great Britain*, London, 1786.

playground on Seward Street, which is ominously two feet higher than street level because of the number of bodies buried there when it served as the St Bart's Hospital Ground for unclaimed bodies and paupers; the graveyard for the inmates of St Luke's Pauper Asylum, which loomed over Old Street and whose gloomy wards were once visited by Charles Dickens.

The dead shadow my steps wherever I go.

You will probably be able to construct a similar account of your locality. Thousands of books and websites make this possible; meanwhile survey maps are dotted with varied marks for graveyards and memorials, for tumuli and round or long barrows, all of them resting places for the dead that have reshaped the landscape and have survived, silent and enigmatic, sometimes for millennia.

above: Francis Frith, *Pyramids of Giza from the south-west, c.* 1857.

below: National September 11 Memorial, New York City, New York.

Consider how many of the world's wonders are memorials to the dead – the pyramids at Giza, the Angkor Wat temples and mausolea, the Paris Catacombs or the Père Lachaise Cemetery, the Taj Mahal in Agra. Crowds still snake in long queues to enter St Mark's in Venice, Westminster Cathedral in London or St Peter's Basilica in Rome, built on the grave of St Peter himself, the early Christian burials beneath the floor built on a prior necropolis even deeper down. The principal national collections and museums of many countries tell their narratives through fragments of grave goods, funerary architecture and other traces of the dead – including, sometimes, bits and pieces of the dead themselves – as much as through their collections of art and sculpture. It is only very recently that museums have started to address the ethics of these displays, and to return the dead to their descendants.

There is a growing trend in travel that specializes in dedicated journeys to sites of death and disaster, often called dark tourism. This might be to sites associated with a lone celebrity (Elvis Presley's Graceland or Oscar Wilde's grave in Père Lachaise), or to places of political violence (Ground Zero, now called the National September 11 Memorial in New York), disaster (the exclusion zone around the Chernobyl nuclear site in Ukraine), mass death (battlefield tours of the American Civil War, the deadly fields of Flanders from the First World War) or atrocity (the Hiroshima Peace Park, built in Japan after the destruction of the city by an atomic bomb in 1945, or the sites of Nazi extermination camps in northern Europe). Such journeys may raise questions

about the ethics and motivations of some travellers, but many forms of travel have *always* been kinds of dark tourism: returns to ancestral origins, religious pilgrimages to sites of martyrdom or journeys to pay respects to fallen soldiers who died on foreign fields.

All of which is to say that to live in human cultures is to exist alongside the dead, to be in a constant relationship with them. To be human, some say, is to be defined by rituals in remembrance of the dead.

There is an influential argument that, over the last century or so, industrial nations have come to 'sequester' the dead and the dying, have hidden death in hospitals or hospices. Displays of mourning have become pathologized, suspicious if they are too overt, go on too long or not long enough. The French historian Philippe Ariès propounded this view in *The Hour of Our Death* (1981), which ended with a section on the secular modern world called 'Death Denied.' The English sociologist Geoffrey Gorer was shocked at the speed of this cultural eclipse, which he argued had accelerated in the twenty years after the end of the Second World War.

But the European and American societies that Ariès and Gorer argued had turned their back on death still produce and circulate vast quantities of cultural reflection on death, burial and mourning. The more sociologists or anthropologists say that some societies bracket off death, the more those very same cultures seem to find new ways to explore the obsession with the dead outside standard traditions or

above: The grave of Elvis Presley, flanked by the graves of his grandmother and father, at Graceland, Memphis, Tennessee.

overleaf: *Night of the Living Dead,* directed by George Romero, 1968.

religious expression. Grief counselling, mourning memoirs, biographies, films and television about death and dying proliferate. The Gothic, that now global form of staging stylized encounters with the dead (and undead), has one of its origins in the gloomy eighteenth-century Graveyard Poets, who indulged their melancholic sensibilities and composed their lines amid mouldering tombstones. There are so many iconic graveyard scenes in horror films: the grave-snatching doctor in the opening scene of *Frankenstein* (1932); the stumbling into view of the first modern zombie in the Pittsburgh cemetery of *Night of the Living Dead* (1968); the hand that lurches from the grave in the last shot of Brian De Palma's *Carrie* (1976). Gorer would have contemptuously dismissed these examples from popular culture, arguing that the suppression of death has led only to a vulgar counter-reaction, a 'pornography of death'.

above: *Carrie*, directed by Brian De Palma, 1976.

Was he right?

Visit virtually any graveyard or cemetery and there will be a guide, either published online or for sale, often researched on behalf of a group that fights to keep the place protected from erasure by development or further decay, and who do their best to preserve the memory of their special dead. Books reflecting on the allure of graveyards also remain popular. You can tell the story of a life through the graveyards that silently shadow it, as the poet Jean Sprackland has done in *These Silent Mansions* (2020), or begin by reflecting on the place of the graveyard as a sanctuary, as Peter Ross does in his *Tomb with a View* (2020). The comfort Ross says he found in his local graveyard on solitary walks during the Covid-19 pandemic reverses a long history of belief that graveyards might be crucibles of disease, places with bad air best avoided. It recalls the fantastic story a friend told me about a large slab in the churchyard in the Scottish village of Nigg, which marks the moment in 1832 when the people of the town saw a dreaded cloud of cholera coming in off the sea, which they trapped in a bag and buried under the heavy stone to contain the deadly infection.

Such singular tales are oddly comforting because they help to individualize the vast weight of the numberless dead: the nightmare of history that presses upon our brief, living consciousness. The implacable fact of our own death is so intrinsic to our existence (and yet so outside it) that the philosopher Martin Heidegger suggested that our Being would be better grasped in the compound word *Being-towards-Death*. We can't ever quite face up to it, though. So, like Sheherazade in the *Arabian Nights*, we postpone death by telling just one more story. Cemetery tours and graveyard books in fact want to bring the dead *back to life*, or back into memory, at least; to rescue a lucky few from the oblivion of the ages.

Rather than focusing on micro-narratives, this book has grand ambitions. Part One sketches out a history of human burial from the earliest archaeological traces to the necropolises of Imperial Rome. Part Two explores the sometimes troubling fascination of burial grounds and practices for anthropologists and tourists alike, before chronicling some of the myriad cultural and religious burial practices that have developed around the world. Part Three focuses on the sheer *number* of the dead in the modern era, the political work that they have undertaken for the living in shoring up narratives of power, and the meaning of communities defined by the dead they commemorate.

Before commencing this history, though, let's just pause a moment to interrogate the motives for writing such an account. I mean, isn't it all a tad *ghoulish*? That's exactly the right word, since 'ghoul' originates in the Arabic term for a spirit believed to hang around graveyards and prey on human corpses. The *ghul* is an evil creature born of the accumulation of wisdom that we should probably not tarry too long among the dead, as it might not be good for us either physically or mentally. Observed rituals give us a cultural framework in which to mourn the dead, but they are also there to stop us being pulled down into the earth with our beloved dead at our rawest moment of grief.

right: Domenico Fetti, *Meditation, c.* 1618.

below: Albrecht Dürer, *St Jerome,* 1521.

This is human pragmatism, perhaps, and yet we often ignore these rules. It's worth remembering that the modern discipline of history-writing has its origins in the work of seventeenth-century scholars, called antiquarians. They were often mocked as obsessives disordered by melancholia, a disease of body and mind that left them too much in the company of dead things and drew them, as one doctor diagnosed in 1639, to

'grots, caves, and other hidden cels of the earth.' Richard Gough, the director of the Society of Antiquaries in London in the 1790s, did nothing to dispel this when he proposed that a full chronological catalogue of the significant monuments of the dead did nothing less than tell the history of the nation itself. He had published his giant, lavishly illustrated *Sepulchral Monuments in Great Britain, Applied to Illustrate the History of Families, Manners, Habits and Arts at Different Periods from the Norman Conquest to the Seventeenth Century* in three volumes in 1786. The Renaissance also gives us the over-sensitive soul contemplating Death embodied by Shakespeare's Prince Hamlet, waxing lyrical on the

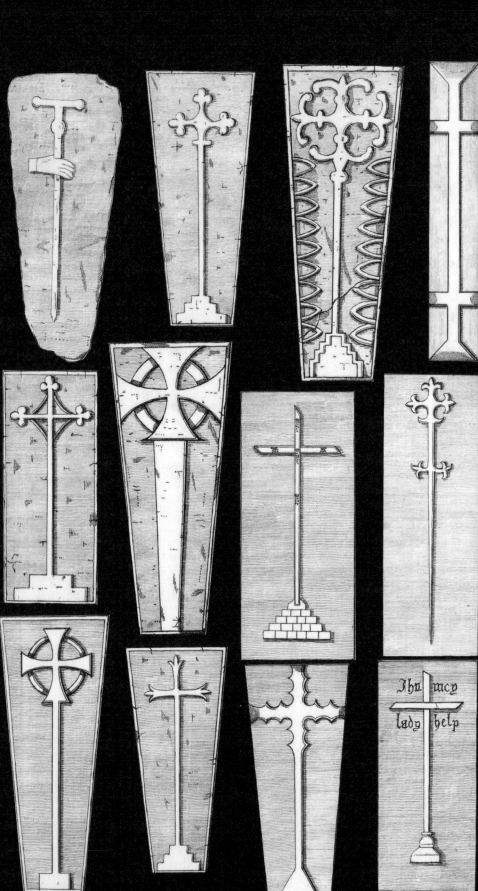

exhumed skull of the court clown Yorick. If we identify too much with this young melancholic, don't we also share his morbid obsessions with 'the witching time of night/ When graveyards yawn'?

You could reach for a high-minded answer. Many religious and philosophical traditions have asked their adherents to reflect intensively on mortality, from Christianity to Buddhism, Greek Stoicism to French Existentialism. It was once very important to study the *ars moriendi*, the Art of Dying, and to prepare for a 'good death' throughout your life. You could read Erasmus's 'On Preparing for Death' (1533) or click through your rosary, some of the beads intricately carved into skull-shaped death heads. A spiritual advisor, shaman or priest might lead you carefully along the path to that good death in the final days and hours. As the living can be directed to observe the correct rites to deal with material remains, so the guides that conduct the soul through the transition to the afterlife can be paid up ahead of time. The Egyptian dead needed a lot of kit stashed in their tombs to help them get through the initial assault course in the first phases of the afterlife. The Greek and Roman dead were sometimes buried with a coin in the mouth, payment for the ferryman Charon to carry the bearer across the Styx. The medieval Christian church

above: *Hamlet,* starring and directed by Laurence Olivier, 1948.

below: An obol coin from ancient Thebes, depicting Heracles battling serpents and Dionysus, *c.* 395–387 BCE.

opposite: Richard Gough, *Sepulchral Monuments in Great Britain,* London, 1786.

happily took payment to ensure their clients were included in daily or weekly prayers, the Offices for the Dead. It's all in the preparation.

In art and culture, the focus on death has fostered a long tradition of its formal contemplation. Many of us might only really encounter poetry these days at funerals, building on its common elevation as a privileged form, given solemn power through recitation in many of life's rites of passage. Christina Rossetti's 'When I am dead, my dearest', written when she was just eighteen, in 1848, asks that the reader

Sing no sad songs for me;
Plant thou no roses at my head,
Nor shady cypress tree:
Be the green grass above me
With showers and dewdrops wet;
And if thou wilt, remember,
And if thou wilt, forget.

In painting, meanwhile, traditions of deathly contemplation such as the *vanitas* or the *memento mori* genres ('vanity' and 'remember that you will die') were consolidated in European medieval and Renaissance art. Transient earthly goods (flowers, candles, fruits) sit alongside a ubiquitous skull as a moral lesson on the inevitability of death, often accompanied by the common legend: I AM AS YOU SHALL BE. Skeletons hold up mirrors to the vain, revealing eternal truth beneath the transient skin. In Hans Holbein's famous painting *The Ambassadors* (1533), now in the National Gallery in London, the markers of the two French diplomats' status are undercut by the smear of an anamorphic skull: an enigmatic eruption of Death amid the grubby reality of Anglo-French politics. Another defining painting is Nicolas Poussin's *Et in Arcadia ego* (c. 1638), which shows shepherds in a pastoral idyll coming across the legend on a tomb, stooping to decipher it, learning of death's insidious presence lurking in paradise.

The contemplation of death in art seems to me very similar to the ambivalent emotions produced by ruins, which on the one hand signify the inevitable triumph of death over man, a stern moral about the vanity of our grand designs, and on the other, animate the human imagination, leading it towards the heights of the sublime. 'Look on my works, ye mighty, and despair!' shouts

below: Nicolas Poussin, *Les Bergers d'Arcadie (Et in arcadia ego)*, c. 1638.

opposite: Caspar David Friedrich, *Monastery Graveyard in the Snow*, c. 1817–19.

the wrecked stone colossus of Ozymandias in Percy Shelley's famous sonnet, inspired by the Egyptian statue of Rameses II. As Denis Diderot put it in 1767, 'The ideas ruins evoke in me are grand. Everything comes to nothing, everything perishes, everything passes, only the world remains, only time endures.'

The graveyard is the ruin, doubled. Graves are both memory markers and sites of decay. And once the grave falls out of living memory, it becomes a ruin itself: a ruin of a ruin. Older sites that give up their bones, millennia old, sometimes leave only the most enigmatic impression of the customs that once animated them, and yet these graves might be the only traces left of entire cultures.

Is there anything that better captures an ambivalent mix of allure and horror than an abandoned graveyard? Michel Foucault once called cemeteries 'heterotopias'. If utopia is the *u-topos*, the ideal 'nowhere space', the cemetery was for him a *hetero-topos*, an 'other space', standing alongside ordinary society yet separate from it, out of normal time, sometimes with its own distinct laws. Heterotopias often reveal productive tensions with the dominant social order, perhaps acting as a space from which to launch critique.

In contemplating graveyards or burial grounds, we join a quintessential tradition of exploring what it means to be human: reflecting on what the dead mean to us, how they remain animate in us and how we might best memorialize our fleeting passage on this Earth.

We've been doing this for a very long time. Since before, in fact, we were human. Let's start there.

PART

O N E

†

T H E

O R I G I N S

O F

B U R I A L

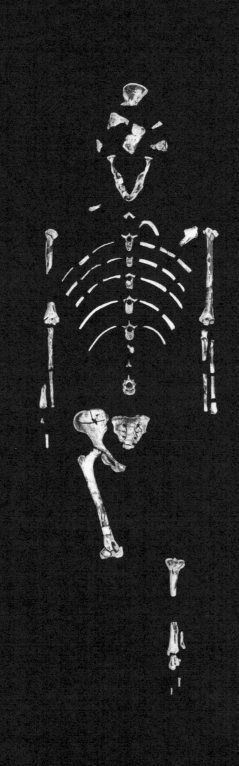

GRAVES BEFORE GRAVEYARDS

In 1907, Robert Hertz, a French sociologist of religion, published an influential essay called 'A Contribution to the Study of the Collective Representation of Death'. He argued that in most human cultures, death unfolds in two stages. First is the physiological death, the blunt organic event. What follows is an interval in which the death passes into the social realm, leading to a secondary, symbolic death staged in funerary rituals. The phase between these two deaths is a difficult transition for both the corpse and the social organization that must shift the newly dead into a different realm of being – or being-after, not-being. The secondary ritual is often followed by another transitional set of rituals of mourning and remembrance that may extend for days, weeks or years.

The following year, Hertz's colleague Arnold van Gennep elaborated on this, suggesting a three-stage structure to all rites of passage: separation, transition and incorporation. In the case of customs or rituals, separation is physiological death, transition the liminal phase between physiological and cultural death marked by funeral rites, and incorporation the phase when the corpse is relocated in the social order and the mourning family are reintegrated back into the world of the living.

There is a compelling simplicity to these structural descriptions, even as they allow for maximum variety. In Hertz's two deaths, the first is biological and universal; the second is representational and open to infinite cultural variation. It is these variations in rites of passage – what Hertz called their 'collective representations' – that give cultures of death some of their fascination. Each is a kind of answer to the metaphysical quandary posed by the fact of physiological death. The variety of cultural responses to this question is what this book hopes to convey. To do that, it first traces some of the significant sites and stages in the very early history of human burial. The practicalities and metaphysics of dealing with the dead have deep roots.

opposite: 'Lucy', a 3.2-million-year-old partial skeleton that forced a revision of theories about the evolution of *Homo sapiens*, discovered in Ethiopia in 1974.

Care for the dead has long been a way of defining what it means to be human. There is always an 'Other' to be considered 'savage' in their treatment of the dead. Greek and Roman texts both mark out the civility of their own culture in this way. In war, as a text like Homer's *Iliad* suggests, one's own soldiers are elevated to sacrificial victims, glorious in death, while the enemy's dead are demeaned and denied the rites of proper burial. Victory is over both the living and the dead.

When anthropology began to emerge as a body of knowledge in the nineteenth century, care for the dead was again used as an important way to define humanity. Humans, it was argued by theorists like John Lubbock or Edward Tylor, were the only creatures on the planet who did not abandon their dead, but *intentionally deposited* their physical remains, developed customs and rituals around these deposits and belief systems about the passage of a surviving spirit or soul into a place beyond mere physical death. This journey often needed the care and aid of the living. Charles Darwin's ideas about the evolution of species across millions of years might have disturbed biblical beliefs in the special creation of man and the fate of individual souls, but it also allowed grand histories of humanity to chart a linear narrative of human progress.

While Darwin was plucking up the courage to publish his theory of natural selection in *On the Origin of Species* (1859), the emerging discipline of archaeology was excavating new finds that also disturbed assumptions about the origins of man. In the Neandertal valley in Germany, remains were discovered in 1856 that gave the name to a species of hominid that pre-dated, overlapped with and was eventually replaced by modern *Homo sapiens* about 45,000 years ago. This find and others like it disturbed not just biblical timescale and narrative, but also suggested that intentional deposition of the dead was not, after all, a distinctive mark of the human. These boundaries began to unravel in deep history.

Human bones can be preserved for millennia in the right conditions, and so it is burial sites that often hold the most traces of hominid cultures and practices. Biochemical advances in dating artefacts and remains continue to push back the date of the earliest intentional deposition. This very early history is in an almost constant state of radical revision.

What bones cannot do, of course, is speak directly about the cultural meanings or beliefs that constitute much of the activity in the liminal phase between actual and symbolic death, or the later phases of memorialization. These meanings have been inferred from evidence, and are often fiercely debated: so much is speculative projection. What the evidence does suggest is that there is no linear progression of burial practices and the development of burial grounds or cemeteries. There is no single timeline. Funerary practices are multiple and various even within the same cultures. Instead, we need to think about patchworks of customs that emerge with local variation, responding to their specific environments.

THE EARLIEST BURIALS: HADAR, ETHIOPIA

The earliest remains of hominids to date, long pre-existing *Homo sapiens*, were found in Hadar, Ethiopia. They are three million years old. Several hundred hominid remains were found at this site, probably deposited there as a result of the action of the river in this delta region, although the clustering of some of the bodies has been interpreted as more meaningful than mere geological accident. As Donald Johnson details, since its beginnings in 1970, research about the Hadar site has offered a tension that will keep recurring in this history. On the one hand, a nearly complete skeleton of a female *Australopicethus afarnesis* hominid found in 1974 was named 'Lucy', humanizing the remains and pulling us towards identification across aeons. On the other hand, there are signs of what Paul Pettitt, an expert in Palaeolithic burials, calls 'carcass processing': cut marks and striations on the bones that suggest defleshing, the deliberate removal of soft tissue after death using stone tools. This might have been ritualistic, or to prepare the bodies for eating – or both. These marks are found again on remains at Gran Dolina in Spain. The ten bodies there were placed in the same location: does that imply intentional depositing of the bodies, or was it just a pit for the discarded bones of consumed carcasses? The spectre of cannibalism marks out another edge of what it might mean to be human.

BURIAL IN CAVES

Caves, which provided natural shelters for nomadic groups of hunters, give some of the earliest known indications of 'structured abandonment' or 'funeral caching': the deliberate depositing of the dead in features of the landscape. The discoveries at Gran Dolina and associated sites in northern Spain were made in cave systems that have been dated, using the remains excavated there, to over 600,000 years. The sites' seemingly narrow selection of bodies – young male and female adults – suggests that they were used intentionally. Can we yet think of such places as 'cemeteries'?

top: Work on the Gran Dolina archaeological site in the Atapuerca Mountains near Ibeas de Juarros, Spain, in 2015. These caves contain remains from hominids that lived in Europe around a million years ago.

bottom: Remains in the Nahal Mearot Nature Preserve, near Haifa, Israel, where four caves show evidence of burial practice by hominins, now extinct relatives of humans.

In the period in which several members of the hominid species co-existed, the evidence for intentional burial becomes more secure. Four caves in the Mount Carmel region, now in Israel, contain half a million years of evidence of use by different hominid groups. The discovery of the remains of ten near-complete individuals, seven adults and three children, in the Es-Skhul cave in the 1920s have since been dated to between 100,000 and 130,000 years old. Initially categorized as perhaps a 'missing link' between Neanderthal and *Homo sapiens*, these are now considered very early humans. Four of these bodies seem to have been deliberately buried in shallow scoops in the earth, with some evidence of formal placement. Early burials are often placed in a flexed position: a foetal crouch, lying on one side, one arm sometimes under the chin as though to mimic sleep. At Es-Skhul, the remains are mixed with animal bones. One body was found with a wild boar mandible placed on its chest. Shells from the site were, writes Paul Pettitt, probably introduced as decorative objects for the body, since the coast where they were collected was miles away. A lot of these elements could be claimed as early 'grave goods': items with specific meanings chosen to be inhumed with the body. Evidence like this asks us to infer the start of structured beliefs about death and burial.

In the Qafzeh cave in the same region, a cache of thirteen early *Homo sapiens*, between 90,000 and 100,000 years old, was first excavated in 1934, with associated bodies discovered at the site over the next forty years. Some graves contain perforated shells, perhaps worn as a necklace, stone implements and a mix of animal bones, including in one case antlers placed on top of the body. Antlers, suggesting an association with hunting, are common presences in early graves. The remains at Qafzeh were stained with red ochre, now recognized as a distinctive mark of burials in this era. The meaning of the red ochre, a clay ground into a pigment, is debated: did it dye clothes or head-dresses, or was it more symbolic, suggestive of blood or fire or rebirth?

below: Shells from Qafzeh cave, now in Israel, thought to be among the earliest displays of human adornment from the Middle Palaeolithic, 250,000–45,000 years ago.

bottom: William Golding, *The Inheritors*, 1955.

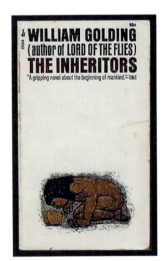

Another significant find was made in the Shanidar Cave in the Kurdistan region of northern Iraq in 1951. The bodies in the cave were a mix of late Neanderthal and early *Homo sapiens*, and show signs of defleshing. Then-new excavation techniques detected the presence of several kinds of pollen with the remains of one Neanderthal body, Shanidar 4. In his popular account of the excavation, the lead archaeologist, Ralph Solecki, famously argued that these were evidence that funeral flowers had been placed in the grave, and that 'in Neanderthal Man we recognize the first stirrings of the concept of man caring for his own, a sense of belonging and family.' This blurred the boundary line of human beginnings and recast previous characterizations of Neanderthals as brutish creatures. Just in time for the counter-cultural 1960s, the Neanderthals were declared 'the first flower people', a pacifist group who were likely killed off by their violent, warring competitors, *Homo sapiens*. This thesis was pursued in William Golding's novel *The Inheritors* (1955), which sympathetically imagined one of the last bands of Neanderthals, sensitive mourners of their own dead, killed off by the relentless encroachment of vicious humans. The popularity of this 'flower burial' thesis suggests an investment in humanizing these origins, but Solecki's theory is widely disputed. A decidedly less romantic explanation of the pollen is that seeds were left behind in the excreta of burrowing animals that fed on the bodies.

In the Dordogne, less than a kilometre from the famous rock paintings in the caves at Lascaux, another Neanderthal skeleton was found in the Regourdou Cave. Cave art in this area is often used as another marker of the exceptional nature of hominids, and this discovery added another element to knowledge of early burials: the use of stones carried from elsewhere to build a tumulus over the body. The well-preserved skeleton was surrounded by bear bones, hinting at a pattern involving animals, feasts at burial and sacrificial offerings. Paul Pettitt proposes that this site might be not just a very early grave marker, but effectively an early tomb construction.

above: Shanidar Cave in the Kurdistan region of northern Iraq, where conceptions of Neanderthals were transformed when pollen was found with remains in 1951.

EARLY CREMATION

The oldest known site of a cremation is at Lake Mungo in New South Wales, Australia. Found in 1968 on the shore of the lake – a symbolic place of transition between land and water – the remains of a woman show evidence of having been burned post-mortem, the remaining bones smashed into fragments, further burned and then gathered and buried in a shallow pit. The remains have been dated to around 26,000 years old and imply several stages in the interval between physical death and the final burial. A second, older skeleton of a man was found nearby in 1974. The estimate of how old the male body is has increased to over 40,000 as new dating techniques have emerged.

These remains were significant as archaeological evidence of Indigenous Australians' long presence on the land mass. Mungo Man and Mungo Lady were taken to Australian National University, where they were held until, after long years of negotiations, they were repatriated to the traditional owners of the Willandra Lakes region, the Barkandji, Ngiyampaa and Mutthi Mutthi – Mungo Lady in 1992, Mungo Man in 2015. The remains were reburied at Lake Mungo in 2017. Different systems of knowledge and belief tangle in these bones.

Cremation is anathema to some religious beliefs – Jewish and Muslim cultures tend to prefer burial, as did Christianity for many centuries. But there is rarely a fixed rule to be found, and many cultures have switched preferences over time. Decisions and norms can drift slowly into new practices, or undergo sudden shifts of taste or symbolic meaning that can be very hard to recapture.

EARLY MUMMIFICATION

In northern Chile, at the mouth of the Azapa and Camarones Rivers, the group burials of bodies that emerge from the Chinchorro culture (*c.* 7000–1700 BCE) show a striking set of posthumous interventions. They are thought to be the oldest mummified bodies in the world, pre-dating their more famous companions from Ancient Egypt by 2,000 years. Mummification offers a wholly different solution to the enigmatic question posed by death.

This coastal fishing culture came to mummification through the natural preservative properties of the earth and desert in their region. The oldest naturally 'mummified' body in the area has been dated to 7000 BCE, and was found in the extremely drying, salty, preservative sands of the Atacama desert. Thousands of years later, the same desert was used to conceal the bodies of leftists murdered under General Pinochet's military dictatorship. The Chinchorro burials have been widely exoticized, perhaps because they represent an extremely active instance of the post-humous processing of bodies in ways that have seemed decidedly 'alien' to other cultures. Ideas of Indigenous South and Central Americans as 'savage' and a fixation on practices like head-hunting were particular features of European popular culture in the early

opposite: The 40,000-year-old remains of Mungo Man were carried in a casket made from a 5,000-year-old red gum tree. The remains were returned for burial in a ceremony with Aboriginal Elders and visitors in 2017 after forty years in the Australian National University.

below: Mummified body from the Chinchorro culture in the Chilean Museum of Pre-Columbian Art in Santiago, Chile.

twentieth century, the same period in which these mummified remains were documented by the German archaeologist Max Uhle. Chinchorro bodies were initially buried to dry out naturally, then recovered and put to posthumous use in the culture. From about 5050 BCE, techniques for artificial mummification began to be developed. The bodies of the newly dead were heat-dried with fire before skin and soft flesh were removed. Arms and legs were detached and defleshed, and the main body cavities emptied and filled with vegetable matter or clay. The head was decapitated, the skull split and brain removed before being recreated. Some were covered by wigs woven from human hair; some have heavy mask-like layers built up over their facial features. Finally, the body was reconstructed. A new skin was made, sometimes from clay, sometimes from sea lion skins and other animal elements such as whalebones. The body was then painted in a thick black tar (sometimes tinted red), which strengthened it for energetic rounds of communal display or procession. The Chinchorro also made 'statuette mummies' from foetal remains or very young infants.

Mummified remains circulated in Chinchorro society before being buried again, for the final time, in clusters that constitute cemeteries (in 1983, over 100 burials were found in one site in Arica during building works). These practices evolved over millennia, their variations aiding the dating of bodies.

The transformation and extension of the life of the physical remains suggest the dead moving among the living, perhaps in processions or displays, although their use remains largely open to speculation. Only a small group underwent this process of posthumous modification: fewer than 300 mummies of this type have been recovered, and other burials from the era show more straightforward practices of inhumation. The Chilean anthropologist Bernardo Arriaza has suggested that these bodies underpin continuity and social reproduction, rather than the concerns with social hierarchy or status reflected by the later Inca practice of mummifying and displaying leaders or heading into battle with effigies of their dead warriors.

†

This very early history suggests that many core elements of the treatment of the dead emerged on the cusp of the appearance of human cultures. Ritual processing can be evidenced from about 30,000 years ago, and the origin of cemeteries – distinct places for the dead, spatially separated from the living, recognized communally and used repeatedly over time – are currently dated to between 11,000 and 14,000 years ago.

The millennia after the Ice Age are rich in evidence of burial customs, yet in many cases these physical traces remain hauntingly silent: sometimes uncannily familiar, sometimes disturbingly alien, more often both at once. How these remains are interpreted often speaks more to our contemporary concerns, read into the barest traces in the physical record.

The end of the Last Glacial Period and the turn to more settled communities is often associated with the development of agriculture and the domestication of animals. These sedentary cultures had a new problem: the steady accumulation of the dead, and what to do with them. A pairing of the city of the living with the city of the dead began to develop. Cemeteries arrive with settlement.

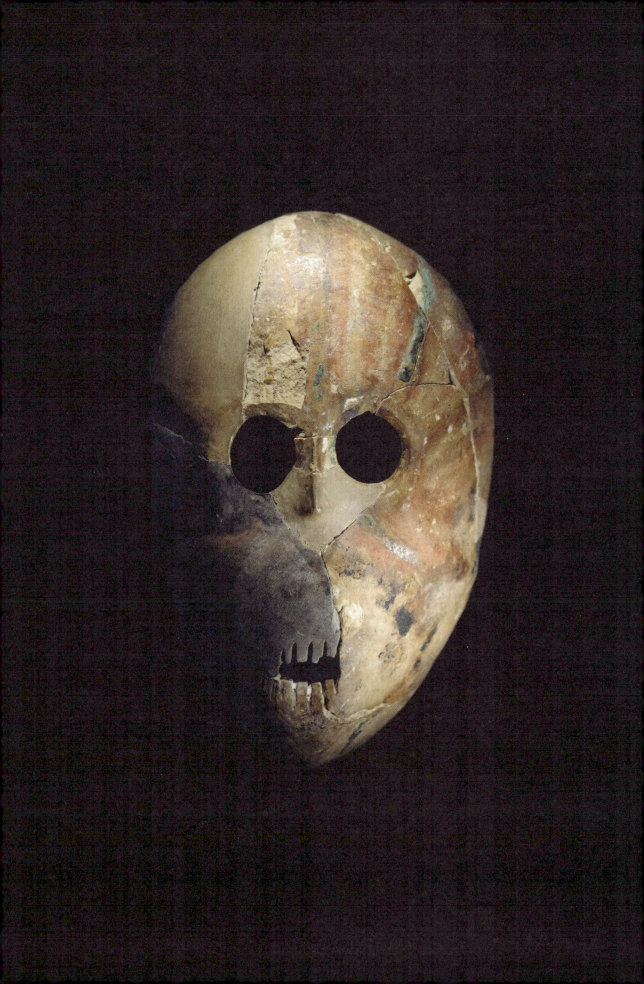

THE EMERGENCE OF THE NECROPOLIS

SKULL CULTS AND RITUAL SITES

Some of the oldest human cultures emerged from West Asia, where very early traces of post-mortem rituals and the circulation of human remains have been found at various sites. In 1985, at the Nahal Hemar cave now in Israel, archaeologists found a significant group of decorated human skulls, limestone masks and human figurines, carefully collected and stored in one place. The skulls, which date to around 7000 BCE, were all male, their lower jaws removed and face areas showing signs of the application of ochre-tinted plaster. The domes of the skulls were decorated in patterned strips of asphalt, taken from nearby natural sources. Researchers speculated that these were involved in a post-mortem reanimation of selected members of the community's dead, the masks and skulls manipulated in various ways. Skulls become cult objects, in the sense of being used as repeated ritual vessels to cultivate some greater, perhaps divine, force.

The precise meanings and practices that surrounded these objects are elusive. Plaster-modelled skulls created between 8000 and 6000 BCE have been found at Jericho in Palestine, Ayn Ghazal in Jordan, and other sites in the region. Similarly augmented skulls have been found at Wadi Faynan in Jordan, their grave markers easing posthumous access to them. Some rest in their graves on 'pillow' stones; others may have protruded above ground after burial, acting as their own grave markers. At Çayönü Tepesi, Türkiye (c. 8630–6800 BCE), a complex site includes the 'Skull Building', possibly the beginnings of an ossuary or bone store, in which 200 skulls were found.

These instances all indicate an ongoing fascination with the severed head: the 'skull cults' of the Neolithic. Such burials suggest a complexity of practice that extends from biological death to first burial, and beyond that to the use of physical remains. The dead appear to have circulated in formalized ways, resting in sacred places where they could be accessed and reanimated as participants in what may have already become cyclical ceremonies or

opposite: A stone mask found in Nahal Hemar Cave in the Judean Desert, located in the occupied West Bank, from the Middle or Late Pre-Pottery Neolithic period, c. 7900–7100 BCE.

above: Burial in the crouched position at Wadi Faynan 16 in south Jordan, from a Neolithic settlement c. 11,500 to 10,200 years ago.

celebrations. These 'special dead' often have characteristics in common: at some sites they may be exclusively men or women, while at others they bear signs of developmental anomaly or are predominantly infants. The logic of selection remains opaque.

One of the oldest survivals of a place suggesting ritual is at Göbekli Tepe in south-eastern Türkiye. Its significance was noted in the 1960s, but it is now recognized as one of the earliest Neolithic earthworks in the world, about 11,000 years old. The mound, obviously chosen for its

significant location in the mountains, was later found to hold a structure of stone columns. This is the earliest megalithic structure of monumental standing stones in the world. The lead excavator of the site in the 1990s, Klaus Schmidt, declared it the world's first temple, centred on two T-shaped columns that are based on the human figure and decorated with images of birds, snakes and scorpions. These are placed in a circle of smaller standing stones, creating an enclosure.

Skull fragments found at the site appear to confirm the sense that this was an important centre for worship of the dead, perhaps a central location for a cult in the region. Was this place built in the transition from nomadic hunter-gatherers to more sedentary communities that invested time in constructing fixed spaces for the dead?

The emergence of systems of writing meant that some cultures began to leave texts with details of how and why they distributed their dead, as well as records of belief around death and the afterlife. Although my accounts of these burial cultures are largely chronological, they also overlap and run parallel to each other: no graveyard history can ever be linear or exhaustive.

ANCIENT MESOPOTAMIA

Mesopotamia is the place where early human settlements first developed into complex city states, and where, in around 3400 BCE, writing emerged from accounting records. Many of its crucial sites are now in Iraq, the invention of European powers after the First World War dividing up the territory that had once been part of the Ottoman Empire.

In the 1840s, Paul Botta, the French consul at Mosul and a naturalist and historian, identified what he believed was the site of the Assyrian city of Nineveh in the north, and a few years later his rival, the Englishman Austen Henry Layard, uncovered both Nineveh itself and a vast library of cuneiform stone tablets at Nimrud, most of which he shipped back to the British Museum. The older cities of Babylon and Ur, further to the south, proved harder for archaeologists to locate; built from mud-brick rather than stone, they had left less obvious ruins.

But by the 1870s, Sumerian culture had begun to be revealed through systematic digs. In 1930, a chronology of ancient Mesopotamian history was agreed, starting in about 5000 BCE and ending with union under Sargon, the first emperor of the Akkadian Dynasty (2350–2100 BCE).

The archaeologist Susan Pollock notes that burial in cemeteries seems to have begun in the late Ubaid period (from 4500 BCE). Fixed settlements required communal solutions to the problem of the dead; the larger the concentration, the more organization was needed, and so spatially distinct necropolises – cities of the dead – were used. Necropolises were typically located on the edges of development, and often in the same location as city rubbish dumps. Some corpses may have been disposed of *as* rubbish, suggesting a distinct hierarchy of persons. Most adults were buried in these necropolises, while infants and children were usually buried under or near family houses in the flexed, foetal position. This was a shared practice in many distinct cultures, tending to imply that infants or children were not considered to have achieved full personhood, and therefore did not need a full burial. This is not to say that burials of children were casual – merely much more common in cultures with high infant mortality rates.

above: The Royal Cemetery at Ur, now in Iraq, photographed during excavations by Leonard Woolley in 1934.

below: Mesopotamian stone vase depicting a sacrificial procession from a sanctuary to the goddess Inanna, *c.* 3200–2900 BCE.

At necropolises excavated at the cities of Eridu, Ur and Susa, bodies were buried in earth pits, some in boxy brick coffins, mostly extended flat on their back. The graves do not cut across each other, suggesting that there may have been surface markers, although none have been found. Most of the dead of this period were provided with a rudimentary set of pottery vessels and occasionally tools for their journey onward. But then, through the millennium of the Uruk period (4000–3100 BCE), all traces of burial seem to vanish – which might suggest a wholly other way of dealing with the dead that left behind no evidential trace. The necropolis returns in the following epoch. These profound and seemingly sudden shifts in cultural practices are typical of burial history, making it hard to tell a simple story.

The Third Dynasty of Ur (*c.* 2112–2004 BCE), which followed the collapse of the Akkadian Dynasty, gives us the first texts of the *Epic of Gilgamesh* and *The Death of Ur-Nammu*, the latter an account of the death of Ur Nammu, the dynasty's first king, and his journey through the Sumerian vision of the underworld, that 'House of Darkness where those who enter do not come out.' This is one of the earliest cultures in which religious beliefs about the afterlife can be reconstructed. We can also begin to reconstruct funerary customs – accounts tell us the costs for funeral food and drink, the hire of lamentation priests, details of the procession carrying the deceased from the city of the living to the city of the dead and the fees for professional weepers at the graveside. Every culture everywhere, from the beginning of time, complains about the cost of putting on a funeral.

The most famous burial site of Mesopotamia is the Royal Tombs of Ur, also from this period, which were uncovered and excavated in the 1920s and 1930s by the British archaeologist Leonard Woolley. The excavation rivalled that of the unlooted tomb of Tutankhamun; the sensational narrative of ancient curses reaching down aeons to smite the modern grave-robbers vied in the press with the discovery of systematic human sacrifice at Ur. The thriller writer Agatha Christie was drawn out to Woolley's dig in Iraq, where she met his assistant, Max Mallowen. They married soon after. In 1936 she published the Poirot novel *Murder in Mesopotamia*, capitalizing on the sensation surrounding the site.

In the wake of the First World War, as Britain sought to consolidate its influence and control in the new territory of Iraq, Woolley's excavation became one of the cultural arms of the colonial project. He began systematic digging at Ur in 1922, using large teams of local workers to dig exploratory trenches and clear the temple ziggurat of rubble. By 1926, they had uncovered a large-scale necropolis that had been used over centuries. After several seasons of digging, the teams eventually cleared nearly 2,000 individual graves. In one specific area, deep shafts led down to large-scale tombs: Woolley termed these sixteen graves the Royal Tombs.

These tombs were, in many respects, atypical of what was known of Mesopotamian culture. They were large, vaulted stone chambers, the main tomb occupied by a single person, surrounded by grave goods including precious metals, jewels and highly decorated tools, weapons and vessels. The intricate gold headdress of Pu'abi (First Dynasty of Ur, *c.* 2600 BCE) is the most famous of the many items removed from the tombs. Woolley speculated that the shafts must have been covered at ground level with temples or altars for offerings to the dead.

Notoriously, the ante-chambers and the pits leading down to these Royal Tombs were packed with human and animal bodies, seemingly killed on site. At one grave, known as the 'Great Death Pit', seventy-three bodies, five men and sixty-eight women, were found. One tomb seemed to include six soldiers, who presumably acted as a posthumous protection squad, two wagons with three oxen and their drovers and a further fifty-four bodies of women, some of them musicians with their instruments, others perhaps the retinue of mourners often paid to attend funerals. It was originally assumed that they had all drunk poison to continue their service after death, but later research shows some

signs of blunt force trauma to the bodies. Although many aspects of the burials remain enigmatic, including the identities of many of those buried, the evocative quality of these scenes, reconstructed in the European mass illustrated press of the 1920s and 1930s and in Woolley's vivid account of the excavation from 1934, has meant that these burials stand in for much popular understanding of Mesopotamian culture.

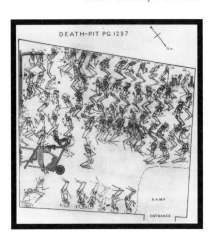

ANCIENT EGYPT

opposite: 'The Standard of Ur' excavated at Ur. Wooden box inlaid with reliefs, one side depicting scenes of war, the other scenes of peace. Sumerian culture, *c.* 2500 BCE.

top: The *Illustrated London News*, depicting the golden head-dress of Queen Shub-ad, excavated at Ur, 30 June 1928.

above: Woolley's sketch of the placement of human sacrifices in the 'Great Death Pit' at Ur.

In the nineteenth and twentieth centuries, Egypt was a space of both realpolitik and Orientalist fantasy to vying groups of European explorers and occupiers. After invading in 1798, Napoleon brought his *philosophes*, an army of scientific men determined to catalogue every aspect of the country's ancient civilization and collect materials for the new, post-Revolutionary museum of world history at the Louvre. Soon there was competition for the spoils: in 1802 the English diverted the collection of the defeated French to their own British Museum.

The dry heat of the desert beyond the narrow Nile valley preserved the temples, tombs and bodies of its ancient cultures with often uncanny perfection across millennia. 'Egyptomania' has periodically gripped the Euro-American world, a fascinated appropriation of Ancient Egypt's styles and cultures that has often narrowed to an evocation of a civilization read solely through its monumental commemoration of the dead. The English novelist and traveller Amelia Edwards wrote in 1891 that 'all Egypt is but the façade of an immense sepulchre'.

1

2

3

4

5

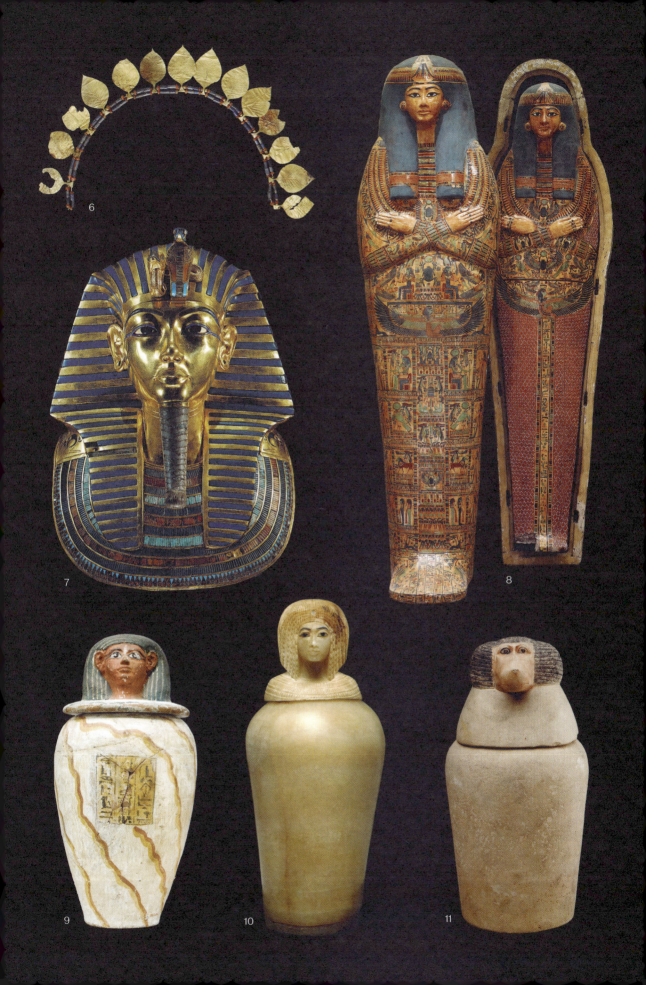

6

7

8

9

10

11

There is evidence of settlement along the Nile and its delta back to the late Neolithic period (4350–3750 BCE), with the first organized cemeteries, separated out from living communities, having developed in the fifth millennium BCE. There are signs of the burial of rulers in underground chambers at Hierakonpolis from around 3700 BCE, but it was the First Dynasty in 3085 BCE that began to establish the process of monumental commemoration of each pharaoh. The city of Abydos became the locus of both political and religious power, with temples that focus on the presiding deity of the underworld, a figure consolidated under the name of Osiris. The earliest known hieroglyphs appear there, and the mythos of the journey through the underworld seems to have begun to be elaborated there, marked out in this world by symbolic passage from living city to necropolis.

At Abydos, from Aha onwards, rulers are memorialized in their own tomb complexes, each with a set of carefully arranged subsidiary burials, suggesting a practice of sacrificing others to accompany their pharaoh into the afterlife. Later, symbolic retinues in statuary form replaced these co-interments, along with grave goods to assist the dead.

The Early Dynasties (3100–2650 BCE) began to build *mastabas*, flat-roofed rectangular tombs with stepped sides made from mud-brick, which developed into the pyramids of the Old Kingdom (2686–2181 BCE). The largest of the cluster at Giza, the Great Pyramid, was built for Khufu in *c.* 2570 BCE. These monumental tombs articulate authority and the continuity of dynastic power, and embody decades of intense labour. Cemeteries built up around them, drawn to deified pharaonic power. The pyramids were built to tower over the low-lying Nile delta region, but this came at some cost: a threat to the entombed bodies of the royal family. Pyramid builders began incorporating complexity into the passageways built to the burial chamber, hoping to conceal and preserve the body and the grave goods within. But the builders of the pyramid for Khafre, second largest in the cluster, did not anticipate a grave-robber like Giovanni Belzoni, who in 1818 simply used dynamite to blast his way to the central chamber. When I visited the central chamber, his graffitied signature of possession was still visible on the wall.

The Middle Kingdom (1991–1786 BCE) and the New Kingdom (1570–1083 BCE) shifted their cultic centre to Thebes, located 500 miles south of the Mediterranean, on the east side of the Nile, a crossroads of the expanded power and territorial reach of the pharaohs. The grand ruin of the temple of Karnak is also situated there, in sight of the river, a theatrical stage for the daily passage of mythic time from life to

top: Mural of King Seti I at his temple in Abydos, Egypt.

above: Tomb of King Djer, pharaoh of the First Dynasty, which includes over 300 burials of the king's retainers. Abydos, *c.* 3000 BCE.

previous spread:
(1) Wooden boat with oarsmen, placed in the tomb to allow the deceased to travel on the Nile to Abydos. (2) Shabti figurine of Pharaoh Seti I, *c.* 1294–1279 BCE. (3) Shabti of Wahneferhotep, Middle Kingdom, Egypt. (4) Queen Pu'abi's headdress, with cap and jewellery, excavated from the Royal Tombs at Ur, Mesopotamia. (5) 'Queen of the Night': a winged goddess flanked by owls with lions at her feet. Old Babylonian culture, *c.* 1800–1750 BCE. (6) Sumerian headdress with gold leaves, lapis lazuli and carnelian beads, from a female attendant in the 'King's Grave' at Ur, *c.* 2600–2500 BCE. (7) Golden funerary mask of Tutankhamun (1347–1338 BCE). (8) Mummy board and inner coffin of Amun-Re Henettawy, who died when coffin decoration was at its height, *c.* 1000–945 BCE. (9–11) Mummification rituals included the removal and placing of vital organs in canopic jars to ensure survival of the complete body in the afterlife.

death and back again. On the west, the side of sunset and death, rock walls veer up at the edge of the valley. Elaborate mortuary temples were built at the base of the mountains: the temple to Hatshepsut (*c.* 1478–1458 BCE) is the most evocative of these sites. Further into the massif, the royal cemeteries, known as the Valley of the Kings and the Valley of the Queens, were sunk deep into the twisting rock to protect the precious physical body. The pharaohs had by then worked out that a pyramid was nothing more than a giant advert for a body and its riches. Burials were kept secret, under the control of a privileged priesthood.

above: Temple of Hatshepsut, Queen Regnant of the Eighteenth Dynasty at Deir el-Bahri, across the Nile from Karnak near the Valley of the Kings and Queens, 1479–1458 BCE.

below: Francis Frith, *Valley of the Kings*, *c.* 1857.

The tombs rediscovered there by European tourists from the eighteenth century onwards were sensations. Hidden for millennia, they blazed with coloured reliefs, depicting the passage of the body into the afterlife and the panoply of gods that oversaw the process. But nearly all had been raided of their contents, their occupants apparently long gone. At Thebes, Belzoni looted

remaining stone statues and grave goods with abandon. As rival European powers went to almost any ends to secure antiquities for their collections, the rediscovery in 1881 of the Royal Mummy cache in the Theban necropolis at Deir el-Bahri caused a sensation. At some point the guardians of the bodies of the pharaohs had decided to shift the royal mummies out of the tombs in the Valley, where raiders continually probed for valuable grave goods. The bodies had been hidden in a rock-face tomb until they were found by illegal traders; once rediscovered, they were secured from further destruction by the French Egyptologist Gaston Maspero. Until recently, the unwrapped faces of the Eighteenth Dynasty pharaohs rested uneasily in cases in the Egyptian Museum in Cairo.

The most famous of the spate of rediscoveries in the Valley of the Kings was the tomb of Tutankhamun, which was excavated by the English archaeologist Howard Carter from 1922. A young, minor king from a disreputable branch of the family, placed in a small, incomplete tomb meant for somebody else, the news of Tutankhamun's untouched grave goods and sarcophagus nevertheless flashed around the world. And when Carter's patron, the Earl of Carnarvon, died six weeks after the formal opening of the tomb in 1923, the 'curse of the mummy' became a shivery Gothic tale with an afterlife all its own.

MUMMIFICATION

top: The world's press gathered in the Valley of the Kings to record the procession of grave goods from the tomb of Tutankhamun in 1923.

right: Harry Burton, Howard Carter and his team looking through the doors of the four shrines towards the sarcophagus of Tutankhamun, 4 January 1923.

below: Reproduction of a ritual of purification in the tomb of Nebamun and Ipuky, New Kingdom, Egypt, c. 1390–1349 BCE.

opposite: Mummy from Roman Egypt, typified by painted panels, c. 80–100.

There is an array of evidence, both material and textual, about the Egyptian process of mummification. Accounts of the physical process still rely on the descriptions written by Herodotus in his fifth-century BCE *Histories* and by the later Roman author Diodorus. Early dynastic Egyptians learned to submerge bodies in natron baths, the high salt content desiccating the remains over a strict period of seventy days before being wrapped. By the Fourth Dynasty, before this natron treatment, embalmers would remove the viscera from the body through an incision on the left side. This was a much tabooed but necessary breach of bodily integrity (as in many cultures, those who tended to the dead often existed outside respectable society). The process eventually evolved at the highest level to placing internal organs in four separate canopic jars for the liver, lungs, stomach and intestines, each presided over by a specific god. The heart was left in place, as it was needed for final judgment by Osiris, god of the underworld.

The body was washed and anointed with spices inside and outside, the cavities packed to retain their shape and the whole then wrapped in bandages dipped in resin or naturally occurring bitumen (*mumia*, which gives us the word 'mummy'). The wealthiest would have protective amulets and

charms woven into the wrappings, overseen by the chief embalmer, who dressed as Anubis to preside over the ritual recitation of sacred texts. A mask would then be placed over the face, later extended to become a wooden cartonnage representation of the whole body – these are sometimes called 'mummy boards'. Wooden coffins would then be placed inside stone sarcophagi, creating wrappings within wrappings to preserve the physical body necessary for spiritual survival. The vast majority of the population, however, went into the ground unadorned after natron treatment in bitumen-soaked wrappings or shrouds.

Texts recording the beliefs associated with this process tell a different story to that of the continuation of pharaonic power. The religious *Book of Emerging Forth into the Light*, often (melodramatically) translated as *The Book of the Dead*, was a guide to spiritual passage through the stages of the afterlife. A loose array of rules rather than a rigid protocol, developed from the 'Pyramid' or 'Coffin' texts of earlier dynasties, personal papyrus copies of the text were stashed in tombs to be consulted. Successive rounds of judgment after death build towards the ceremony of the Weighing of the Heart on the scales of Justice, overseen by Osiris. Success allowed passage into the Field of Reeds or Rushes, an idealized, eternal life that followed the rhythms of the Nile seasons. Failed hearts were consumed by Ammut, the Devourer, and cast into darkness. Dramatizations of this perilous passage play out on the walls of the grandest tombs.

The mummification practices of Ancient Egypt have been seen as grotesque by subsequent eras and cultures, a shiver of revulsion still evident in the parade of mummies through the horror and thriller genres. But the later uses of mummies are without doubt much weirder. In 1634, the French doctor Ambrose Parey noted that ground-up mummy was a much sought-after medicine in Europe, since it was believed to help reduce bruising or inflammation (or sometimes to help with toothache). In the nineteenth century, it is thought that some Egyptian mummy rags were exported to America to make paper during the Civil War cotton shortage. Perhaps worse still was the commercial use of mummy to make a paint colour often known as 'Egyptian Brown' or 'Caput Mortuum' ('dead man's head'). When the Pre-Raphaelite painter Edward Burne-Jones was told exactly what he was painting with, he is said to have conducted a burial ceremony in his back garden with a tube of the paint as an appeasement for this awful

top: Outer stone sarcophagus of Wennefer, carved with texts from *The Book of the Dead* and depictions of the journey through the underworld. Thirtieth Dynasty, 380–332 BCE.

below: Papyrus roll depicting scenes from *The Book of the Dead* for Nauny, chantress for Amun-Re. The scene shows the Weighing of the Heart. Nauny stands on the left, flanked by the goddess Isis. The scales are overseen by Anubis, the jackal-headed god, and Thoth, who sits on the beam of the scales. Osiris, god of the underworld, sits on the right, *c.* 1050 BCE.

misuse of the dead (a story told with some relish by his nephew, Rudyard Kipling). Unbelievably, Mummy Brown was still manufactured as a form of paint pigment into the 1960s, after which the supply of human remains seems to have stopped.

Mummy curse tales, however, have continued to circulate. Boris Karloff's reanimated Imhotep first walked into Hollywood in 1932, the year the term 'horror film' was coined. 'Mummy curses' are a complex product of differing beliefs overlaid onto the region as it was occupied by successive powers: Greek, Roman, North African Muslim, Mamluk, Ottoman and Christian. That these tales really only arrive in English literature after the British colonial occupation of Egypt in 1882 says much about their function of turning floating superstitions about the transgression of burial places into allegories of undead vengeance for violent occupation. There are no actual 'mummy curses' in Ancient Egyptian culture, at least as Euro-American popular culture has depicted them. This fantasia speaks instead of the guilt and fear of later occupiers, spooked by their passing existence in these monumental necropolitan spaces.

top: A tube of 'Egyptian Brown' paint, which was mixed with mummy remains and commonly used by painters long into the twentieth century.

right: *The Mummy*, directed by Karl Freund, 1932.

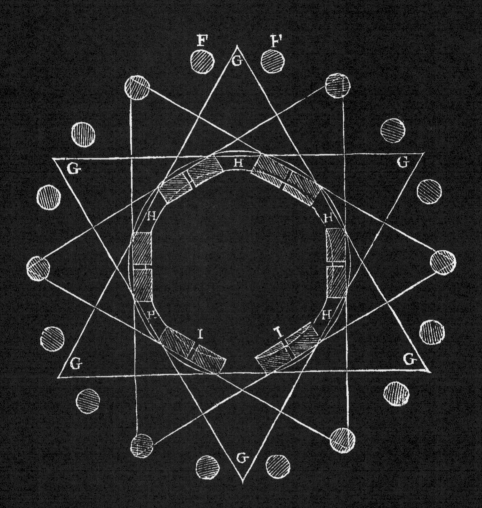

MEGALITHS, PASSAGE GRAVES
AND BARROWS

The practice of placing giant stones (megaliths) and creating large earth mounds and barrows to mark sites of spiritual import, including burial, has developed separately in different cultures and periods all over the world. Such features survive in Abyssinia and Sudan, southern India and Japan. The earliest concentrations of barrows and megaliths are found in north-western Europe. In southern England, sites follow the path of inland rivers, including, most famously, the standing stone circle and associated burial mounds and barrows at Stonehenge and Avebury in Wiltshire.

Many of these spaces remain profoundly enigmatic; there is no written culture to accompany the silent stones and earthly remains. For centuries they have been sites for fantasy and the projection of competing meanings, and even the secure dating of key sites remains contested. The current view is that from about 5000 BCE a population migrated out of the eastern Mediterranean and began to settle in north-west Europe, moving into the Danube River valley and then further east. They addressed the problem of burying their dead in this new, settled context by turning to monumental forms.

At first, they built small stone structures similar to coffins, called *cists* (derived from the Welsh *cist faen*, 'box of stones'), which were created by laying two large stones on their sides, then capping them with a single slab. Inside these structures, bodies were placed in the flexed position, sometimes singly, although many sites reveal bones deposited over time. Repeated return for acts of communal burial suggests that part of the import of these sites was as resting places for the dead. The bones at these sites are often incomplete and jumbled, which may imply posthumous use and later reinterment. Some inhumations include cremated remains. Burial chambers were then covered over with earth to create small mounds, also known as tumuli and long barrows. Some are marked by standing stones, though not

opposite: Inigo Jones, diagram of Stonehenge, 1655.

above: William Blake, Stonehenge, the text explores the 'stony Druid temples' of Albion, from *Milton: A Poem*, 1811.

49

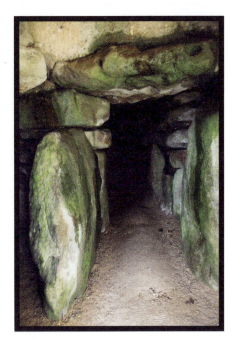

above: Entrance to the Neolithic long barrow at West Kennet in Wiltshire, England.

all standing stones are associated with burial. What survives, after the soil has eroded away, are around 40,000 of these striking, balanced or collapsed stone structures across Europe.

At some point these cists began to cluster and grow into more elaborate barrows, extensions that give these places the function of larger 'cemeteries', although for dead selected in ways that are opaque to us. At Barnenez in Brittany, a famous stone barrow overlooks the water on a headland, with eleven passage graves – stone passageways leading to an interior burial chamber. This prominent structure was started around 4850 BCE and added to for over 500 years. Chris Scarre suggests that this culture used coastal zones as a meaningful place of time and tide, the twice daily influx of tidal water symbolizing a liminal space between land and sea, life and death. He notes that the higher water level millennia ago would have routinely made islands of some of these chosen sites at high tide. 'If the sea itself was regarded as the world of the dead, then burial close to the sea edge will have been a symbolic practice of particular power,' Scarre writes.

There is later evidence that human sacrifices were made on these symbolic edges, votive offerings from the land to the watery other-world. Bogland is one such watery environment considered ritually important. Bogs have unique properties that preserve the bodies of the dead very well. During the Iron Age, household objects, weapons and bodies, many presumed to have been ritually killed, were buried in bogs across north-western Europe. Tollund Man, a sacrificial victim discovered preserved in peat in Jutland in 1950, is a famous example of this. Other scholars have speculated on the role that barrows might have played in declaring territorial owner-ship of land, the ancestral dead acting as guarantors of rights or the boundaries of rule. There are sites across England and France – for instance at Passy or Balloy – where whole clusters of long barrows sit in symbolic landscapes on the edges of rivers or on flood plains.

Inland sites might have been chosen for symbolic reasons: in the chalky terrain of Wiltshire, for instance, the long barrows glitter in the moonlight, and may have been part of what Aubrey Burl, one of many obsessive mappers of the megaliths over the last century, called an 'astronomy of death', oriented on the paths of celestial bodies. There are theories that some passages in barrows were aligned to be lit by sunbeams at key moments of seasonal change, suggesting a pattern of cyclical annual celebrations. Others have suggested that long barrows were shaped to echo the long wooden houses of settlements, mirroring houses for the living and the dead.

Long barrows develop variations and different functions, partly dependent on local materials. Some were low, unchambered artificial rises of soil, perhaps used as platforms or raised walkways rather than for burials. Some have traces of internal and external use of wood – but only elusive post-holes survive, sketching out the shapes of vanished structures. More elaborate barrows made with stone have survived better. A number contain long passages, sometimes leading to multiple and partitioned chambers, and clear evidence of sorting and circulation of bones. There is also evidence that some of the entryways had a large stone for a doorway that could be moved aside both for new interments and for the later removal of bones, possibly for rituals conducted within the wooden palisaded enclosures that were once built around the entrances. For the true meaning of these sites, we only have the haunting shapes of an absent culture, onto which have been projected many different theories. Druidic rites were a favourite of eighteenth-century antiquarians such as William Stukeley; in the nineteenth century, the worship of pagan gods, perhaps a single fertility goddess, came to the fore. Ronald Hutton has suggested that Victorians such as James Fergusson and John Lubbock, who first sketched out this prehistory with some historical discernment, tended to imagine the era as a 'chamber of horrors'. The Canadian novelist and science writer Grant Allen produced a (supposedly) non-fiction piece about the Ogbury Barrows in Wiltshire, which he claimed marked the burial of a 'cannibal king of the newer stone age.' He then turned this into a fever dream of meeting with these murderous spectres in his short story 'Pallinghurst Barrow' (1892), in which the protagonist is only saved from stone-age monsters by wielding his tempered iron sword – the blade marking his modernity. While some bones do bear marks of violence from the arrowheads or axe wounds that finished them off, in reality these are relatively small in number.

Long barrows were followed by more circular mounds, some with exquisitely constructed internal passageways and corbelled chambers with recesses built off the central chamber. At Newgrange in Ireland, built around 3200 BCE, the stone passageway is over sixty feet (just

above: The uncanny remains of the 'Tollund Man', likely a victim of ritual murder given to the marshes as a sacrifice, survived intact from the Iron Age to its rediscovery in 1950.

below: Grant Allen, 'Pallinghurst Barrow', illustrated by Amédée Forestier, *Illustrated London News*, Christmas Number 1892.

under twenty metres) long and heads to a central chamber with a forty-five-foot (13.7 m) high corbelled roof where bones and cremated remains were found. In the 1960s, it was discovered that a 'roofbox' aperture let in a beam of sunlight at sunrise on the winter solstice. The circular mound itself is surrounded by a megalithic stone circle, and forms part of the larger Brú na Bóinne complex in County Meath, a site of several passage grave mounds, circular henges and standing stones. In Orkney, at Maeshowe, built in *c.* 2800 BCE, the central chamber has a roofbox aligned with the winter solstice. Formal clusters of round barrows, suggesting demarcated spaces for burial, began to emerge around 1850 BCE.

Smaller, round barrows associated with more 'heroic' burials of noted individuals appear in the second millennium BCE. Grave goods have been found with the bodies – beakers (liquid for the thirsty dead) and arrowheads, suggesting warriors buried with weapons, and later copper and bronze daggers. The monuments to these special dead seem to have attracted associated burials of bones or cremated remains, tucked in close to their residual power. Sometimes they seem to be laid out in linear trajectories across the landscape, interpreted by some as a pattern of burials marking out ancestral lineages.

Circles of standing stones, and the henge structure of stone trilithons unique to the British Isles, arrived late in megalithic culture. Although Stonehenge is the show-off survivor of this era, it is only one small and belated aspect of a larger ceremonial site. Understanding of Stonehenge is subject to continual

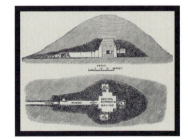

revision, but between 2009 and 2012 there was a major systematic survey of its environs. The oldest Mesolithic traces suggest that the river was the initial focus of activity. The long barrows appeared 3,000 years later, nine within the current designated World Heritage Site and more beyond (John Lubbock counted 300 burial mounds in a three-mile radius of the henge in 1865). The largest in the area, Knighton Barrow, is on a ridge that looks down on Stonehenge. Not all of the long barrows were used for burial, but at the village of Winterbourne Stoke, buried remains have been dated back to 3630 BCE. Next came the so-called Greater Cursus, a gigantic earthwork that created a causeway enclosure over three kilometres long. This was constructed by digging ditches and raising earthworks in long sections. The Greater Cursus was built between about 3600 and 3375 BCE; a Lesser Cursus, largely lost to the plough, was also constructed a bit further north.

above: 7,000-year-old array of standing stones that align with the rising sun in Carnac, Brittany, France.

below: Stereoscopic image of Stonehenge, 1860s.

Stonehenge itself arrived in stages. It was initially a circular earthwork of about 330 feet (100 m) in diameter, constructed of ditches and banks, with irregular openings, built between about 3100 and 2920 BCE. Banks and ditches were sometimes used to bury the dead. Inside this earth circle are the fifty-six Aubrey Holes (found by John Aubrey in 1666), burial pits with evidence of the removal and reinterment of bones and cremated remains. This makes this earthwork and its enclosed pits, for Ronald Hutton, 'the largest cemetery yet found in Britain from the late Neolithic.' Was this place a sacred space for visiting the dead?

Henges made of wood and wooden palisades came next. Stones circles followed, and the henge itself was started in about 2500 BCE. The final construction was the placement of avenues of stone marking out significant pathways. These were constructed between about 2280 and 1930 BCE, meaning that it took about 1,400 years for the place to find its fullest expression.

Stone circles and long barrows saturate the collective imagination of Britain, whether as places of Neolithic origins, Druidic worship, Celticism or subversive pagan or pantheistic worship. Thomas Hardy's tragedy *Tess of the d'Urbervilles* (1892) leads the outcast Tess, with grim inevitability, to her death on the sacrificial stone of Stonehenge – although we can't be sure that it was ever actually an altar stone. Hardy's imagined 'Wessex' has been imprinted over the geography of this terrain. British artists from Samuel Spode to John Constable explored the Romanticism of Stonehenge's ruins in paintings of the site, and their fascination with the magic and enigmatic grandeur of the standing stones has lasted into contemporary art.

Avant-garde filmmaker Derek Jarman's short film *Journey to Avebury* (1971) was made alongside a cluster of horror films that evoke the pagan survivals and occult magic ascribed to standing stones or stone circles. Piers Haggard, the director of *Blood on Satan's Claw* (1971), which features witchery in circles, coined the term 'folk horror' for this renewed fascination with the pre-modern, pre-Christian world, which was appropriated into counter-cultural reactions to the failure of the promise of the 1960s. Modern Druids, hippies and travellers still gather at Stonehenge at midsummer dawn, where in the 1980s and 1990s pitch battles were fought with police. Since the 2010s, the Folk Horror Revival has intertwined with a continuing obsession with tracking every last menhir, dolmen, barrow or stone circle. Websites such as

below: Nathaniel Whittock, 'Druids Sacrificing to the Sun in their Temple called Stonehenge', from a plan of the site by antiquarian William Stukeley.

opposite: Derek Jarman, *A Journey to Avebury*, 1971.

The Megalithic Portal, guidebooks by the pop singer Julian Cope (*The Modern Antiquarian*, 1998) and *The Hellebore Guide to Occult Britain* (2021) document ancient sites that they say thrum with occult energies and communion with the vanished past. The documentary *A Year in a Field* (2022) keeps a steady eye for a calendar year on Boscawen-Ros, a standing stone near Land's End. In these recent appropriations, the power of the ancestral dead, channelled through their monuments, seem to be invoked as leverage against prim English Protestantism and modernity's dull, amnesiac materialism.

Analysis of these material traces has engaged their presence across millennia, but they remain reticent on most of the cultural practices and beliefs that once surrounded them. Such limits create a tempting space into which much has been projected.

THE GREEK NECROPOLIS AND
THE ROMAN CEMETERY

GREEK CITIES OF THE DEAD

Athens, which by the sixth century BCE had become a centre of immense power on the Attic Peninsula, occupies an outsized role in many histories of the world, not least because some 2,000 years later its monuments and texts would become one of the engines of the European Renaissance. Athenian culture, at a crossroads between Europe, Asia and Africa, emerged out of Mycenaean Greece in about 1100 BCE and gained its own distinct identity from about 750 BCE. Athens held a multitude of belief systems and a slow mutation of burial customs over millennia.

The final books of Homer's *Iliad*, a work central to classical literature, written down in the late eighth century BCE, focus on mourning and burial. When Achilles hears of the death of his fellow soldier Patroclus, we are thrown into the disorder of his grief, the horror that his friend's body has been stripped of armour by his slayer, Hector. We read of Achilles's vow both to avenge his death and to give Patroclus's body a proper burial. Patroclus's shade even visits Achilles from the 'murky darkness' where his unquiet ghost is trapped, in order to beg his friend for 'my due rite of burning'. Book 23 depicts his funeral: the construction of a grand pyre, the procession of thousands of soldiers beating their chests and tearing their hair in grief, and the ritual sacrifice of animals and twelve 'noble sons of the great-hearted Trojans' (human sacrifice is a grand gesture of this heroic literature, rather than actual common practice in Greece). The pyre is lit with the help of the gods and burns to the noise of 'ceaseless lamentation'. Funeral games are then played out – the liminal phase of this extended, grandiloquent burial.

The Homeric text gives poetic shape to the rituals around death in Greek culture. The dead must be properly buried, honoured and remembered. Interment is a single act: there is no manipulation of the body and no recirculation of the remains. The corpse was purified in preparation for the funeral, and sometimes a coin was placed in the mouth to pay for passage from this

opposite: Greek ceremonial vase used for funeral rites. Without a bottom, water offered to the dead flowed into the grave below, sixth century BCE.

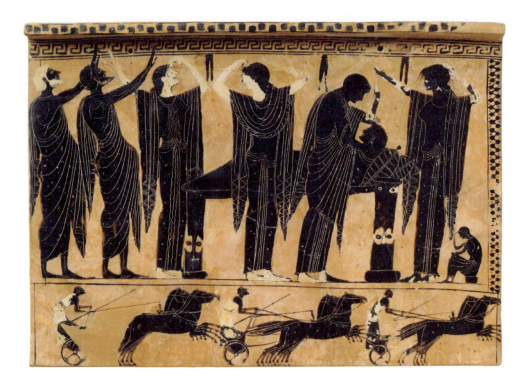

world to the next. The body was washed, as was the house in which the death occurred (the language of 'pollution' is a constant in Greek laws about burial practice). The feet were aligned with the door and surrounded with decorative vessels of scent. The body was then processed on a bier decked with branches from the home to a place separate from that of the living, accompanied with stylized displays of lamentation. Men beat their chests, women wailed and pulled at their hair or tore at their cheeks.

In the *Iliad*, grand cosmic forces come together with the sudden, intimate expression of human grief. We see this also in Homer's *Odyssey*, when in the underworld Odysseus meets figures like Elpenor, recently dead and longing for a pyre and proper rites, and in the great scenes of death, mourning, rage and ghostly visitation in the classical Greek tragedies. Many Greek texts explore a division at death of the material body from the *psyche*, the breath or spirit (not quite a 'soul') that initially stays close to the place of burial, needing sustenance before moving on. There were ways in which the passage of this spirit could be interrupted. Those who died away from home faced risks – especially soldiers like Patroclus, killed in foreign wars. Early or sudden death might produce agitated or restless spirits. Young maidens who died early could return as *lamia*, demonic, devouring sexual predators (in myth, Lamia devours children; later, she preys on young men). Those not given the proper rites or subsequent obsequies became *ataphoi*, unquiet souls, unhappy, haunting and out of place. We can see the shape of modern ghost stories emerging in these beliefs.

These shades were often pallid and weak – as Homer puts it, 'worn out'. They could not do much to intercede directly in the world, but could take messages to those who had gone before; many tablet messages have been found in burial sites, as if graves also served as postboxes or dead letter drops. Later, however, those unjustly killed might persuade the three Furies to avenge them.

Greek beliefs about the afterlife ranged all the way from reincarnation to nothing at all, but some conventional elements began to emerge over the centuries. The initial journey of the dead was overseen by various *psychopomps* (the conductors of souls): Hermes, the messenger of the Olympian gods; Charon, who ferried souls across the river separating the living from the dead (sometimes called the Styx or Lethe, the river of forgetfulness), and led them towards Hades, the god who lends his name to the Greek underworld. The gates were guarded by his fearful dog, Cerberus, and the dead were sometimes buried with treats to win the dog over.

In Mycenaean Greece, from about 1500 BCE, distinctive *tholos* tombs were built: chambers of corbelled stone in a distinctive 'beehive' shape, covered with earth. They have an entrance passageway, a *dromos*, and could be constructed on vast scale according to status, as in the 'Treasury of Atreus' in Mycenae (c. 1300 BCE). This style of building continued into the classical period. *Heroa* – small temple shrines to heroes, sometimes with statuary, often built over the bones of the dead hero – were often clustered around surviving *tholos* tombs to create spiritual complexes. An individual *heroön* could become emblematic of the authority and power of a city or city state, and so a powerful locus of identity – the return of the bones of the hero Theseus to Athens in the fifth century BCE, for instance, was seen as a major symbolic victory for the city. By contrast, invaders might target the bones revered by their enemies for further humiliation.

above: William Blake, 'Charon and the Condemned Souls', for an edition of Dante Alighieri's *Divine Comedy*, 1824–27.

right: Edward Dodwell, 'Interior of Treasury of Atreus at Mycenae', from *Views and Descriptions of Cyclopian, or, Pelasgic Remains in Greece and Italy*, 1834.

opposite: Terracotta funerary plaque, once hung on the wall of a tomb, showing the laying of the dead and, below, a chariot race. Attic peninsula, c. 520–510 BCE.

From about the eighth century BCE, the Greeks delineated specific cemetery spaces outside the city walls. This was not the case for infants, who were buried at home. Corpses were either buried or cremated on a pyre, a choice that shifted according to taste and locale, and was sometimes dictated by city law. The dead were rarely accompanied with lots of grave goods, although Patroclus wanted back his armour, the tools of his trade, for his pyre. For burial, the body was wrapped in a shroud and placed in a stone coffin – the term *sarcophagus* derives from the Greek belief that certain forms of limestone were 'flesh-eating', accelerating the process of physical decay. In the case of cremation, the ashes were doused with wine, placed in an amphora or urn and then buried. In both cases the grave was marked and became a place of commemoration, with posthumous rites conducted on the third, ninth and thirtieth day after death, including libations – offerings of food and water. At the end of thirty days, the commemoration by the family marked the end of the formal mourning period, and the end of the period of pollution death brought to the household.

above: William James Stillman, Stelae from the Kerameikos Cemetery, Athens, early 1880s.

The stone monuments built to mark the dead changed in style and convention over time, shifts that can be tracked in relation to legal edicts issued by city states. In the sixth century BCE, Solon's Athenian funeral laws introduced limits on the timing and expenditure in funeral processions, placed restrictions on exaggerated displays of public mourning and subsequent feasts and curtailed excessive ostentation in grave markers. Cemeteries were meant to become essentially more *democratic*, with large monuments replaced by more modest tombs and *stelae* – simple stone markers with the name of the deceased, the precursors of modern headstones. However, as is evident in the famous Kerameikos cemetery in Athens, which was in continual use from about 2700 to the sixth century BCE, cemeteries continued their work to mark out social distinction and power. In Greece as elsewhere, conduct in the extramural city of the dead helped the intramural city of the living to shape its patterns of political power.

The grand tomb built for Mausolus and his wife Artemisia at Halicarnassus (*c.* 353–350 BCE) was so imposing that it became one of the Wonders of the Ancient World, a monumental meeting point of Anatolian and Greek design. It gave the Romans the word *mausoleum*, used for any grand 'house' tomb that stands above ground. Mausolus built Halicarnassus as the capital of his fleeting empire, using Lycian tombs from Xanthos (now south-west Türkiye) as inspiration for his own tomb. It is thought that he began building it before his death, but it was continued by his wife. Both were buried in the structure before it was completed. On a hill above the town, the marble tomb rose nearly 150 feet (45.7 m) to create a platform on which stood a temple with thirty-six columns, its roof a twenty-four-step pyramid.

The lavish tomb was partially destroyed by earthquakes in the region, the city below left in ruins for centuries. The tomb was finally pulled apart by Christian invaders during the Crusades, who built a fortress using the marble stones. In the mid-nineteenth century, the British Museum sent excavators, who unearthed the last damaged remains of the tomb: sections of frieze and sculpture can now be seen in the Mausoleum Room at the Museum. Five minutes' walk away in Bloomsbury stands St George's Church, its tower modelled on Pliny the Elder's description of the stepped pyramid of the Mausoleum of Halicarnassus. Its architect, Nicholas Hawksmoor, placed the British King George at the apex in Roman dress. The spire is one of many neoclassical imitations of the tomb to be found around the world, from the colossal mausoleum built for American president Ulysses S. Grant in New York City to the Melbourne Shrine of Remembrance, now the Australian national monument to the war dead.

Grandiloquence was for leaders and heroes, but wealthy citizens of Athens or other city-states could still afford smaller house tombs, mausolea or *stelae* decorated with friezes or sculptures in high relief. Amid the classical revival in western Europe, these elements were much admired in purely aesthetic terms,

and were frequently removed and taken from Greece for public and private art collections elsewhere. It is striking, reading Erwin Panofsky's classic lectures on *Tomb Sculpture*, how often the funerary context falls away for a purely aesthetic consideration of the elements detached from graves. But the debt to Ancient Greece in neoclassical designs of churches, cemeteries and grave markers themselves has also been enduring.

7

8

9

AEL·ALEXANDRIA·
AEL·SEPTIMAE·
MATRI·KARIS·
SIMAE·BENE
MERI·FECIT·

11

10

12

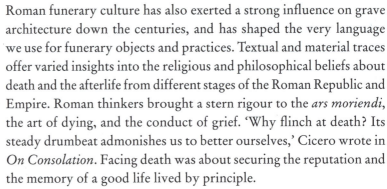

previous spread:
(1) Menorah on a Jewish
burial plaque, 200–300.
(2) Greek jar decorated with
Odysseus and Elpenor in
the underworld, c. 440 BCE.
(3) Lachryma or glass 'tear
bottles', from the Gallo-
Roman necropolis, Alba Iulia,
France. (4) Mask from a Greek
warrior buried in Thrace, sixth
century BCE. (5) Greek Orphic
tablet, appealing for safe
passage in the underworld,
fourth century BCE. (6) 'The
Sarcophagus of the Spouses',
a terracotta Etruscan cinerary
urn reconstructed from 400
fragments, c. 530–520 BCE.
(7) Mourning women, likely
placed around a funerary
couch in lamentation. Canosa,
Italy, c. 300–275 BCE.
(8) A Greek oenochoe (wine
jug), depicting Hercules's
capture of Cerberus.
(9) Female funerary mask,
Ptolemaic or Roman Egypt,
c. 50 BCE–50 CE. (10) Greek
clay lekythos, for oils, depicting
offerings for the dead,
c. 470–460 BCE.

Roman funerary culture has also exerted a strong influence on grave architecture down the centuries, and has shaped the very language we use for funerary objects and practices. Textual and material traces offer varied insights into the religious and philosophical beliefs about death and the afterlife from different stages of the Roman Republic and Empire. Roman thinkers brought a stern rigour to the *ars moriendi*, the art of dying, and the conduct of grief. 'Why flinch at death? Its steady drumbeat admonishes us to better ourselves,' Cicero wrote in *On Consolation*. Facing death was about securing the reputation and the memory of a good life lived by principle.

Funerary practices through the millennium of Republican Rome (510–31 BCE) and Imperial Rome (31 BCE–476 CE) borrowed much from the Greeks and from the Etruscans, whose culture emerged in Italy from 900 BCE. The Etruscans developed strict rules about the separation of the cities of the living and the dead, and built systematic necropolises outside their settlements, with rows of graves marked out in streets cut in grids into soft rock. Their underground stone chambers were elaborately decorated with paintings, some of which survive, as in the extraordinary necropolises of Tarquinia and Cerveteri. D. H. Lawrence visited them in 1927, and in *Sketches of Etruscan Places* describes bed-like niches in tombs with multiple rooms, an arrangement that led some to suggest that the evolution

of Etruscan tombs deliberately follows the pattern of house designs for the living. Unlike 'the weirdness of Celtic places, [or] the slightly repellent feeling of Rome', Lawrence writes, Etruscan burial sites had 'a stillness and a soothingness in all the air, in that sunken place, and a feeling that it was good for one's soul.' Erwin Panofsky, meanwhile, insisted on thinking of the Etruscans a 'weird people' who were 'even more death-ridden ... than the Egyptians.' Their tomb sculpture was 'repellent' to him, it seems, largely because it is a mix of cultural influences from across the region. The Romans did not share his qualms, and continued and adapted a lot of Etruscan material practices.

The laws of the early Republic, written out in the Twelve Tables in 450 BCE, are a helpful guide: the tenth tablet lays down rules on funerary practices. Burial or cremation inside city walls was banned, and constraints on excessive expenditure on funeral clothes, processions and festivities, and over-exaggerated displays of grief (professional mourners, as in Greece, could be hired for a fee) were borrowed directly from Solon's laws for Athens. Musicians playing dirges were limited in number. Ostentation in grave markers

(11) Burial plaque: 'Alexandria set up [this stone] to Ael[ia] Septima, her dearest mother, in grateful memory.' The symbols are offerings: fruits and a ram for sacrifice. Italy, c. 300–400 BCE. (12) Greek terracotta hydria (water jar), depicting a funerary statue of a bride flanked by youthful figures, c. 360–330 BCE.

above: The Etruscan 'Tomb of the Leopards'. Leopards face each other above a funeral banquet scene, Monterozzi necropolis, Tarquinia, Italy, c. 470–450 BCE.

opposite: *Memento mori*. Scales, with wealth on the left and poverty on the right, are balanced against a skull (death) and the butterfly and wheel below represent brevity and fortune. Pompeii, c. 30–14 BCE.

was less easy to enforce: social differentiations emerged quickly in a culture built on enslaved and proletarian labour. In the late Republic and into the Empire, the tombs of emperors became ever grander in scale, borrowing from the giant tumuli, mounds of earth and stone, that they saw at the edges of their imperial reach. The Twelve Tables also forbade the burial of gold grave goods with the dead – although gold teeth were excepted. This aimed to suppress tomb raiders, in part because the laws were clear that once bones or ashes were inhumed they were not to be disturbed again. Punishment for the violation of graves was strictly enforced, although this did not stop the common practice of recycling tombs.

The big arc of Roman burial history is from the predominance of the funeral pyre in the Republic to the later tendency towards burial of bodies in trench graves in wooden coffins or sarcophagi, or above ground in mausolea. As with other cultures, it is not always clear why these customs shifted, although the Romans ascribed a lot of power to the homeland, the very *earth* of home. Even when cremation was preferred, some refer to the custom of *os resectum* – that is, the removal of a finger of the dead from the pyre so that the bone might later be symbolically covered in earth back home. The Latin *humus* (soil) gives the words *inhumation* and its correlates: burial underground was important, particularly so if the death occurred away from Rome. The journey onwards is, after all, through the *under*world, the terrain through which Aeneas travels beyond 'the forests of the Styx, those

right: Paul Nash, *Funeral Pyre and Teeth, Bones and Hair*, designs for Urne Buriall, 1931–32.

below: Roland Brunier, wood engraving of a Roman funeral at the Columbaria of the Caesars, Capena Gate, in Rome, after Louis-Hector Leroux, 1871.

opposite: Funerary mask, Roman period of Egypt, c. 125.

realms barred to the living' in the sixth book of Virgil's *Aeneid*. To be left unburied or simply exposed to the elements was the worst prospect. The *cenotaph*, the empty memorial for soldiers who died overseas, was a stop-gap, a gesture of understanding of a major sacrifice to name and memory as well as body.

The process of preparing the body, the rituals of the funeral and associated commemorative acts can be synthesized from many surviving texts and images. A 'good' death was foreseen, accounts settled, prepared for and met at home. At death, the family closed the eyes of the corpse, laid it on the ground and began rituals of cleansing. The mourning family were now 'polluted' by death until the post-funerary ceremonies were complete, as in Greece. The Roman funeral industry began to differentiate specialists: those who prepared the body, carried the body in procession, built the pyre, dug graves and conducted the inhumation. Such professionals were culturally abject, working as the officials of this polluted liminal space between two deaths.

Processions out of the city took place before daybreak, the mourners carrying torches to light the way, sometimes accompanied by singers and musicians, and for wealthier families by people carrying *imagos* – paintings or death masks of the family's dead. This emphasized the role of family in conducting the funeral; those who could not afford all this could join funeral clubs to share the costs. For cremation, shrouded bodies were taken on a bier to the *ustrina*, a place reserved for pyres away from the living, strictly regulated by city ordinances. Eulogies were pronounced, the eyes of the corpse ritualistically opened to face death, and the body was then placed on the pyre.

The pyres themselves ranged from basic to deluxe – the largest could be elaborate, multi-storey structures. Cremated remains were placed in urns or ash-chests for interment. Animal sacrifices were made, the beginning of a feasting sequence. After interment, feasts were conducted at the burial site, wine and food shared between the living and the dead. The most important of these was on the ninth day after death, after which the immediate family began to emerge from their association with polluting death. Romans returned to make offerings and libations to the dead, sometimes at specially constructed altars. They laid roses on graves as emblems of eternal spring in May and June, and the annual Parentalia festival, a nine-day period for commemorating the ancestral dead, took place in February. This was an ordered and rule-bound civic process.

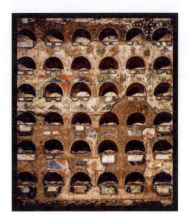

above: The Columbarium of Vigna Codini, Rome. A vast underground burial complex started in the first century BCE and rediscovered in the nineteenth century.

below: The 'Street of Tombs' in Pompeii, commercial print, c. 1890.

Types of Roman burial structure and their designated spaces introduced new elements into funerary language. Monuments built up outside city walls – most famously along the Appian Way, the road that leads out of Rome towards Brindisi. There is also a famous 'Street of Tombs' leading out of Pompeii. Necropolises burrowed into the ground to create the kinds of *hypogea* familiar from Greek and Minoan cultures. These catacombs and columbaria, with niches for cremated remains and tiers of longer, shelf-like structures (*loculi*) for shrouded bodies in coffins, could be extended indefinitely by cutting deeper into the rock. Outside Roman city laws, the early Christians buried their dead and perhaps worshipped below ground in their own catacombs. The Appian Way also contains Jewish catacombs, most famously the Vigna Randanini, which dates to between the second and fifth centuries BCE.

right: Giovanni Battista Piranesi, 'Ancient intersection of the Via Appia and Via Ardeatina', from *The Antiquities of Rome*, vol II, 1756–57.

Because so many travelled along the Appian Way, showy, grand mausolea were built to often mammoth size along the route. They tend to cluster in the first five miles out of the city, but monuments continue for miles beyond that. Other, smaller structures for average, modest citizens included *stelae*, small-scale mausolea or funerary altars. The larger necropolises, such as the Isola Sacra, the Isle of the Dead, south of Rome at Fiumicino, display the social hierarchies of Roman society through the smaller monuments crammed in between larger-scale structures. Other family plots were built as walled cemeteries or funerary gardens, their vines and orchards or meditative pools attempting an 'Elysian' ambience for the living who came to remember.

Sarcophagi with sculpted friezes came late to the Roman Empire and were less favoured by the Republic. By this time, the later emperors had begun to abandon rules about extramural burial and build gigantic monuments in the city, as in the case of Augustus's tomb, which was modelled on round mound tumuli and controversially built on city land inside Rome (and later sacked by the Goths). In Split, Croatia, Diocletian's palace was also his mausoleum. This odd reversion teaches us yet again that burial practice never proceeds in straight, orderly lines.

†

We experience the early histories of human burial as a collapsed simultaneity. Layers are rammed together in a bewildering mélange, often difficult to separate and parse into coherent narratives. The paths taken across this dangerous and alarming interval between two deaths vary enormously and continue to diverge as they head into more recent history.

PART

TWO

†

DEATH

&

FAITH

ANTHROPOLOGY AND
DARK TOURISM

In his 1972 essay 'How Others Die', cultural anthropologist Johannes Fabian suggests that the discipline of anthropology has often focused on the 'ceremonial of death' because it most clearly registers cultural difference. From the beginning of this discipline, which was inextricably linked to the origins of empire, the systematic recording of other cultures' funeral rites has been at the core of distinctions between cultures. Fabian observes that 'fascination with the curious, the violent, and the exotic seems to be the arena assigned to the use of anthropological studies of the dead.' Travel writing and early anthropology in the nineteenth century always showed a particular interest in funerary practices 'that appear irrational, over-ritualised and picturesque.'

MODERNISM AND EXOTICISM

In the nineteenth century, the accounts of travellers and missionaries began to be systematized into the discipline of anthropology. It is no coincidence that this knowledge arrived with the major phase of European empire-building. We might now read late-Victorian accounts of death and burial from the arm-chair anthropologists Edward Tylor or J. G. Frazer with a sense that we have moved beyond such rigidly hierarchical, racist ways of thinking. The arrival of a more openly comparative anthropology, in which researchers left the archive and entered 'the field' in order to understand very different cultures on their own terms is often allied with the rise of radical Modernism and its rejection of nineteenth-century moral hierarchies. Yet Modernists, too, had their 'exotic dead'.

In the early twentieth century, the French Surrealist Georges Bataille cultivated an overt obsession with rituals that involved sacrifice and death. He pored over accounts of Aztec sacrifice and the death and memorial practices of Indigenous people in North America. In the 1920s, he set up a secret society in France with the ultimate hope of one day enacting a human sacrifice. 'Sacrifice

opposite: Pablo Picasso, *Self-Portrait Facing Death*, made in the artist's final year, 1972.

restores to the sacred world that which servile use has degraded, rendered profane,' he wrote. Bataille's fascination was expressed in a mode typical of his peers, including Picasso and his fellow Modernist artists, for whom the 'primitive' – including death rites – offered a riposte to the perceived constraints of 'civilization'.

In 1931 one of Bataille's fellow dissidents, the poet Michel Leiris, joined an anthropological mission through the African continent, the Mission Dakar-Djibouti. His diaries of the mission's fieldwork detail his engagement with practices of ancestor worship among the Dogon people and spirit possession in Abyssinia, but also his queasy complicity with French colonialism, including the looting of sacred sites. His record of the mission was published as *Phantom Africa* – a title that makes evident his fascination with projecting an exoticized African Other.

One of Leiris's associates, the American author William Seabrook, shared his sensational fascination with death cultures in his interwar travel books and journalism. Seabrook notoriously travelled to West Africa in an attempt to join a cult in their ritual of eating human flesh, but was later forced to admit that he could only do so on his return to France, where he bribed someone at the Paris Morgue to take home an arm from an unclaimed body. The anecdote neatly inverts the idea of civilized centre and savage margin: the cannibals are in Paris, not West Africa. Seabrook also travelled to Haiti, where he wrote up a sensationalized account of Haitian Vodou ('voodoo') for his 1929 book, *The Magic Island*, which recounted tales of dead men 'working in cane fields'. Seabrook's book helped introduce the term 'zombie' to American popular culture through his account of voodoo priests raising the recently dead from their graves.

Early twentieth-century Modernists set themselves up as a radical break from the rigid morality and racial hierarchies of the nineteenth century. It is true that there were significant advances in understanding cultural difference, and new models of encounter. Yet there remain many continuities into the present day, in the fascination with the death rituals of those we place as other to ourselves. These have been in place from the very beginnings of the travel, trade and settlement that developed into colonialism.

THE HURON-WENDAT OSSUARIES, ONTARIO

When French traders pushed into the North American continent in the 1600s – in what would become Ontario in Canada – Jesuit missionaries were not far behind. The earnest Catholic priests, eager for souls to save, established a mission called Sainte Marie, one of the first white settlements of 'New France'. The missionaries encountered a confederacy of Indigenous communities they called the Huron

(a pejorative term for 'unkempt' or 'boar-like'). The five nations of Wendat people were a matrilineal society supported by subsistence farming, their power in the region built on trading beaver furs. Their burial practices and bone pits were documented extensively by the Jesuits.

Wendat people who died in their fortified villages were buried outside the palisades in graves after three days, having been watched over in a vigil held by the women, who prepared the body by wrapping it in bark. Then, about every ten years, when the fields were exhausted of nutrients for crops and the Wendat needed to move elsewhere, villages came together for a lavish Festival of the Dead. In preparation, the dead were disinterred then defleshed, cleaned, collected and enfolded in ornate wrappings that were then hung in hierarchy on wooden scaffolds above a large pit. In 1636, the Jesuit Père La Jeune recorded a ceremony, at which the bones were treated 'with a care and affection that cannot be described'. Each family, he wrote, 'feels afresh the grief they had the day of the funeral': an emotional tie the priest recognized, and that appeared to transcend cultural difference. Feasts and ceremonies continued for several days, with the hosting village and visiting leaders offering presents to one another in an escalating spiral of gifting.

above: Skull of St Jean de Brébeuf. The Jesuit was killed in 1649 during his mission to convert the native population of New France, now Canada. The relic is held at Martyrs' Shrine, Ontario.

opposite: 'Huron ancestral feast of the dead', illustration from Jesuit Joseph-François Lafitau's *Fête des morts chez les Hurons-Wendats: Moeurs des sauvages ameriquains*, 1724.

At the end of several days, the bones were taken down from the scaffold and buried in a communal ossuary, with grave goods including tomahawks, beads, clothing and layers of beaver furs. This second burial marked the departure of a portion of the spirits of the dead to a village in the west, beyond the setting sun, and reconfirmed the social and political alliances of the living through the mingling of bones. It also released the living to move to new ground. The Festival often took over a year to prepare and consumed vast resources.

Père Jean de Brébeuf was another Jesuit priest who attended and recorded a Feast of the Dead in the 1630s. In 1649, the Jesuit mission at Sainte Marie was attacked and Brébeuf was killed along with other priests. Nearly 300 years later, a Catholic Shrine Church was built at Sainte Marie to honour the first Christian settlement, and Brébeuf was sanctified by the Catholic Church. In the later nineteenth century his accounts, along with others, were collected in the multivolume collection *Jesuit Relations and Allied Documents*. His skull is one of the holy relics now on display at the church, next to a historical reconstruction of the mission.

By 1651, the Wendat confederacy had been destroyed and dispersed by the encroachment of Iroquois people into Wendat territory, in wars that have been understood as both trade and mourning wars.

Mourning wars were large-scale attacks with the purpose of avenging or replacing members of the Iroquoian community lost to fighting and to the diseases introduced by white settlers. The surviving Wendat migrated to areas outside Quebec and further away, into the American West.

The 'ossuary burial' ritual of the Wendat was considered an example of 'potlatch', a Chinookan word borrowed into the English language to refer to a range of significant practices, including many around death and burial. Potlatch rituals were marked by what the anthropologist Marcel Mauss in *The Gift* (1925) called 'the purely sumptuous destruction of accumulated wealth', an economy that seemed to invert European ideas of exchange, value and scarcity. European Christians and capitalist traders alike tended to regard the practice as immoral. Sir John MacDonald, the first Prime Minister of the newly formed Dominion of Canada, was involved in drafting laws to suppress potlatch practices in the 1880s, calling it a 'useless and degrading custom'. Prosecutions began in Canada in 1919, although the law was revoked in 1951.

The bone pits of the Wendat, over 200 of which have been listed as important burial sites in Ontario, were persistently raided as part of a secondary trade in the sale of human remains and grave goods to museums and private collections. Laws against this trade and policies on the repatriation of remains have since come into operation, but the survival of these sacred places remains fragile. In 2016, it was revealed that the construction of a new commuter rail line in downtown Barrie, approved by the Ontario government, had ploughed through a known burial site under a rail yard.

The history of the displaced Wendat also left a trail of cemeteries in America. In the nineteenth century, a surviving part of the Wendat confederacy known as the Wyandot were repeatedly displaced westward in the hope of finding land and peace. In 1843, they were displaced from Ohio to Kansas City, where they fell victim to a smallpox epidemic. Many Wyandot people were buried at the Huron Indian Cemetery in Kansas City. Now renamed the Wyandot National Burial Ground and given recognition on the American National Register of Historic Places, it was for many years under constant threat of erasure by redevelopment in the city. Finally, in 1990, the Native American Grave Protection and Repatriation Act was passed into American law, which protects burial sites and makes it a legal requirement for museums and archives to return ancestral remains still in 'scientific' collections. Despite this, it was only in late 2023 and early 2024 that major museums such as the American Museum of Natural History and the Smithsonian finally pledged to remove human remains from public display. Repatriation of Native American remains continues to be a fraught and incomplete process. No wonder the American Gothic continues to be haunted by the trope of the unquiet Indian Burial Ground.

AT DRIGUNG MONASTERY

Tibet was for a long time almost entirely closed to European travellers, and colonial fantasies about the region were amplified in early twentieth-century travel writing, in particular James Hilton's novel *Lost Horizon* (1933). Cultural fascination with Tibet has focused particularly on its death practices, which are associated with the particular strand of Buddhism that developed in the mountains over centuries. The Tibetan Buddhist philosophy of death is outlined in the legendary *Tibetan Book of the Dead*.

The practice of *bya gtor*, literally 'alms for the birds', is most associated with the Buddhist monasteries of Tibet, but is also practised in Nepal and parts of China. In the high mountains, where there is no earth to bury the dead, there are several key sites where bodies are taken to ritual grounds in the open air, cleaved into sections with machetes, and then fed to the vultures that cluster around the sites. In 2023, Catherine Jigme, a tourist guide for Tibet Vista, writes 'not one visitor in five hundred is privileged to witness the

above: A 'sky burial' at Drigung Til Monastery in Tibet, one of the main ritual sites.

opposite: Effigies of the dead on the Torajan cliff at the Lemo burial complex, South Sulawesi, Indonesia.

ceremony that I'm about to see' of her time at Drigung Monastery, the most auspicious of these sites. She records that at the decisive part of the ceremony, 'the only sound is tearing flesh and chittering.' After this rapid defleshing, the vultures are chased away and the remaining bones are further crushed down with hammers. The vultures return and complete the process of disposal.

It is a solemn religious ritual but also a joyous one, enacted to free the spirit into the sky from its now useless and abandoned flesh, prayers having guided the spirit through the *bardo* (the space of transition between reincarnated lives) for weeks before the final ceremony. This way of handling the dead has been called 'sky burial' or 'celestial burial' in translation.

The rise in tourism to spectate at these rituals has resulted in periodic attempts to restrict access to the sites since the 1980s, in part to limit the practice, although it has also been claimed that restriction helps preserve the tradition from the pressures of modernization. The Chinese state has been concerned to control the apparent popularity of the ritual with its own tourists as much as visitors from abroad.

There is a deepened engagement and understanding of death and memorial cultures among many anthropologists and travel writers working today, but the concurrent rise of the phenomenon of dark tourism (a term coined in the 1990s) names a growing trend in travel that is explicit about seeking out the most 'exotic' death and burial rituals around the world. Dark tourism suggests that there is a continued investment in and fascination with death practices that mean that we cannot position cruder ethical engagements in earlier, less informed ages.

One focus of the dark tourism industry has been a number of burial sites in the mountains of South Sulawesi, Indonesia: the cliff cemeteries of the Tana Toraja region. As the website for *Atlas Obscura*, an American magazine and travel company, explains, 'the funeral rites of Toraja are some of the most elaborate in the world.' Dotted across the cliff-faces are wooden doors, entries to vaults where coffins are placed. Balconies are carved out of the limestone cliffs and lined with *tau tau*, brightly dressed effigies with appliquéd eyes that stand in for the dead, who peer down on the village and rice fields laid out below. Every few years, the graves are opened and tidied and the *tau tau* spruced up.

'Torajaland' was strategically chosen by the Indonesian government as a carefully packaged off-the-beaten-track experience for the 'authentic' traveller in the early 1970s, when the state wanted to expand its tourist trade. In 1972, *National Geographic* ran a documentary film of the funeral of a nobleman. It, and the accompanying illustrated piece, raised the international profile of Torajan funerary practices significantly; today, the 'Visit Toraja' website promises a 'jaw-dropping' and 'intense' experience. One American tourist cited by the anthropologist Toby Volkman called the whole thing 'really stone age'. In Rantepao, little *tau tau* effigies made for tourists can be purchased. Many of the original hardwood decorated effigies on the cliff itself

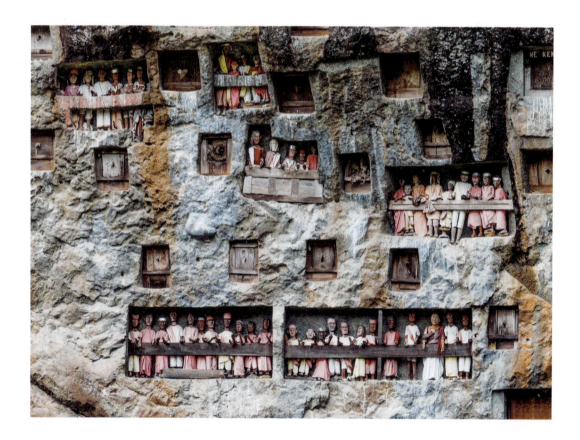

above: Manene ritual in the Lokomata Stone Graveyard, Toraja, South Sulawesi, Indonesia. Family members clean the graves and change the clothes of their relatives to honour their spirits during the ritual, which is held every three years.

are now fakes; the originals were moved into more accessible positions for tourists to photograph and subsequently stolen, some even ending up in art galleries in New York.

Thousands of members of the Torajan diaspora travel from across the world back to South Sulawesi to attend funerals, which begin with the sacrifice of buffalo and pigs. These are gifted at immense and escalating cost by family members and guests (the higher the status, the more sacrifices are made). Some meat is handed out or sometimes auctioned off to relatives and guests, while some is understood to be carried by the dead into the afterlife to sustain them and mark out their status among the ancestors. The expense associated with this burial ritual has continued to rise even after the Asian financial crisis in 1997, its cultural and spiritual value far outstripping any narrow economic calculation.

The public rituals of sacrifice are only a small part of a longer post-mortem process that can take up to a year. Before this final funeral ceremony, which lasts over several days, the Torajan dead are often kept at home. The bodies are injected with preservatives to prevent decay and rest in a temporary coffin; previously, they were 'smoked' with pine or aromatic leaves. They are considered only 'sick' at this stage, and are served with food and drink at every meal along with the rest of the family (the traditional religion of the Torajans, pa'kandean nene', can be translated as 'feeding the ancestors'). 'Torajans literally live with the dead, and there seemed to be "no life without the dead,"' the Dutch anthropologist Edwin de Jong observed during a fieldwork stay with a Torajan family that was heavily involved in arranging and overseeing mortuary practices.

After the final ceremony and interment of the bodies, subsequent rituals ensure that the spirit of the dead travels westwards to Puya, the afterlife. This journey itself is still only one stage of a process that conducts the spirit through several levels of transformation, until it might reach the status of ancestor.

For many years, the colonial occupiers of the island, the Dutch, who consolidated their occupation in 1906, sought to suppress these burial practices. They tried to make a distinction between custom, which was acceptable, and religious practice, which was not. The distinction never worked, because the two are of course inextricable. In the 1910s the Dutch Reform Missionary Church made a further attempt to Christianize the Torajan region and thus outlaw these religious rituals. Yet they are now valued as authentic expressions of Indonesian multicultural diversity, with the most significant funerals attended by government officials from Jakarta.

There is a certain melancholia about the recording of Torajan culture among the anthropologists that document these ceremonies and their changing nature. Roxanna Waterson, who returned to the same area for over twenty years from the late 1970s, tracks a rapid transformation of the region by aggressive modernization, outmigration, and the continued Christianizing of the population. Village life and mortuary culture have been significantly altered by the very tourists seeking a taste of the 'authentic'. This now partly includes the diaspora of Torajans who return to the region to participate in their own cultural practices.

†

The treatment of the dead has commonly been used throughout human history as a way to measure cultural difference. What most diverges from assumed funerary norms becomes othered. In colonial eras, practices marked as 'primitive' or 'savage' can be used to justify settlement and the suppression of local customs. Even very minor differences in burial practice seem to produce a *frisson*, a shiver somewhere between attraction and repulsion. Within Christianity, for instance, Protestants have been suspicious (but also perhaps secretly admiring) of Catholic death practices – including the culture of ossuary-display of bones and the veneration of bodily holy relics. The American custom of embalming and displaying the body at funerals clearly appalled the English aristocrat Jessica Mitford, who wrote *The American Way of Death*, a satirical exposé of what she disdained as a cynical industry, in 1963. It is too easy to suggest that contemporary cosmopolitanism and the democratizing of global travel have made humans more liberal and tolerant: the emergence of death tourism shows that there is still an impetus to exoticize how 'others' die.

DEATH AND FAITH

Perhaps death itself must always remain a rupture from the absolute outside. If death cannot be experienced in itself, it is left for those living in its aftermath to frame a meaning for this discontinuity, and to smooth the perilous passage from life to whatever follows. These formalizations of ritual practice and theories of death are frequently conducted through religious frameworks, which still encompass billions of human lives across the planet. Theologies have often been inferred from the earliest intentional depositions of bodies in caves, even if there is scant evidence of how they may actually have operated. The meanings ascribed to death and the passage from life to death burst from some of the earliest fragments of marking, memorialization and writing that we have.

The following chapters on death and faith use the comparative grouping employed by some historians of religions, looking at the so-called Abrahamic religions in the order of their emergence: Judaism, Christianity and Islam. These are monotheistic religions that share a founding-father figure called Abraham. Even as their histories are always entwined, they have very different systems of belief and practice, and their cemeteries reveal these divergences. This section then tracks the polytheism associated with Hinduism in India and ends with some burial places that reflect Buddhist beliefs. This range is covered by moving from graveyard to graveyard, with the aim of understanding each of these spaces on their own terms.

THE MOUNT OF OLIVES, EAST JERUSALEM

The Mount of Olives – Har ha-Zeitim in Hebrew and Jabal az-Zaytun in Arabic – is an ancient necropolis that serves the holy city of Jerusalem below. The soft, chalky ground of the Judean mountains is easy to dig: underground chambers, tombs and monuments have been carved out of the rock face for millennia. Some of the oldest surviving monuments stretch back to the ninth century BCE, but this is within a broader area of West Asia that has revealed some of the earliest human burials. The dead continue to be buried in the cemetery on the Mount of Olives, making it one of the oldest active graveyards in the world. It is also one of the most politically and religiously fraught places on Earth, a site both overdetermined and splintered. It is here that each of the Abrahamic religions find crucial elements of their origin stories.

To the Jews, whose founding patriarch Abraham struck a Covenant with the one true God, it is a landscape filled with originary significance. Jewish burials have taken place there for at least 3,000 years, with an estimated 150,000 graves on the site. Zechariah prophesied that YHWH would stand on the Mount of Olives and effectively split the world between north and south; the necropolis was also exactly the place where the resurrection of the dead would begin with the arrival of the Messiah. Some of the highest-ranking officials of the kingdom of Judah were buried there between the ninth and seventh centuries BCE. In sections known as the Silwan necropolis, their graves now largely lost to quarrying, reuse or settlement, some of the prophets of the Tanakh (the Jewish scriptures) are also customarily believed to have been buried there. The Tomb of the Prophets is named for Haggai, Zechariah and Malachi (three prophets in the last book of the Nevi'im, the second division of the Tanakh, and also the final three prophets in the Christian Old Testament). These significant burial places are typically marked by a *nefesh*, a grand funerary monument above ground, with burial chambers below.

The Temple at the centre of Jewish worship was built in the city below, and after the destruction of the Second Temple by the Romans in 70, the Mount of Olives, from which its site can be seen, became a place of Jewish lamentation. After the establishment of the state of Israel in 1948, it gained huge political significance. From 1948 to 1967, this territory, earmarked under a UN resolution for a Palestinian Arab state, was annexed by Jordan. During this period, Jewish graves were deliberately cleared or demolished, and Jewish pilgrims were barred from the site. After the Six Day War in 1967 and the annexation of East Jerusalem by Israel in 1980, restoration work on the Jewish cemeteries on the Mount of Olives began. It is now a key part of Israel's politics of memorial, paired with Mount Herzl, which it faces across the Old City.

previous spread: Francis Bedford, the Tomb of Absalom and Tomb of Zechariah, Kidron Valley, Jerusalem, 1862.

The Mount of Olives is also one of the holiest sites in Christianity, the location of the last phase of Christ's ministry, as recorded in the New Testament. The tomb of Mary lies in the valley below (with a chapel built over an ancient rock-carved tomb). At the base of the Mount is the Garden of Gethsemane, where Jesus met with his disciples and Judas betrayed him to the authorities. There Jesus experiences 'the agony of the Garden', his moment of anguish for the suffering to come between the Last Supper and his arrest and crucifixion.

The Christian churches and monuments in this necropolis bear all the marks of its splintered ecclesiastical history. There are Greek and Russian Orthodox churches alongside Roman Catholic churches, a Lutheran Protestant church and a Church of Jesus Christ of the Latter-Day Saints, the Mormon church founded by Joseph Smith in upstate New York in the 1820s.

The Mount is also a holy site for Islam, which regards Abraham and Jesus as part of a line of prophets of the one true God that comes to include the seventh-century Prophet Muhammad, the founder of the religion. The southern part of the Temple Mount in the Old City of Jerusalem contains the earliest surviving Islamic building, the Dome of the Rock at the centre of the Al-Aqsa Mosque compound, first built in the seventh century around the rock where God created Adam, Abraham placed his son Isaac to be sacrificed and the Prophet Muhammad began his visionary Night Journey in 620. The Dome is also built on the site of the lost Second Temple, and so rests in a deeply conflicted space, in which several religions compete for exactly the same territory. In recent history, Muslim access to the Mosque has been subject to passing through checkpoints and restrictions by the Israeli police force; any change to restrictions there causes major rises in tension.

opposite: The Chapel of Ascension, Mount of Olives, Jerusalem. The central structure survives from a twelfth-century church built by Christian crusaders, which was repurposed as a mosque by Saladin after 1189. It covers a burial crypt significant to all three Abrahamic religions.

Violent possession and dispossession of the sites of Jerusalem have taken place between the Abrahamic religions for millennia, intensified by the Crusades, the first of which captured Jerusalem for Christian forces in 1099, only for it to be retaken by Muslim rulers in 1189. There was some attempt to establish a system of mutual respect for different religious sites under the decree of the Ottoman sultan Osman III in 1757. Almost a century later, an international diplomatic agreement proposed that 'religious buildings and sites in Palestine should be protected and free access to them assured, in accordance with existing rights and historical practice.' This hope was built on in the early years of the United Nations in a Conciliation Commission for Palestine, which advocated for the 'internationalization' of holy sites in Jerusalem and elsewhere after the 1948 Palestine War. Cemeteries have always been part of this politics; grave dust constitutes both memorial continuity and the very soil of what is understood as 'home'.

This complex overlaying of different histories and faiths is typified in the structure and burial chamber at the top of the Mount of Olives, the site where Christ is believed to have delivered his last words on Earth and ascended to heaven (Acts I). Built as a church and monastery by a wealthy Roman convert to Christianity in the fourth century, it surrounds a rock that is held to bear the imprint of Christ's last footprints on Earth. After the twelfth century, in its Romanesque form, it became part of the Zawiyat al-Adawiyya mosque complex. The associated crypt is claimed by three faiths with three different accounts of the woman it once contained: Saint Pelagia in the Christian version, the prophetess Huldah in the Jewish version and Rabi'a al-Adawiyya in the Islamic version. The Mount of Olives necropolis is a place where multiple communities of the dead are asked to work hard to shore up each living faith.

JUDAISM

THE BRADY STREET JEWISH CEMETERY, LONDON

If you turn into Brady Street off the Whitechapel Road in London's East End, you quickly leave the joyous chaos of the street market and start to follow an unbroken high brick wall. As this boundary turns a corner, through a grilled gate can be glimpsed the serene sight of gravestones on slightly raised ground under mature trees. This is the Jewish cemetery of the New Synagogue, which was in operation between 1761 and 1857. It is one of several surviving inner-city cemeteries for the Jewish population of London. They are often bounded by high walls, all clearly well-tended and maintained, and closed to the casual visitor.

In 1891, Isabella Holmes rushed to document London's abandoned, precarious burial grounds in order to prevent their destruction and preserve them as parks. She did not need to worry about the Jewish grounds because, she wrote, 'the Jews ... are particularly pledged to preserve their burial-places'. The Chief Rabbi had explained to her that this was not a law as such, 'but a binding obligation handed down from the most ancient times, and any disturbance of the burial-grounds which now exist was not permitted.' Hence the archipelago of small Jewish grounds across London – in Alderney Street, further east, or on the Fulham Road, where a tiny single-acre ground is hemmed in by walls and shops.

Brady Street's headstones stand upright, in the custom of northern European Ashkenazi Jews. A few streets further east, the campus of Queen Mary University has preserved a section of the Novo, or New, Cemetery where the grave markers are flat ledger stones, laid horizontally on the ground in the tradition of Sephardic Jews. These cemeteries are located on a main artery out of the old City of London, because Jewish custom states that the dead should be buried outside the boundaries of the city. The Jewish community had been allowed to resettle in England after the Civil War in the 1640s, after centuries of exclusion, but had not at first been granted separate burial grounds. They were excluded from Church of England burial grounds and interred in Dissenting grounds. Eventually, in the eighteenth century, the growing community was able to establish separate burial grounds as Jewish custom

opposite: The Wailing Wall at the Old Jewish Cemetery in Remuh, Krakow, Poland, constructed in 1959 from fragments of the gravestones broken up during the Nazi occupation.

below: The Novo or Nuevo Beth Chaim Cemetery, a Sephardic Jewish cemetery, Mile End Road, London. The surviving section is on the campus of Queen Mary University of London.

bottom: Tombstones at the Jewish cemetery at Brady Street, Whitechapel, East London.

89

preferred. In London each synagogue purchased its own space. Later, as the Jewish population grew, shared cemeteries emerged.

Jewish observances and practices around death and burial are derived from the Tanakh, the Halakah (laws and ordinances that have evolved since biblical times) and Talmudic commentaries. They are therefore largely the product of codification in exile and diaspora, which makes for customs that have room to flex within different expressions of Judaism. Burial was long the rule, with cremation forbidden. Graves are mentioned throughout the Old Testament, some of which, it is argued, are still identifiable on the Mount of Olives. Markers memorialize the name and the genealogy of the tribes of Israel that are ruled by the covenant between God and Abraham. On the river gates of the Beth Haim cemetery at Ouderkerk outside Amsterdam, which opened for the Sephardic community exiled from Portugal in the early seventeenth century, there is a quote from Ezekiel: 'Behold, O my people, I will open your graves and cause you to come up out of your graves, and bring you into the land of Israel.' The symbolic import of burial is evident in this vision of bodily return in the messianic age. Even so, some branches of Judaism have allowed cremation.

Jewish funerary customs that emerged in the diaspora dictate that, if possible, the funeral should be conducted within one day of death. It is conducted in an Ohel, a hall inside the cemetery. Bodies are washed and purified but not embalmed, and dressed in traditional burial clothes. The coffin is meant to be a modest, unadorned wooden box (in Israel, burial is often only in a shroud). The grave might be dug by the mourners; the ritual of mourners placing a shovel of soil on the coffin at the end of the funeral, or filling the grave, still carries weight. Conventional practices after the funeral involve sitting shiva, observing seven days of reclusive mourning for the immediate family, during which others visit. A longer thirty-day period is also observed, in which study of religious texts may be encouraged. There are also rituals of remembrance at the synagogue, including the recitation of the Kaddish, a prayer in praise of God rather than lamentation for the dead. The first anniversary of the death is an important moment in the cycle of mourning and remembrance.

above: Detail of a headstone at Beth Haim of Ouderkerk aan de Amstel, the oldest Jewish cemetery in the Netherlands.

opposite: Bette Blank, *Kaddish*, 2001.

A key aspect of Jewish law is a rejection of all idolatry ('Thou shalt not make unto thee any graven images'), so grave markers are often very simple, in contrast to both classical and Christian conventions of funerary sculpture. The early use of wooden markers means many have not survived. Simple stone markers became the norm, with some rudimentary signs allowed, often to indicate the name or profession of the person. Occasionally, a significant person was marked by a larger chest tomb or stone sarcophagus protected under a stone canopy: a significant rabbi, holy scholar, or leader. There are a small number of these in Brady Street – tombs for members of the Rothschild banking dynasty; a monument that carries the likeness of an important community figure, Miriam Levy, a very rare honour.

A mark of memory and respect for the dead is to place a small pebble on their grave. The tradition is perhaps another tie to the symbolic importance of the soil of the homeland. But Jewish respect for the dead is perhaps most exemplified by the fact that Brady Street was never abandoned, as so many inner-city burial grounds were. Even after the Jewish community had largely moved out of the East End of London, the memorials to the dead are still maintained.

THE OLD JEWISH CEMETERY, PRAGUE

For centuries, anti-Semitism was institutionalized across Christian Europe. Jews were held to refuse to assimilate, although they were often not allowed to, being forbidden from key aspects of public life and forced to live in separate areas. The word 'ghetto' is thought to derive from the Italian *getto*, or foundry, the small quarter in Venice where from 1516 onwards Venetian Jews were ordered to live. Christian dogma conventionally blamed the Jewish people for the death of Christ, and related prejudices and superstitions grew up around diasporic Jewish communities. They were often persecuted, subject to murderous pogroms or violent expulsion.

The history of the persecution of Jewish populations in Europe shapes the space of many Jewish cemeteries. Brady Street, for instance, is elevated above ground level in some places because the small space was soon full, but no more ground was granted. Against religious custom, another layer of soil was layered on top for double burials, and there are still some 'double' headstones placed back-to-back to mark the two burials below.

Dramatic heapings of stones are characteristic of one the most famous Jewish cemeteries in Europe, the Old Jewish Cemetery in Prague. This tiny space has graves dating from 1437 to its eventual closure in 1787. Since Jews were only allowed to live in demarcated spaces in cities across Europe, and forbidden from burying their dead outside these ghettos, graveyards like that in Prague had to keep piling up soil, creating a wild and wayward terrain with over 12,000 grave markers clustered in the tight space. It is thought that over 100,000 bodies were buried here before its closure along with all other inner-city cemeteries. Prague's New Jewish Cemetery was established in 1890, on a much larger parcel of land.

above: Headstones at the Old Jewish Cemetery in Prague.

opposite: The Wailing Wall at the Old Jewish Cemetery in Remuh, Krakow, Poland.

The Old Jewish Cemetery in Prague is picturesque, but only because of this history of ghettoization. Where so many Jewish cemeteries were deliberately smashed up and erased during the Second World War, it is said that the Nazis wanted to maintain Prague's Jewish quarter, including the cemetery, for a proposed museum of 'Extinct Races'. The genocidal elimination of Jewish people and culture was central to National Socialist ideology in the 1930s and 1940s, culminating in the construction of a vast network of prison camps first to 'concentrate' and then to systematically murder them. The treatment of the bodies of the dead – dumped in mass graves or reduced to ashes – was the final, intentional violation of Jewish custom. In the places from which Jewish populations were eliminated, their cemeteries were also destroyed.

In Poland, many Jewish cemeteries were targeted to be erased. Under Nazi occupation, headstones were smashed and the fragments used to pave roads or ground up as rubble for the foundations of new houses in deliberate acts of erasure. In some places these broken fragments have been recovered to create new kinds of memorials. At the Old Jewish Cemetery in Remuh in Krakow – one of the oldest Jewish cemeteries in Poland, established in the 1530s – headstones were torn up, reduced to rubble or bulldozed underground. Over a decade after the war, a cache of over 700 stones was uncovered and used to create a mosaic wall as an emblem of the surviving shards of a shattered community. In the New Cemetery, established in 1800, a monument to the memory of murdered Jews has been built from recovered headstones. Areas of systematic vandalism of older graves still persist, its own eloquent reminder of the history of European anti-Semitism.

Elsewhere in Poland, the destruction of graveyards begun by the Nazis was completed by incoming Soviet and Communist Party forces. In Brest, on the border between Poland and Belarus, a Communist-era sports ground keeps revealing fragments of the Jewish gravestones below, with a large cache unearthed in 2014. Pieces have also been recovered in local building works, collected and displayed. There are ongoing attempts to reconstruct a small area of the graveyard as a memorial to a doubly erased Jewish community.

YAD VASHEM AND THE NATIONAL CEMETERIES, WEST JERUSALEM

The modern Jewish memorial and funerary complex on Mount Herzl faces the ancient Mount of Olives across the Old City of Jerusalem. Designed to resist a narrative of tragic victimhood, the National Civil and Military Cemeteries of Israel and the memorial complex of Yad Vashem bind the dead into a symbolic landscape of the national rebirth of *eretz Yisrael*, the land of Israel, after the establishment of the new state in 1948.

Modern Zionism is strongly associated with the Austro-Hungarian Jewish writer and activist Theodor Herzl. When he died in 1904, his will directed that he be buried in the family plot in Vienna, but reinterred once a homeland for the Jews had been established. In August 1949, he was reburied on the southern slopes of the heights overlooking

Jerusalem, a place renamed Mount Herzl. The remains of his immediate family, children and grandson were moved more recently, in the twenty-first century. His grave, now marked by a black granite stone, soon became a locus for the burial of other key figures, and after 1952 the area became the National Civil Cemetery. The memorial area for Great Leaders of the Nation includes many former presidents and prime ministers.

On the northern slopes of Mount Herzl, the National Military Cemetery is the place where soldiers who have died in the service of the state of Israel are buried, the first burials taking place in 1949. It is protected by a low wall, and the graves initially followed a rigorously uniform style regardless of rank, much like those of Imperial War Graves. The markers sit low to the ground to encourage obeisance. The cemetery is approached through a long avenue of trees, the site carefully laid out by the landscape gardener Haim Gilandi, who wanted to create an environment of shelter and protection, with shadows above and ivy vines and rosemary bushes below. Graveyard keepers are employed to tend specific sections of the graves, and come to know individual mourners. Part of their task is to assure the bereaved of the continual remembrance of these national dead.

above: The Mount Herzl National Cemetery, a key element of Israeli national identity, Jerusalem.

below and opposite: The Hall of Names, dedicated to preserving the memory of the six million Jews killed in the Holocaust, Yad Vashem, Jerusalem.

At the top of Mount Herzl is the Yad Vashem memorial complex. The Hebrew name translates as 'a monument and a name', taken from a verse from Isaiah 'I will give in mine house and within my walls a place and a name ... I will give them an everlasting name, that shall not be cut off.' This complex houses an archive centre, several specific memorial sites and the Museum of the Holocaust. At its core, Yad Vashem works to name, recover what traces can be recovered and remember the six million Jews murdered in the Holocaust. There are memorials to children, to particular acts of resistance such as the Warsaw Ghetto uprising, and also monuments to 'Righteous Gentiles' who helped save Jewish lives. The historian James E. Young suggests that the site wrestles with 'how to remember the Holocaust without allowing it to constitute the centre of one's Jewish identity.' Thus Yom HaShoah, Israel's Holocaust Remembrance Day, is carefully placed into a sequence of the Hebrew Calendar, so that this day – dedicated as much to recalling Jewish resistance – is rapidly followed by national Independence Day. It is designed to create a narrative of national rebirth and renewal, the dead both remembered and recruited to affirm a national identity.

CHRISTIANITY

CHRISTIAN BURIALS: FROM CATACOMB TO CHURCHYARD

Under the Roman Empire's occupation of the territories of West Asia, Christianity moved from a small, persecuted religious sect of Judaism, centred on the martyrdom and bodily resurrection of Jesus Christ, to a recognized and eventually official religion – an epoch marked by the conversion of Emperor Constantine in 312. Christianity has always had an eschatological vision centred on burial and resurrection, the Bible being full of prophetic visions of tombs opened and the righteous returned bodily to life. The Old Testament describes the creation of man from 'the dust of the ground' (Genesis 2:7) and insists 'from dust you are and to dust you will return' (Genesis 3: 19).

THE CATACOMB OF CALLIXTUS

Along the Appian Way, where Romans built mausolea for the great and good, the early Christians buried their dead in catacombs. The most important of these was the Catacomb of Callixtus, enlarged from an early *hypogea* for members of wealthy Roman families who had been early converts to the church. Below ground, the community excavated a large system of galleries from the rock to place their honoured dead in simple white shrouds – a mark of the equality that death was supposed to bring. It became known as the 'Crypt of the Popes' because it originally contained the early church leaders from St Zephyrinus (d. 218) to St Eutychianus (d. 283) – although Pope Callixtus himself was buried in a catacomb elsewhere.

It is sometimes claimed that catacombs were used by Christians for clandestine acts of worship, a practice that closely tied the living to the dead – but this is not entirely clear. The Romans certainly allowed both Christian and Jewish burials to be carried out without suppression. However, the classical world had kept worship of the gods and the burial of the dead strictly demarcated. The Christian intermixing of the two was a broken taboo; indeed, commentators on the early church saw it as a rather repellent cult of dead bodies. In the fourth century, the Greek writer Eunapius of Sardis objected

opposite: Hans Holbein the Younger, 'The Abbess', from *The Dance of Death,* c. 1526.

97

that Christians 'collected the bones and skulls of criminals who had been put to death [and] … made them out to be gods.' In the same period, Emperor Julian (known as 'Julian the Apostate') objected that the Christians had 'filled the whole world with tombs and sepulchres'.

In a sign of how important the bodies of the dead were to Christians, many shrouded corpses from the catacombs were later shipped out to form the founding relics of new churches. One of the bodies to emerge from the Catacomb of Callixtus was that of St Cecilia, said to have been martyred for her faith in 177. After an executioner used up all three of his legal blows to her neck, she is said to have remained in a position of supplication and prayer, her neck split open, dying later holding out three fingers – her undying commitment to the Holy Trinity. In 822, Pope Pascal I was led to Cecilia's body in the catacombs after her appearance in a vision. He had her body reburied as the founding holy relic of the basilica of Santa Cecilia in Trastavere in Rome, which was being substantially rebuilt. Tradition has it that the church was built on the site of the Roman villa where Cecilia had been martyred. In 1599, 777 years later, an ancient Roman sarcophagus was found during a renovation of the church and opened: it supposedly held the body of St Cecilia, witnessed by many present as holding the same position of supplication and holding out the same three fingers. This moment was recorded in a famous baroque sculpture of her rediscovered body by Stefano Maderno.

St Cecilia is regarded as the first of the Incorruptibles, miraculous bodies in Catholic belief who are held to have resisted decay because of their purity and virtue. They are found days, weeks, months or years after their death to be still vibrant, lifelike, often emitting a heavenly scent – the odour of sanctity – or leaking fresh blood, tears or holy oil. These signs are a miraculous inversion of the inevitable stages of bodily death, a mark of the eternal life that is promised by the church evidenced in its holiest bodies. Incorruptibles remain part of Catholic belief: Joan Carroll Cruz's capsule biographies of those 'blessed with this unusual dispensation' end with the nun Maria Assunta Pallotta, who died of typhus in China in 1905, emitting a heavenly scent of violets and incense in the days after her death.

As a result of the recirculation of these early martyrs, the locations of many of the first catacombs in Rome were eventually lost. In 1578, vineyard workers came upon the opening of the Coemeterium Jordanorum along the Via Salaria out of Rome. This rediscovery produced a whole new wave of church martyr relics that, over the course of the seventeenth century,

above: The shrine of St
Konstantius, Rorschach,
Switzerland. The skeleton
of a presumed martyr from
the Roman catacombs
arrived in the town's
church, St Kolumban, in
the 1670s.

opposite: The statue
placed at the grave of St
Cecilia in the Catacombs
of Callixtus, Rome, second
to fourth century.

were sent across the Alps to shore up the waning influence of Catholicism in northern Europe. Recovered bodies were declared saintly by official Vatican excavators simply by virtue of having been buried in the catacombs. Remarkable displays of these weirdly bejewelled and decorated catacomb saints exist across Austria, Switzerland and Germany, skeletons that found a second life between the sixteenth and eighteenth centuries as ostentatiously displayed relics in the religious wars between Catholics and Protestants. The entrance to the Catacomb of Callixtus, meanwhile, was not relocated until 1854.

Holy bodies attracted others to be buried in proximity. Augustine of Hippo wrote up his reflections on this in his letter to Bishop Paulinus, 'On the Care to be Had for the Dead' (*c.* 422), concerning a woman who wanted her son to be buried in the basilica of St Felix in Nola, near Naples. Augustine wrestled with the Christian message that the soul transcended mere mortal remains, yet understood the power of memory and prayer that holy relics attracted. He acknowledged that tombs of martyrs could be associated with miracles, but was reluctant to ascribe these to the remains themselves: they must be thought of as *conduits* of divine intercession. This seemed to sanction proximate burial.

Burial inside churches became an established Christian practice, another decisive break with Greek, Roman and Judaic law. Christian practice brought the dead inside the core of the living city, the memorials growing up around the church and its relics another mark of the Christian imbrication of living and dead.

Despite the Christian insistence that death was the great leveller, social hierarchies among the dead were marked out inside the church by proximity to the altar, where any holy relics were typically built into the predella. Intramural burials were marked by ledger slabs and wall memorials; crypts allowed many more to be buried inside the foot-print of the church. Prominent figures, often church patrons, began to be marked by chest tombs with stone effigies or even separate side chapels dedicated to their memory. A complex calendrical sequence of remembrance developed, with masses – Offices for the Dead – said on the third, seventh and thirtieth day after burial, and then on the yearly anniversary. The wealthy could pay for this mass to be said long into the future, even in perpetuity. After the eleventh century, as the intermediary state of Purgatory became part of Christian orthodoxy, prayers could

below: Willem Vrelant, 'Office of the Dead', *The Llangattock Hours*, Bruges, *c.* 1450.

be sought on behalf of the deceased, the living working to atone for the sins of the dead.

Purgatory was envisaged as a transitional state where the burden of sin and thus the soul's final destination, Heaven or Hell, hung in the balance. The need for the living to redress this balance through prayer further bound them to their dead. Henry II, for instance, endowed dedicated altars and priests in perpetuity at Rouen Cathedral to pray for the souls of his dead sons. The financing of churches through their monopoly on these burial and post-burial offices for the dead was the subject of bitter satire in the medieval period, as in Chaucer's 'Pardoner's Tale' in the *Canterbury Tales*, and were later central to the schisms that sundered the Christian Church.

Outside the church, the churchyard was initially used for anonymous burials, usually in shrouds rather than coffins and without any permanent memorial marker; headstones only developed in the seventeenth century. There was a strict spatial organization in the Christian churchyard. The church, oriented east–west, usually had its main churchyard on the south side. Funeral processions paused with the body on the threshold of the consecrated ground, under the lychgate (literally the 'corpse gate'), where vigils were held by mourners until the time of the funeral. Social status might be marked by proximity to the church's main walls. A famous verse carved in stone for a Devonian gravedigger known as Bone Phillip in 1793 runs: 'Here lie I at the Chancel door, / Here lie I because I'm poor, / The forther in the more you'll pay, / Here lie I as warm as they.'

As church burial practice was consolidated, space became a perennial problem. Strict time limits for burial before removal are still observed in some European countries; in Italy, wall tombs, known colloquially as *forno*, 'ovens', are leased for a fixed period before removal of remains and re-use, a tradition that has been maintained and even modernized, as in the 'high-rise' tombs of the unfinished San Cataldo Cemetery in Modena. Exhumed bones are moved to charnel houses either in or at the edges of graveyards. These bone houses or ossuaries, some with elaborately patterned displays of human bones and sometimes even mummified corpses for effect, first emerged in the small graveyards of monastic communities, but became more common in churches from the twelfth century.

In a history of these charnel houses, Paul Koudounaris observes that 'human remains were part of the ritual landscape' across Europe for over 500 years. Some sites steadily accumulated thousands of bodies over time: the Michaelskapelle ossuary in Oppenheim, one of the

above: Woodcut depiction of purgatory, Germany, fifteenth century.

below: The scornful inscribed tablet commemorating Robert 'Bone' Phillip, St Edmund King and Martyr Church, Devon, England, 1793.

overleaf: Stereoscopic cards from the crypt of the Santa Maria della Concezione dei Cappuccini Catacombs, Rome, 1890s.

Corridor in the Cappuccino Catacombs, Rome, Italy.
Copyright 1897 by Underwood & Underwood.

1

1979 — Catacombs of the Capuchins, Rome, Italy.

Copyright 1896 by B. L. Singley.

2

5112. Corridor in the Cappuccino Catacombs, Rome,
Italy.

8763 Main Corridor of the Cappuccini Catacombs, Rome, Italy.

4

43-e Capuchin Catacombs, Palermo, Sicily Rome
Copyrighted 1899 by C. L. Wasson

5

3303—Capuchin Church, Cemetery of the Friars, Rome, Italy.

6

largest surviving in Germany, is estimated to contain over 20,000 skeletons. Later instances of ossuary displays were also ideological assertions. One widely visited ossuary belonged to the Confraternity of Orazione e Morte, who buried Rome's indigent poor. Another, the crypt of the Santa Maria della Concezione, was begun by the strict Capuchin order in 1631 and rapidly became a dark tourist attraction not just for the devout to think on death, but also for northern Protestant travellers who wanted to shiver at the Catholic obsession with relics and remains.

Traditionally, the north side of the Christian churchyard was reserved for problematic bodies: strangers, paupers, criminals, unbaptised infants, suicides. In Britain, supplemental burial sites were needed for non-Christians, dissidents, non-believers, executed criminals and other orders of the already-damned. The Irish countryside is dotted with hundreds of *cillíní*, burial sites for infants who had died before being baptised and were thus technically unable to be buried in consecrated ground and so denied salvation. Across North America, there were mandated separate graveyards

above: San Cataldo Cemetery, Modena, Italy, designed by Aldo Rossi, 1971.

below: Tommy Weir, *A cillin in Ballydawley,* County Sligo, 2018.

for Indigenous populations, for enslaved people, for African American populations and for those who died while incarcerated in madhouses or correctional facilities. Death was not the great leveller for these communities.

Some of these places of burial are only now being recovered and their shadow histories acknowledged. The African Burial Ground National Monument in downtown Manhattan became a national monument only in 1993. The Dozier School for Boys in Florida, where an abusive regime led to the deaths of African American youth sent there for 'reform' from 1900, had its own graveyard, but since 2012, forensic archaeologists have discovered undocumented mass graves in the grounds of the school. African American writers including Colson Whitehead in *The Nickel Boys* (2019) and Tananarive Due in *The Reformatory* (2023) have sought other ways to hold these disremembered lives in collective memory. In 2021, the confirmation of over 200 similarly unmarked burials on the site of Kamloops Indian Residential School, once the largest of a system of Canadian boarding schools for the forced assimilation of Indigenous children, became a national scandal. It is one of a number of such findings in Canada, which have prompted a wave of grief and memorialization led by the Indigenous communities affected by the residential school system.

DANSE MACABRE

There was a notable turn towards the physical details of death and decay in fourteenth-century Christian Europe. This is sometimes held to be a response to a sequence of famines, wars and the devastation wrought by the outbreak of the Black Death in 1348, which killed millions across the continent. In Christian literature, there was a renewed focus on the *ars moriendi*, instruction manuals on the art of the good death, and injunctions in prayer books and devotional Books of Hours to *think on death*. The penitent Spanish writer Miguel Mañara urged his readers to 'consider the vile worms that will eat your body, and how ugly and abominable you will be in your grave.' Ivory rosary beads (already made of bone) were shaped into death's head skulls, to aid the reflection on death in prayer; pious patrons were painted holding skulls.

In churchyards, a new element was added to charnel houses: the Danse Macabre, or the Dance of Death. The origin of the word 'macabre' is unclear, some relating it to St Macarius, who miraculously raised the dead, or to the Arabic *maqabir*, meaning graveyard. It was first recorded in a French poem that begins 'I did the dance of the Macabré/who leads all men to his dance/and directs them to the grave,/which is their final abode.' These renditions of the Danse Macabre became popular after 1424, when a mural

above: Memorial artwork for those buried in unmarked graves at the Kamloops Indian Residential School, Canada, on Tk'emlúps te Secwépemc First Nation land. This was one of the largest schools in the forced assimilation of indigenous children, established in 1893 and closed in 1979.

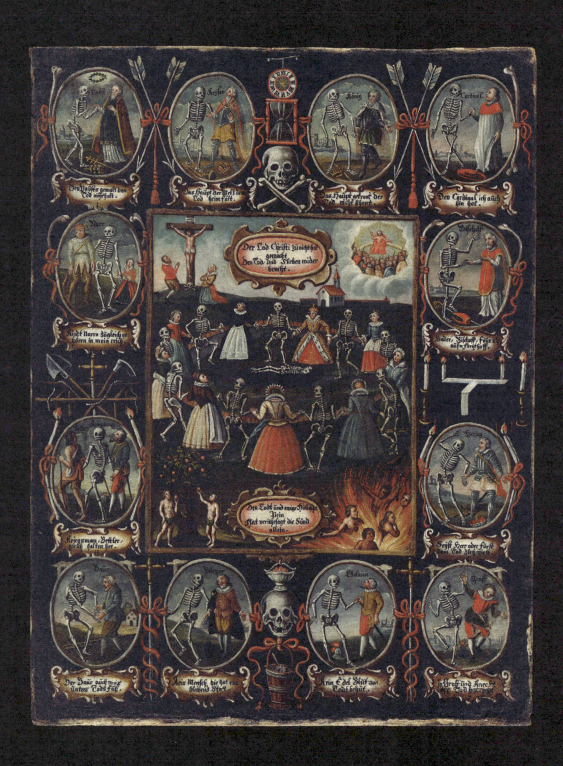

with a poem called 'The Dance of Death' was drawn in the arcades underneath the charnel house in the cemetery of the Church of the Holy Innocents in Paris. It echoed a fresco called *The Triumph of Death*, painted in around 1340 along the inner walls of the Camposanto cemetery in Pisa, with phantasmagorical scenes of the fates of the saved and the damned after death. The mural in Paris depicted the skeletal personification of Death taking up a merry jig with a succession of people representing every aspect of society, from emperors and kings to the lowliest peasants, none of whom could escape his clutches.

The English monk and poet John Lydgate likely visited the Church of the Holy Innocents in 1426, when he worked on a free English translation of the poem. A version of his Danse Macabre was added to the cloister walls of the Pardon Churchyard in the grounds of the Old St Paul's in London in 1430, recalled in John Stow's *Survey of London* (1598): 'About this Cloyster was artificially and richly painted, the dance of Machabray, or dance of death, commonly called the dance of Pauls.' That it was known as the 'dance of Pauls' suggests how commonly the image was copied in other churches and churchyards. Early printed book culture also embraced the Dance of Death, heavily illustrated with dramatic woodcuts. Hans Holbein published his *Dance of Death* in 1538, and Lydgate's poem was first published in illustrated book form in 1554.

For Stow, the Pardon Churchyard's Dance of Death was only a memory, because it had been pulled down in 1549 as part of the English king Henry VIII's move against the power and wealth

above: Buffalmacco, *The Triumph of Death*, Camposanto, Pisa, Italy, 1336–41. Postcard, 1902.

below: Hans Holbein the Younger, 'The Noblewoman' and 'The Shop-Keeper', from *The Dance of Death*, c. 1526.

opposite: *The Dance of Death*, where the central dance is surrounded by death's encounters with all, from aristocrats to the lowliest children and fools. Germany, seventeenth century.

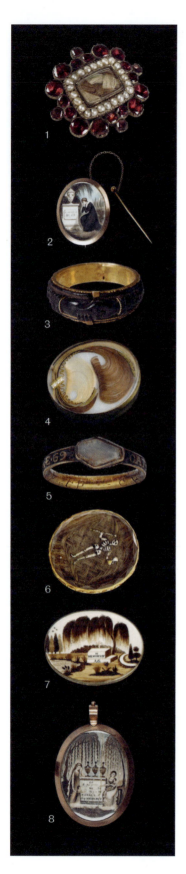

of the Roman church, dissolving the monasteries through the 1530s and 1540s and redistributing their lands and money to his aristocratic supporters. Theological justification came from the growing Protestant movement in northern Europe and from Reformation figures such as Martin Luther and John Calvin, who took particular aim at the cult of saints and 'popish' superstitions about the power of holy relics, which they regarded as dangerous forms of idolatry. This schism in the Christian Church is clearly marked out in the divergence of death and burial practices. Only two ossuaries survived in England – at St Leonard's in Hythe and Holy Trinity in Rothwell – and these mainly by accident.

THE COUNTRY CHURCHYARD

In the eighteenth century, the classical revival began to secure the familiar shape of the modern Christian churchyard. Trench graves were marked with headstones, a revival of the Greek or Roman stele, with stone curbs marking out the plots to avoid intercutting. The Christian cross was fixed in stone, rather than the more temporary wood. A lot of stone funerary architecture borrowed from classical sources but was a neoclassical invention: the Greek temple in miniature, the Roman cinerary urn (sometimes draped or veiled), the laurel wreath, the scroll, the pedestal, the broken Greek or Roman column to symbolize a life cut off in its prime. These conventionalized emblems fuse ideas of modern Christian restraint with classical stoicism: a restricted sculptural language that contains grief inside a strict semiotics. As undertaking emerged as a profession in eighteenth-century England, the industry was soon producing pattern books for these conventional grave-markers. Concurrently, a whole 'black stuff' industry of mourning silks and jewellery in jet sprang up.

During the nineteenth-century evangelical revival, grave markers were increasingly policed to ensure they communicated appropriate Christian values; wayward pagan influences were to be avoided. But echoes nonetheless arrived from beyond the Christian and Hellenistic traditions. Obelisks became particularly popular in the wave of Egyptomania that came after Napoleon's defeat by the British in Egypt in 1802. Models for grand mausolea or family tombs were familiar from Roman culture, but there was also an infusion of influence from India, where the Mughals had for centuries built large family mausolea. Rival British and Dutch trader communities had copied these structures in the seventeenth century, most

opposite: Mourning jewellery
(1) Nineteenth-century
brooch containing the hair of
the deceased. (2) Memorial
family brooch, 1796. (3) Fede
mourning ring (the name
derives from the Italian
mani in fede, 'hands clasped
in faith'). (4) Mourning
brooch with human hair,
eighteenth or nineteenth
century. (5) Mourning ring
with human hair, 1733.
(6) Mourning brooch with
a skeleton and human hair,
nineteenth century.
(7) Brooch with graveyard
scene, nineteenth century.
(8) Miniature of grave scene
with woven hair on the
reverse, *c.* 1800.

dramatically in the colonial graveyards in Surat. The writer and architect Sir John Vanbrugh, who saw these tombs during his own brief career as a trader, brought the idea back to England for his aristocratic clients.

Another major neoclassical influence on burial was the ideal of the rural churchyard or garden, which evoked Elysian fields or Arcadian paradise ('paradise' derives from the Persian word for garden). Eighteenth-century landscape designers placed memorial structures in idealized rural settings, and memorial gardens with elaborate temples and tombs (real or fake) became common in the landscaped estates of the British and French aristocracy. Parc Monceau in Paris was laid out at the height of this fashion in the 1770s as a 'bois des tombeaux' (woodland with tombs), complete with fanciful pyramids and fake grave markers that can still be found among the foliage there today.

These picturesque deathscapes fed directly into one of the most famous poems in the English language, Thomas Gray's 'Elegy Written in a Country Churchyard' (1751). The poem commemorates the churchyard of St Giles in Stoke Poges, a once-rural village church now swallowed up by the conurbations west of London. Gray used the neoclassical Penseroso figure to reflect on Death the Leveller in a solitary rural setting, rather than staging the stark physiological confrontation with Death typical of the medieval period.

This meditative poem is often considered the culmination of the so-called 'Graveyard School' of poetry. Its earliest expression came in 1728, when David Mallet published *The Excursion*. This flight through a 'blasted Heath, a Place of Tombs' prompted others, including Robert Blair's 'The Grave' (1743), which went through fifty editions by the end of the century. Even more successful was Edward Young's poem in nine books, *The Complaint; or Night Thoughts on Life, Death and Immortality* (1742–45), which was widely admired, translated and excerpted across Europe, with an enduring influence on the melancholic iconoclasts of French and German Romanticism. The favoured episode was the burial of Narcissa, a melodramatic account of the death and burial of Young's teenage daughter-in-law in Catholic France. The Protestant Youngs were horrified to be 'denied a grave' by the Roman Catholic authorities (laws restricting Protestant rites for burial were only revoked in 1787), and the poem confesses: 'With pious sacrilege a grave I stole; With impious piety that grave I wrong'd …'. Hints

above: Grand tombs of English
settlers in Surat, Gujarat, in
imitation of Mughal mausolea.
Photograph, *c.* 1855–62.

below: Egyptian pyramid in
picturesque miniature, Parc
Monceau, Paris, 1778.

(14)

And when blind man pronounc'd thy bliſs compleat!
And on a Foreign Shore! Where Strangers wept!
Strangers to Thee, and more ſurpriſing ſtill,
Strangers to Kindneſs, wept : Their eyes let fall
Inhuman Tears ; ſtrange tears! that trickled down
From marble Hearts! obdurate Tenderneſs!
A Tenderneſs that call'd them more ſevere,
In Spight of Nature's ſoft Perſuaſion Steel'd ;
While *Nature* melted, *Superſtition* rav'd ;
That, mourn'd the Dead ; and *This* deny'd a Grave.

Their Sighs inceſt ; Sighs foreign to the Will!
Their Will the *Tyger* ſuckt, outrag'd the Storm :
For oh! the curſt Ungodlineſs of Zeal!
While *ſinful Fleſh* relented, *Spirit* nurſt
In blind *Infallibility's* embrace,
The *Sainted Spirit* petrify'd the breaſt :
Deny'd the Charity of Duſt, to ſpread
O'er Duſt! a charity their Dogs enjoy.

What

(22)

Reaſon, the Sun that gives them Birth, the ſame
In either Clime, tho' more illuſtrious *There*.
Theſe choicely cull'd, and elegantly rang'd,
Shall form a Garland for *Narciſſa's* Tomb ;
And, peradventure, of no fading Flowers.
Say on what Themes ſhall puzzled Choice deſcend?
" Th' Importance of Contemplating the Tomb ;
" *Why* Men decline it ; *Suicide's* foul Birth ;
" The various *Kinds* of Grief ; the *Faults* of *Age* ;
" And *Death's* dread Character——invite my Song.
Firſt, be th' Importance of our End ſurvey'd.
Friends council quick Diſmiſſion of our Grief ;
Miſtaken Kindneſs! our Hearts heal too ſoon.
Are *They* more kind than *He*, who ſtruck the Blow?
Who bid it do his Errand in our Hearts,
And baniſh Peace, till nobler Gueſts arrive,
And bring it back, a true, and endleſs Peace?
Calamities are *Friends* : As glaring *Day*
Of theſe unnumbred Luſtres robs our Sight ;
Proſperity puts out unnumber'd Thoughts
Of Import high, and Light divine to Man.

of grave-robbing led to fantastical accounts of a secret dash with the dead body from Lyon to a grave in Montpellier. The rumours were not true, but the Youngists, as Young's followers were called, erected a memorial in Montpellier's Jardin des Plantes anyway.

Gray's poem seems to bevel the sharp edges off this lurid imagination. Critics have suggested that this was a deliberate act of displacement: the diffident poet had just before attended the trials of the last Scottish Stuart rebels, one of the final, doomed attempts to restore a Catholic to the throne of England. Gray left London in disgust before the public executions were carried out. The judgment ordered: 'you must be hanged by the neck, but not till you are dead; for you must be cut down alive; then your bowels must be taken out, and burnt before your face; then your heads must be severed from your bodies, and your bodies must be divided into quarters; and these must be at the King's disposal.' The pastoral scene in Stoke Poges is the dialectical opposite of this grizzly exercise of sovereign power over life and death taking place in London.

The 'Elegy' was published in an era corresponding to the emergence of the European Enlightenment, a movement associated with a new legitimacy given to scientific knowledge and sometimes aggressive dismissal of superstitious belief and the clerical authority of the Christian Church. European modernity produced a whole series of crises that would challenge the pastoral scene of the churchyard described by Gray's poem, yet Christianity has remained one of the key ritual frameworks in Europe to manage the transition from life to death.

opposite: William Blake, for an edition of Edward Young, *Night Thoughts*, 1795–97. The upper page is from 'Night Third', which describes the events concerning the illicit exhumation and reburial of the girl Narcissa, who was denied burial by the Catholic Church. The lower page shows Narcissa's tomb visited by the poet.

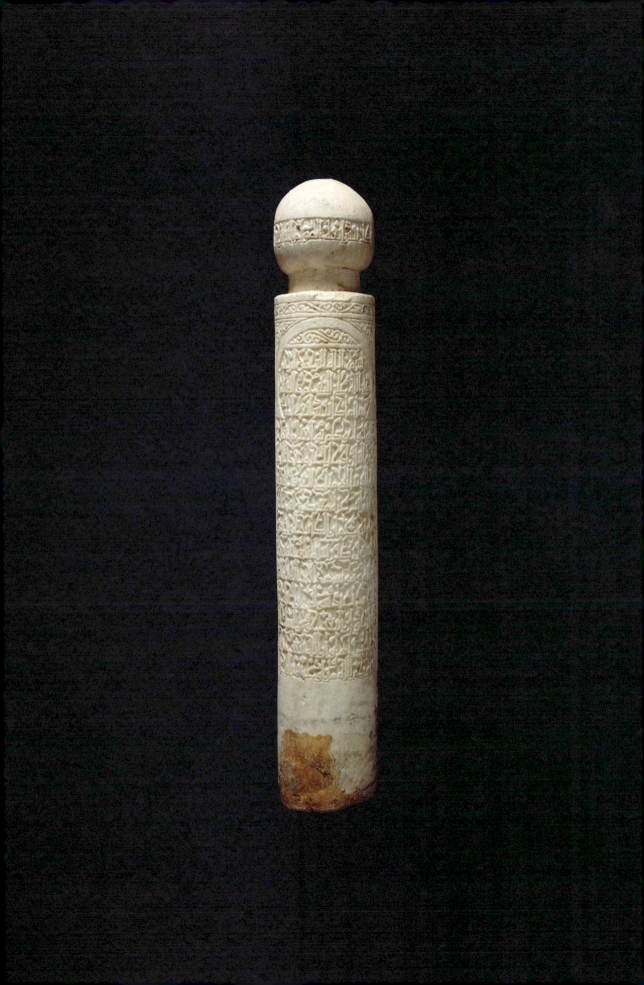

ISLAM

Islam was founded by the Prophet Muhammad, who was born in Mecca in about 570 into an Arabia of cultic and local polytheistic beliefs. The Prophet affirmed one true God and received a series of divine revelations from the Angel Gabriel, which were written down after his death in 632 in Medina in the 114 *suras* that form the Qur'an. Muhammad saw himself in a line of prophets coming down through Abraham, Moses, John the Baptist and Jesus, but with a truer grasp of the teachings of Allah than either Judaism or Christianity. Importantly, Allah is a unity; Muhammad rejected the Christian understanding of Jesus as Son of God.

After Muhammad's death, splits began over who should be appointed the next caliph, the spiritual and political leader of the faith. The Prophet's son-in-law, Ali, was the closest male relation (he had married the Prophet's daughter, Fatima), but the first three caliphs came instead from Muhammad's trusted group of Companions. This is the origin of the split between Sunni Islam, the larger 'orthodox' group, and Shia Islam, which followed the bloodline of Muhammad's descendants for its appointed religious leaders. In the seventh century, struggles over religious leadership were bound up with a rapidly expanding empire or caliphate. The Sunni majority extended over much of the terrain of the Islamic empire, with Shia groupings consolidated mainly in Persia, in what is now Iran, but with pockets across the whole region.

BURIAL CUSTOMS

The teachings of the Prophet Muhammad insist on simplicity and speed in funerary practices. In expectation of resurrection, bodies must be buried, preferably in cemeteries of fellow believers and if possible before sundown of the day of death, to minimize the contact with the dead. Hastening the burial is logical in hot climates, but it has created

opposite: Islamic tombstone, Tunisia, eleventh century.

ثم أعقب المؤلف رحمه الله ترجمة الأسماء بترجمة صفة الروضة المباركة والقبر والمقدسة موافقا في الأوقات والمشايخ تاج الدين بن بقائها فإنه عقد في كتابه الفجر المنير بابا في وصفة القبور المقدسة ومن أراد ذلك أن يبرز في المثال لمن لم يكن من زيارة الروضة وليشاهده ويزداد فيه حبا وشوقا وقد استنبأنا بأمثال النعل الشريف من النعل المنفة وجعلها له من أجلّ الكرام والأحترام ما لا يوصف كراماته خواصا وشوقا وقد جرت بركات به أشعار كثيرة أتقوا في صوره ورذوه بالأسانيد وقد قال القائل إذا ما النشوق قلتني إليها ولو أظفر تبطئو نورها نقشت مثالها في الكفت فتنا وقلت لناظري قصر عليها ولا تنبر مذ كذ وذا الكتاب في ثلاثة مواضع أولها وربعة وفي الأخير ذكر في قبره صلى الله عليه وسلم وقبر صاحبيه رضى الله عنهما ولم في ذا ذا الكتاب يشتمل على جملة من وصفها هرة صلى الله عليه وسلم وباطنه وسيرته وأحواله ومعجزة وثناء الله وهذا ما قد تعلق بذلك وقد ورّح بعض المؤمنين في السير وكيفيتهم وجعلوا مجامعتهم بذلك وقد ذكر بعض من تنكم على الأيام كما درى كيفية الرتبة بها الله لا إله الا الله محمد رسول الله فلينتصر في عينته ذاته الكريمة بشرية من وجود في ثيابه ومراعاة لحقيقة بشريته وتبعية ثيابه لكمال المعجزة يعني لينطبع صوره صلى الله عليه وسلم وجوانبه وثياب للفنع ما لا لغايتكن به من الاستفادة من أساده ولا قنا سمن أنواره صلى الله عليه وسلم فال فان لم يبرز ويخص صوره ورته وفيه وكان جا به سبحه فيء قبره المبارك بشير إليه ميا ذكره فإن القلب من اشتغله بما تغيره في الوقت الى هكلامه ويحتاج الي تصوير الروضه المشرفة والقبو والمقدسة لبعرف صوره وجوانبها ويختص بها عينيه من لم يعرف فهم من المصلين عليه وهذا الكتاب يين كان حاله ما ذكره وهو مثاله وجمهور درهم وقد كثرت ثنا رتب في تأليف بعض المشارقة يقول عليها التي ينبغي أن يرسل الخلال أن كنا من المريدين الركبة ويرقم ويجعله بضرب عينيه فإذا صام قارئ وهذا الكتاب بلو وصنة صوره حسنة بالوان حسنة حضوصا بالذهب فهو من غني انه والله أعلم

وهذا صفة الروضة أمثالها والروضة في اللغة أرض ذات كان مطمئن ذات أشجار ورياض وميا فاستعمرت المروضة فانا الانوار والرحمة والبركة وكثير الافضال بها مع المحسن والنشره والاتباج ويحتمل أنه يعنى بصفة القبور في الروضة ونسبة بعضها مروضة وهوانا ا هو من اشكال الموجود في أنس المقدمة العتيقة وصفة الروضة على ما هى عليه الأن بعد انشائها عام ستة وثمانون على ما ذكر بعض المشارقين حما أسا اخبره به الشيخ أبو مركا ن ابو محمد بن بركا بالخطاب بغي والده وقد حضرنا انشاءها بها لم يكن لاعقود الشريفة ليس بها علامة سوى ارتفاع الأرض فيها بعل بعض الرضاع انشا بها في ذا الرضاع عثلاثة الاسانيد مربعة ولا محمسة مطمئنسة بالبنيا من أسفل ومن فوق ولوجين لهما طاقة في أعلاها يخرج منها النور كهذه ترى على القبة المذكورة قبة اخرى اعظم من ذه القبة الى التجنيس وترى قبة طباق لابغ على القبة الأولى

التي الى الاساس وهى الاساس منشا بمجارة سود ملبس بالرخام الابيض غير الرخامة التي فيها المسمار لقصى فإنها حمرا جدا والطبقة الثانية من لاجر والطبقة الثالثة من العود بينها في فيها ربط الكسوة وكست بخمسة منها وهى مربعة على اركان اربعة وسواء وعشرة غير الروضة الصغيرة وارضها مفروش بالرخام غير الموضع الذي يذكر في عيسى عليه السلام في الشهوة وهو معروف عند الخدام ومن شاهد هذا ذلك واها اربعة ابواب القبلية وهو وقبلة المسيح في شباك النجاس يشع نزول الشاداش ليس لا وبابا لو وقد بقيفة لو ليلة وفي المصابح وباب فاطمة رضى الله عنها ليلة والجراحت كل ليلة وفي ليلة الجمعة وفضله صلى الله عليه وسلم والشفاء لسبه المواجهة لراسه صلى الله عليه وسلم وغيره من التقييد فيصبحه أكثر من الحجرة في وبين تارة وبتارة في وفى الجمعة ايسا حتى الخيرا المشبة

نقول هذه ه من ايما ع فى أعلى مرجمه فى احس الستر المشبة

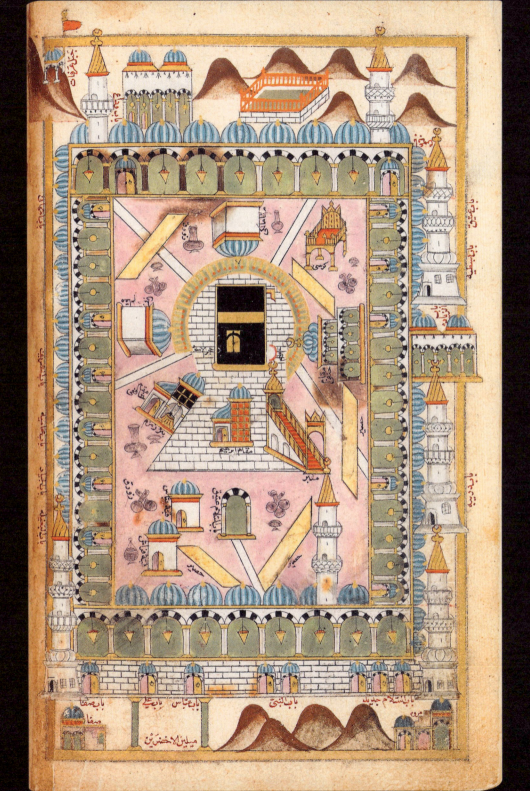

logistical problems for the Muslim diaspora and those living through conflict, if relatives want to bury in a particular family plot or a holy ground such as Wadi Al-Salam. The Syrian writer Khaled Khalifa's black comedy *Death is Hard Work* (2019) follows a grim attempt to transport a body back to the family plot, a journey that extends for days across the fractured and deadly terrain of Syria's civil war.

The dead body is washed and shrouded, often by professionals whose abject status – a common cultural unease – is evoked in Sinan Antoon's grief-stricken novel set during the Iraq War, *The Corpse Washer* (2013). In a simple shroud, preferably plain white, the body is laid with the head facing east, in the direction of Mecca. The funeral ceremony and prayers are held at the mosque, with minimal ritual at the graveside and strict rules about over-emotional displays of grief. Ostentation in grave markers is not encouraged, and as in Judaism, representational funerary architecture is forbidden. There is a short period of formal mourning and withdrawal from public life for the immediate family. Muhammad initially forbade visiting graves, particularly those of non-believers, and said 'the most beautiful tomb is the one that vanishes from the face of the Earth.' There was early suspicion of annual commemorations or pilgrimages to anywhere other than Mecca (the Prophet's birthplace), Medina or Jerusalem. Arabic superstitions – not necessarily specific to Islam – about *ghul*s that begin to menace those who spend too long moping around in graveyards is suggestive of this belief in affirmation of life, rather than melancholic tarrying with the dead.

Modesty and simplicity are at the core of these directions for burial, but the history of Islamic culture across millennia also includes some of the most magnificent and elaborate funerary architecture ever built. Many were built principally in the service of political power rather than in the name of strict religious observance, although early, significant mausoleum complexes were built by followers of Shia Islam in commemoration of Muhammad's descendants, teachers and martyrs.

The history of Shia Islam is marked by moments of massacre and martyrdom, and it frequently commemorates its special dead – its lost leaders, saints and venerated imams (religious teachers). Mosques with complexes of caravanserai and religious schools attached, and even whole cities, were sometimes built around these mausolea. A tradition of pilgrimage to these Shia holy sites has developed, among them the largest cemetery in the world, the Wadi Al-Salam.

The Wadi Al-Salam (Valley of Peace) is located in the region of ancient Mesopotamia, just a few miles from the ruins of Babylon. It has been in continuous use for Muslim burial since the eighth century. The six million occupants of the necropolis make it far more densely populated than the living city to which it is attached, Najaf, which lies ninety-nine miles south of the capital of Iraq, Baghdad.

The cemetery is located on land traditionally understood to have been purchased by Abraham, and it is where the fourth Islamic caliph, Ali Ibn Abi Tabib, the son-in-law of the Prophet Muhammad, is believed to have been buried after his assassination in 661. His place of burial was marked and the city founded in 791, with the Old City building up

right: 'The Coffin of Imam 'Ali', depicting the first Shia imam escorting his own body on the back of a camel as his sons look on. Folio from a *Falnama* (*The Book of Omens*), c. 1550.

around his shrine. The land around his grave is considered holy land, and became both a desirable burial place and a place of pilgrimage for the followers of the 'Party of Ali', the Shia sect of Islam. This is where the souls of true believers will gather and be resurrected to ascend to heaven in the apocalyptic end days of revelation shared across the Abrahamic religions.

Many prophets and religious leaders have been buried in Wadi Al-Salam, some in grand tombs, but most people are buried in simple shrouds in the earth, their resting place marked by small chest tombs built from baked clay and plaster, some with domes to announce their status. The older tombs cluster close to the mosque and tomb of Ali, where funerals still take place; some crypt spaces in this area share as many as fifty bodies. Bodies are transported from all over the world to be buried in this holy site.

Since the American-led invasion of Iraq in 2003 and the toppling of the dictator Saddam Hussein, who suppressed the Shia minority in Iraq, the shrine has returned as a place of pilgrimage. But in a turbulent era of invasion, civil war and brutal sectarian violence, the cemetery around it has also been considerably expanded by tens of thousands of burials each year. The cemetery itself has been entangled in those wars, with sections of it bulldozed to prevent its use by Islamic State militants in 2014, and illicit burials crammed into the winding routes through the graves by desperate families.

below: Wadi Al-Salam Cemetery, built around the shrine of Ali, Najaf, Iraq.

opposite top: Worshippers visit the tombs of relatives on the first day of Eid al-Fitr, marking the end of Ramadan, Wadi Al-Salam Cemetery, Iraq.

opposite bottom: Fatimid Cemetery, Aswan, Egypt.

Najaf is an island of minority Shia belief surrounded by a Sunni majority, but through centuries of imperial rule from afar (from Damascus, Baghdad, Istanbul and London, under the British colonial mandate that created Iraq in 1920), the shrine of Ali and the necropolis attached to it have remained the third holiest site in Islam, after Mecca and Medina.

DYNASTIC FUNERARY HISTORY

The early Umayyad caliphate (661–750), the second established after the death of Muhammad, focused on building mosques and extending the territory of their rule. The Dome of the Rock, the central shrine of the Al-Aqsa Mosque complex in Jerusalem, was constructed under the fifth Umayyad caliph, Abd al-Malik. The Dome encloses the rock from which Muhammad is believed to have risen to heaven on his visionary Night Journey in 620; the Bab al-Rahma cemetery, with its earliest burials dating to 650, runs along the eastern wall of the compound. The slightly later Great Mosque at Damascus, also built by the Umayyads on a site long used as a place of worship (a temple of Jupiter and a Christian cathedral had both already stood there), is believed to be the burial place of the head of Yahya ibn Zakariya (John the Baptist), an important prophet in both Islam and Christianity, making the shrine a place of dual pilgrimage. One seventh-century *hadith* locates the mosque in Damascus as the place where Jesus will return to Earth at the Second Coming. The mosque also contains the shrine of the Prophet Muhammad's grandson and martyr, Husayn ibn Ali, so is extremely important to the Shia.

The Abbasid Dynasty (750–1258) recentred their Islamic caliphate in the city of Baghdad and built extensively there, but it was the Shia Fatimid rulers, claiming direct lineal descent from Muhammad's daughter, who began to innovate with funerary architecture and grand mausolea during their reign in north Africa and beyond (909–1171). Beginning in Tunisia, they conquered Egypt and in the tenth century founded the city of Cairo amid the vast necropolises of Ancient Egypt. Perhaps the Egyptian landscape influenced their early cemeteries: the Fatimid Cemetery in Aswan was described by the

overleaf: (1) Stereoscopic photograph of Mameluke tombs, Cairo, *c*.1908. (2) Inscribed tombstone of Shaikh al-Husain ibn Abdallah ibn al-Hasan, buried in Yazd, Iran, 1110. (3) Certificate marking a visit to the Prophet's Mosque in Medina, *c*.1930s. (4) Mosque lamp bearing the name of its patron Amir Qawsun, Cairo, Egypt, *c*.1329–35. (5) Gravestone of the martyr Shaykh Muhammad ibn Abi Bakr, Nishapur, Iran, 1138. (6) Tombstone inscribed with Qur'anic verse and dedicated to a ship's captain from Gujarat, India, 1459. (7) Architectural plan of the twelfth-century Toghrol Tower from *Monuments Modernes de la Perse*, 1867. (8) Funeral scene from *Maqamat*, illuminated by Yahya Mahmud al-Wasiti in 1237. (9) Central piece of an 'Alam', a standard carried in Shia religious processions to commemorate the martyrdom of Husayn ibn Ali, who died in the Battle of Karbala in 680, India, late sixteenth century.

1

2

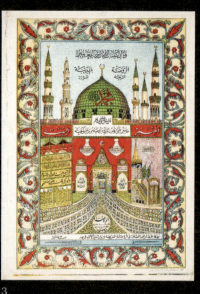

3

4

5

6

TOUR RESTAUREE

7

8

9

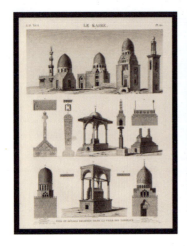

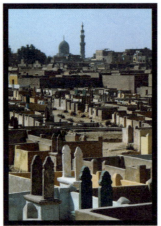

Orientalist scholar Edward Lane in 1820 as a picturesque ruin among rocky terrain, with 'several large sepulchral mosques.' Many of these baked brick and clay structures have not survived, their grave markers moved, destroyed or imperfectly preserved by nineteenth-century archaeologists. The Fatimids also took over the existing necropolis in Fustat, which became the centre of Cairo; some of the oldest Islamic structures in al-Qarafa necropolis have origins in the Fatimid era. The mausolea, headstones and memorial complexes in al-Qarafa trace the history of rule by the Abbasid and Fatimid dynasties, the Mamluks and Ottomans, all the way to the present day.

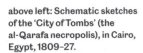

above left: Schematic sketches of the 'City of Tombs' (the al-Qarafa necropolis), in Cairo, Egypt, 1809–27.

above right: Tomb enclosures in al-Qarafa necropolis, Cairo.

Later sultans and governors, particularly during the era of Sunni Mamluk rule (1250–1517), developed walled complexes around their family mausolea that began to attach mosques, religious schools or *madrasas* and places for pilgrims to stay or study. The extent of these complexes perhaps makes it less surprising that populations of the living began to occupy the city of the dead. By the 1980s it was estimated that the population of 'tomb-dwellers' in al-Qarafa had reached over a hundred thousand, as poverty rose in the busy city. Some are the paid caretakers of *hawsh*, enclosures of family tombs, while others are long-term squatters. Meanwhile, the government of Cairo vies for space with its necropolitan other, bulldozing its historic tombs to build dwellings for the living.

From the Fatimid period on, dynasties and regional rulers had begun to fuse local architectural traditions with Islamic styles in their elaborate funerary complexes. The Seljuks and the Mamluks, in particular, elaborated some extraordinary syncretic tombs and memorials.

below: Ruin of the Mausoleum of Sultan Ahmad Sanjar, a Seljuk ruler of Khorasan, now Merv, Turkmenistan. The UNESCO World Heritage Site has since been rebuilt and restored. Photographed 1911.

During the Abbasid extension of empire, in what is now Iran, local governors were installed by the distant imperial centre and often ran semi-autonomous statelets. This gave space for the fusion of Islamic belief with Persian, Zoroastrian and other cultural traditions. In funerary architecture, the most striking impact was the giant brick towers built as mausolea to assert posthumous princely power, which relate visually to the Zoroastrian *dakhma*, or towers of silence, circular towers used for the ritual exposure of corpses.

The tomb tower built for Qabus ibn Wushgir, who died in 1012, is nearly 200 feet (*c.* 60 m) high: a hollow tower of tapering brick on a flanged circle or pointed-star pattern, topped with a dome pointing up to the heavens. Panels record the name of the amir who ordered the structure built in 1006, in the last years of his reign. It is a mathematical and engineering marvel, designed to be visible for miles, and it still stands, having survived the destruction of the surrounding city of Gurgan by Mongol invaders.

above: Gonbad-e Qabus, the tomb tower built for the ruler Qabus ibn Wushgir, who died in 1012. Iran, 1933.

The mausoleum contains no body, but local legend proclaims that the corpse may have been displayed in a glass coffin suspended from the roof, making Qabus the master of all he surveyed (one biographical entry calls him a poet who innovated in rhyming patterns, a devoted patron of the arts, but also 'a bloodthirsty tyrant'). It is more likely that the body was placed on a platform inside the tower, a customary marker of status also sometimes used in burials in the classical era. No traces of these internal structures remain, making all the tomb towers across the region empty graves. This mode of burial is neither wholly Islamic nor wholly Zoroastrian, but a product of both traditions.

Later in the tenth century, Seljuk sultans took up power in the region. Oghuz Turk invaders who had converted to Sunni Islam and carried influences in from the Steppes, their innovations included new styles of funerary architecture. The squat, octagonal twin mausolea at Kharraqan, built in 1067 and 1093, are much smaller than the Gonbad-e Qabus (though still a monumental 40 feet, or 12 metres, high). Each of the eight exterior walls is decorated with intricate

geometric designs effected by brick patterning in as many as seventy
different repeating designs, suggestive of expansive, infinite repetition. Each building also carries inscriptions from the Qur'an in
Kufic script. The twin tombs also survived for a millennium, but
were severely damaged by an earthquake in 2002.

THE AMIR TIMUR TOMB COMPLEX
(GUR-E-AMIR), SAMARKAND

Timur was a ferocious Turco-Mongol empire-builder and warrior who ruled
across territory that stretched from Türkiye to the fringes of China in the
fourteenth century. His reputation for exaggerated cruelty and slaughter was
stoked as far away as Britain, where Christopher Marlowe's play *Tamberlaine*
was first performed in London in 1587. The name Tamberlaine was a corruption of 'Timur the Lame' (he moved around on crutches). He, along with
other rulers such as Saladin, the Sunni leader who took back Jerusalem from
Christian crusaders in 1187, was demonized in Europe as a heathen, even
demonic invader, intent on the destruction of Christianity.

At Samarkand, now in Uzbekistan, Timur constructed a funerary complex initially intended for his grandson and heir, who had died suddenly in 1403. After his death in Otrar in 1405 meant that he could not be returned to his prepared tomb in time, Timur himself was also buried at Gur-e-Amir (which means 'Tomb of the Ruler'). The Samarkand complex eventually contained his sons, grandsons and his spiritual advisor, Sayyid Baraka, said to be a descendant of the Prophet Muhammad. It was completed by another of Timur's grandsons, Ulugh Beg, in 1434. It is surrounded by tombs built in later centuries, including the Ruhabad Mausoleum (which contains a holy relic of a strand of the Prophet's hair) and the Aksaray Mausoleum, part of a grand necropolis.

An entrance gate of intricately carved brick work and mosaics, opening onto a courtyard in front of the mausoleum itself, is all that survives of the Timur complex, which once had a madrasa and other buildings attached. The octagonal mausoleum building itself is framed by tall, symmetrical columns and is topped by a single-ribbed azure dome, the sixty-four ribs supposedly equating to the age at which Muhammad died. The exterior is decorated with blue and white tiles of intricate design, the interior with onyx slabs, painted plaster and high-relief cartouches. The inner room of the mausoleum has ornate carved headstones that indicate the location of the tombs of the dynasty that lie directly below, in the crypt.

Famously, Timur's tomb is topped by a block of jade, a trophy ostensibly taken from a Chinese emperor's palace and added later by Ulugh Beg. It is supposedly the largest single block of jade ever discovered. This was a mark of the ambitions of the Timurid Dynasty in East Asia: jade was associated with immortality, power and protection in Chinese burial practices at the time. Later, in 1740, long after Samarkand had lost its place on the Silk Road from China and fallen into ruin and neglect, Nader Shah, a ruler of the Iranian Afsharid Empire who had modelled himself on Timur, tried to move the jade and cracked the block. Considered a sign of ill-omen, it was returned to its proper place.

above: The block of jade that sits atop the tomb of Timur.

The power allegedly exercised by Timur's tomb extends into the twentieth century. In 1941, a team led by the Soviet scientist Mikhail Mikhaylovich Gerasimov opened Timur's grave and, remarkably, was able to confirm from the skeleton that it was likely his body. The tomb has the inscription in Arabic: 'When I rise from the dead, the whole world will shake', and during the Soviet exhumation, a curse was rumoured to have been found – the warning against disturbing the grave already a typical flourish of 'mummy curse' stories. Just two days after the exhumation, it is said, the Nazis began their invasion of the Soviet Union; only once Timur's remains were reburied with proper Islamic rites in 1942 was the siege of Stalingrad finally ended. Since 1991 and the formal end of the Soviet Union, Samarkand and Timur's tomb have been a locus of Uzbek national identity, and the site has been extensively restored.

The influence of the single-domed mausoleum, set in a symmetrically arranged formal setting, was extensive. The Mughals who moved into northern India drew upon precisely this design, and its echoes are evident in some of the most important large-scale mausolea built in India: Humayun's tomb, constructed in 1570 in Delhi, and the white marble Taj Mahal, built in Agra between 1631 and 1648.

MUGHAL MAUSOLEA:
HUMAYUN'S TOMB AND THE TAJ MAHAL

From 1526, the Mughal Dynasty moved into northern India and established an empire that secured the place of Islamic belief in South-East Asia. In 1570, a gigantic mausoleum for the second Mughal emperor, Humayun, and his dynasty was commissioned by his widow, Bega Begam. She was Persian-born and brought in architects and designers trained in Persia to create an influential design, the central domed mausoleum borrowed from Samarkand but placed in a *charbagh*, a garden in symmetrical quadrants divided by flowing channels of water. This is a Persian rendition of paradise and its four rivers,

above: Tomb of the Mughal ruler, Humayun, an influential instance of Mughal architecture, which took nine years to complete. Delhi, India, sixteenth century.

below: Humayun's tomb complex contains separate resting places for members of his family. Over 100 people were buried in the complex.

as described in the Qur'an, and it was the first time a formal garden like this had been seen in India. The central structure sits on a raised platform, so that it appears to float above the water and gardens.

The chosen site was near the burial place of the Islamic saint Nizamuddin Auliya, an important figure in the Sufi mystical tradition in Islam. Proximity to the saint's grave and the association that this built between dynastic political power and religious authority made this area an important necropolitan space for the establishment of Mughal rule in Delhi, and other tombs and memorial mosques were constructed nearby. Humayun's mausoleum became known as the 'dormitory of the Mughals', with well over a hundred family members buried at the site.

The design clearly influenced the construction of the Taj Mahal in Agra, built sixty years later by the Mughal emperor Shah Jahan for his favourite wife, Mumtaz Mahal. The perfectly symmetrical, single-domed mausoleum, built from almost uncannily white marble, sits in another paradise garden, this time at the far end of the vista of symmetrical gardens and waterways. The whole central structure is again raised on a platform, framed by four tall corner minarets. At the core of the building is the central chamber holding raised marble chest

tombs for Mumtaz Mahal and Shah Jahan. As at Samarkand, these monuments locate the burials in the crypt beneath. Other tombs of the dynastic family are situated in rooms situated at the four corners of the chamber. The building is often held to be the finest surviving example of Indo-Islamic sepulchral architecture.

Status communicated through grand mausolea – if on a considerably smaller scale – became established practice among local rulers, wealthy traders and administrators in places like Lahore under the Mughal Empire and the Sikh Empire. In the eighteenth and nineteenth centuries, during the periods of indirect rule by the British East India Company and direct rule by the British Empire, British and other European traders borrowed the architectural language of the mausoleum for their own assertion of status, and began to import this style back to family vaults in the new garden cemeteries that were emerging in Victorian Britain. Meanwhile, for Muslims in Victorian and Edwardian Britain, burial was frequently in pauper or dissenting grounds. A section dedicated to Muslim burial was opened in

above: The Taj Mahal, the mausoleum for Mumtaz Mahal, c. 1900.

Brookwood cemetery, or the London Necropolis, in 1854, the earliest of several multi-faith grounds at which formal Islamic rites could be conducted. Such occasions were rare enough to make the news; the funeral and burial of Michael Hall, a Muslim convert, in Liverpool Necropolis in 1891 made national newspapers.

Brookwood also has a number of Muslim war graves, twenty-seven of which were moved in 1969 from Woking Muslim War Cemetery on Horsell Common in Surrey. Begun in 1915 as a burial place for Muslim troops who had died fighting in France, it was built in the same 'pseudo-Mughal' style as the nearby Shah Jahan Mosque, established in 1889 and the first purpose-built mosque in Britain.

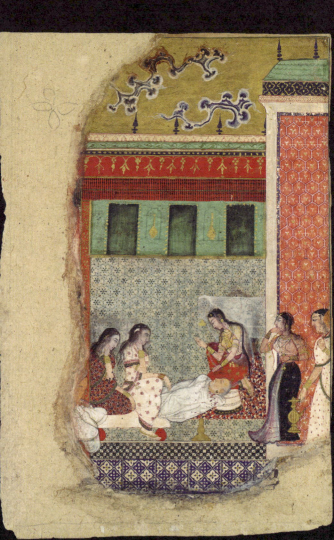

HINDUISM

Varanasi is the most sacred place in Hinduism, and a holy city for Buddhists and Jains. Locally named Banaras or known by its holy name, Kashi, the 'City of Light', it is one of the oldest continuously occupied cities in the world. Hindu religious texts suggest that it is where the god Vishnu created the cosmos, making it the place where time begins and ends, a site that exists in and out of the world. It is a *tirtha* – a crossing place between sacred and profane realms – and pilgrimages there trace the circumference of the city as well as the seven concentric circles that surround the centre, to emphasize the movement towards the holiest place. India's most sacred river, the Ganges, flows through the city, and on its banks are the famous *ghats* (steps). Manikarnika and Harishchandra *ghats* are the most important cremation grounds for Hindus in northern India.

opposite: The death of King Dasharatha, who died of grief after exiling his son, Rama, *c.* 1605. Rama becomes the major deity in Hinduism, as recorded in the epic, *The Ramayana*.

below: Varanasi, a key funerary location in northern India, where funeral pyres are lit and bodies released into the sacred river Ganges. Uttar Pradesh, India.

Many thousands of pilgrims come to immerse themselves in the holy water of the Ganges at Varanasi's *ghats*, in acts of atonement and purification. The sacred water is believed to multiply the remittance of sins many times over. Others make pilgrimages to Varanasi to prepare to die there, since to breathe one's last within the city boundaries brings one closer to immediate salvation. Hospices located near the cremation grounds aid these pilgrims in their last months or days. 'Varanasi is the Great Cremation Ground,' writes Gavin Flood, a scholar of Hinduism, 'which reflects the cremation ground which is the universe.'

Along an extended waterfront that contains many kinds of ritual space, the Manikarnika and Harishchandra *ghats* are dedicated entirely to funerals. The 'last sacrifice' of cremation at the end of life mirrors the birth of the world and the shaping of every child in the fire of the mother's womb, and so completes the cycle of birth, death and rebirth. Funerals are supposed to be conducted within a day of death, so time is always pressing. As a result, at

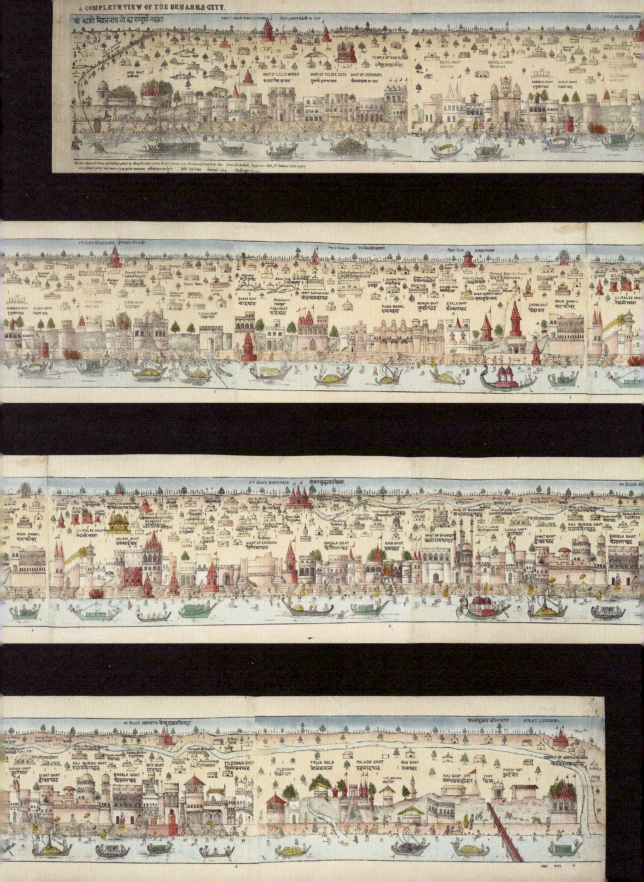

opposite: Panoramic scroll of the city of Benaras (Varanasi), showing the *ghats* along the Ganges riverbank where funerary rituals take place, 1901.

the funerary *ghats*, every stage of the funeral process is under way simultaneously. Funeral processions arrive, carrying the dead in shrouds on a bier, their groups led by musicians. Funeral priests negotiate the cost of the pyre and the supervision of the ceremony. Nearby, halfway through the ritual, the eldest son might be performing 'the rite of the skull', striking the head of the body being consumed by fire with a bamboo stick to finally separate and release the spirit

from its vessel. This is the true moment of death for the devout. Another group, still further along in the ceremony, might be breaking a pot filled with water from the river, a symbol of the now useless and corrupted material body being left behind. Other families might have returned after the funeral to submerge the ashes of the dead in the river, so that they can be carried north on the sacred current, merging with the vast, unceasing flow of spiritual life. Many people travel a long way to release ashes into the river in Varanasi.

Cremation is standard practice in Hindu belief, which is tied together by rituals of holy fire. But many people are not cremated, including very young children, some members of the lowest caste, ascetics or holy men who have already renounced the world and may be buried in a shrine by devotees, and those who have died suddenly or unpropitiously of diseases such as leprosy. Childless people, who may fear they are breaking a long line of ancestors or the cycle of birth and death, can also ritualistically stage their own funeral by burning an effigy, but cannot then be cremated upon their actual death. The bodies in these categories are buried, or their corpses are submerged or launched on floating biers in the Ganges.

The cliché about Varanasi is that it is a place where life and death chaotically intermingle: that children play and crowds bustle just feet away from the pyres that burn the dead. Death is intensely present, whether in the form of shrouded bodies being carried through the streets towards the river, or in the presence of Aghoris, a sect of ascetics who follow the god Shiva, who smear themselves with the ashes of the dead and make use of bodily remains, including consuming human flesh, inverting the frequent logic of dead bodies as pollutants to be avoided. Frequently exoticized and sensationalized in Indian and Euro-American media, Aghoris in fact surround themselves with death in order to better renounce the world.

above: The Burning Ghat, the Manikarnika, one of the holiest sites in Varanasi, c. 1890.

below: The Aghoris in Varanasi live in close proximity with the dead, smearing their bodies with cremation ash, fashioning skull cups and ritualistically eating the flesh of bodies post-mortem.

Hinduism has no single founder, sacred text or god. It emerges from a wealth of religious texts, stories, epic poems, laws, treatises and ritual practices that spread out of the Indus valley from about 2500 BCE onwards. The oldest texts are the sacred *Vedas*, which established the place of sacrificial fire and the tradition of relinquishing the material body into smoke and ashes on death, and also codified the caste system. Later additions include the codification of laws and customs in the *Dharamshastra*, philosophical reflections in the *Upanishads* ('secret teachings') and the allegorical stories of the *Mahabharata* and the *Ramayana*, both written down in around 400 BCE. The complex mythologies and genealogies of the gods were collected much later in the *Puranas*, which are important for the folk versions of Hinduism that always rub alongside stricter codifications.

Jainism is believed to have originated between the seventh and fifth century BCE, with austere rules and laws including a fundamental tenet of non-violence. Cremation is also standard in Jainism, but ashes are customarily collected and buried, rather than released into the river. Buddhism emerged in the same region of east India in the sixth century BCE, from Prince Siddhartha's rejection of certain beliefs enforced by the Brahmin (priestly) class. This created a palimpsest of texts and beliefs and a polytheistic culture that both Muslim and Christian invaders of India variously

denounced as 'primitive' or worse. Ideas of a Hindu identity were constructed in negative terms, to point to what Islam or Christianity were not. But Hinduism is now a faith professed by over one billion people on the planet, with many divergences in custom and belief. In India, meanwhile, Hindu nationalism has become a potent political force.

Funerary practice in Varanasi includes manuals for proper mortuary practice, but competing beliefs, contradictions and constant mutations make rules hard to fix. The anthropologist Jonathan Parry has outlined the following sequence, which begins at death. The death is announced on the same day and the body is visited by the extended family, with specific tasks divided between men and women. The women wash the body and wrap it in a white shroud – although many other brightly coloured shrouds and garlands can adorn the body for its journey through the streets. The face is exposed and smeared with *abir*, a red powder with ties to the god Krishna that is also used to mark the mourners. The men carry the bier towards the cremation ground, led by musicians and followed by the women. Certain ritual actions take place at points along the route, partly to propitiate the gods and partly to prevent lonely spirits from following the family home: malign spirits can be distracted by rice-balls and seeds and so lose their way. Traditionally, the women of the family were sent back before arriving at the cremation ground, leaving the men to be led by the eldest son at the funeral itself, although this gender divide is no longer strictly enforced. The body is carried into the cremation ground, feet pointing south (the direction of the place of

death). Officials examine the death certificate and allow the body to pass onto the *ghat*, where funeral specialists take over supervision of the body. The location of the pyre marks out status in a distinct social hierarchy. The body is carefully positioned on the pyre, feet still to the south, and the ritual fire is lit, the wood sometimes treated with ghee to intensify and purify the flame. The 'rite of the skull', mid-way, marks a turning point at which the spirit is released from the vessel of the body. The head mourner breaks an earthen vessel to signal the broken attachment and leads the mourners away without looking back.

After the funeral, there are several days of observances intended to propitiate the spirit of the departed, which wants to return home and must be dissuaded from doing so. It is a period of potential danger – the possibility of an imperfect departure turning into a malign haunting if rites are not correctly observed. Bad deaths or poor observances can have consequences that ramify misfortune inside the family. A feast on the twelfth day after death marks the end of the official mourning period and the procedures for ushering the spirit into the next stages of its spiritual journey begins.

There is a tipping point in this sequence where the material body shifts from a holy object into mere polluting matter. Outside observers – the Mughal leaders who invaded from the north, or the East India Company who took over direct control of Varanasi in 1775 – were often appalled by what they perceived to be the casual treatment of the dead, and offended by the cremation that contravened their own burial customs. British colonial policy was generally to not intervene in local practices, but in 1829, British officials outlawed the funeral practice of *sati*, a rare sacrificial ritual in which the widow steps into the flames of her husband's funeral pyre. From the eighteenth century, studious Orientalists began to study and translate sacred texts and to build an understanding of the theologies of the region, some in language that came to idealize (and exoticize) its lofty spiritual ambitions. This happened particularly often with the forms of Buddhism that had been carried east from northern India.

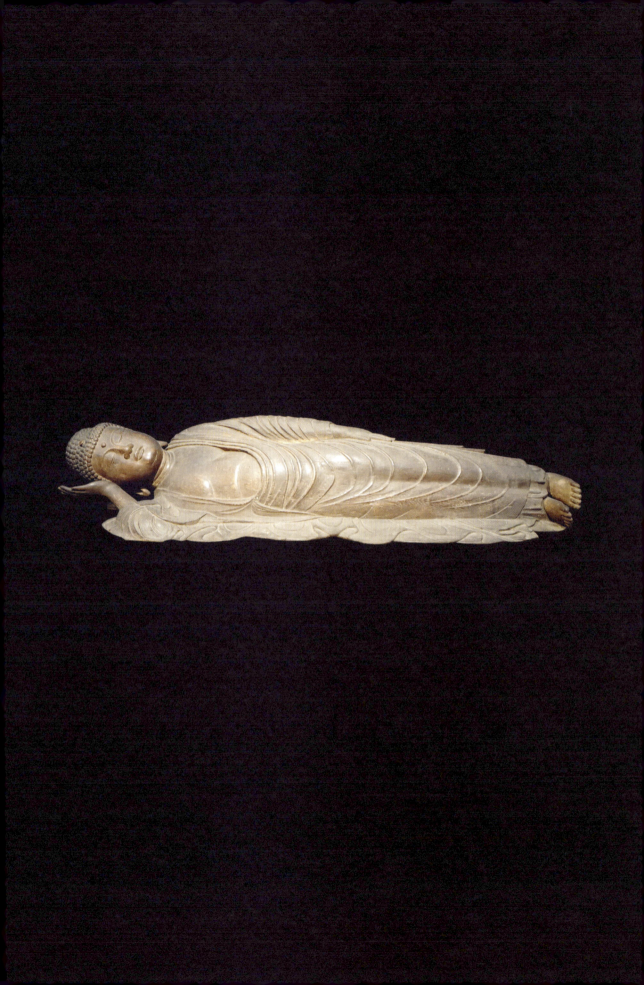

BUDDHISM

THE BIRTH OF BUDDHISM: DHAMEK STUPA

Only seven miles north-east of Varanasi, at Sarnath, stand the ruins of a complex of buildings. The site is dominated by the Dhamek Stupa, a rounded monument of brick and stone, 100 feet high (30.5 m; much reduced from its original size) and lavishly decorated with carved stone reliefs, which marks the place where Siddhartha Gautama, born around 623 BCE, offered his first teaching, the 'Discourse on the Four Noble Truths', to five followers. This event effectively founded the Buddhist religion, as his listeners formed the first *sangha* (assembly). Siddhartha, having renounced his royal lineage, spent the next fifty years as an itinerant preacher travelling through northern India, spreading teaching that proposed a way out of the endless wheel of life, death and reincarnation described in the *Upanishads* by aiming to achieve the pure, enlightened state of *nirvana*. Nirvana was arrived at through a strict way of living and a series of practices and techniques for contemplation on the transience of life. This was not a religion of saviour gods or holy leaders, but a path to enlightenment.

At the age of eighty, Siddhartha announced he was approaching death and, at Kushinagara, lay down on his right side under a tree and issued the anti-instruction: 'Decay is inherent in all things. After my death each of you must work out your own liberation.' This has prompted many different schools of Buddhism to develop across the millennia, with local variations emerging as it travelled further east from India through Java and Indonesia, and along the Silk Road to Nepal, Tibet, China and Japan.

Buddhism has often been regarded as an ascetic practice of meditation, and has been absorbed into Euro-American esotericism and 'New Age' thinking as such. The usual Buddhist

opposite: Wooden sculpture depicting the death and passing into Nirvana of Sakyamuni, the historical Buddha, thirteenth century.

below: The Dhamek Stupa at Sarnath, which commemorates where the Buddha gave his first sermon. Sarnath, Uttar Pradesh, India, 1814.

funerary practice of a modest ceremony of cremation – or the much earlier practice of simply leaving the body in a charnel ground out in the open to decay naturally – makes manifest the idea that the body is an impermanent vessel to be discarded in the spirit's journey. While Buddhism does focus on the spiritual, often meditative ascent towards *nirvana*, it is also a movement that is unusually invested in the bodily remains of its dead.

above: Francis Frith, detail of the Dhamek Stupa, nineteenth century.

below: Sacred hair relic of the Buddha in the Botahtaung Pagoda, Yangon, Myanmar.

Siddhartha became the originary Buddha, the awakened one, upon his death. His remains were initially to be divided between four sites, where they would be installed in memorial reliquaries called *stupas* (Sanskrit for 'mound'). These four stupas mark the Buddha's birthplace in Lumbini (now in Nepal); the place where he first achieved enlightenment, in his famous meditation under a tree at Bodh Gayā; the site of his first teaching at Sarnath; and his place of death. But legend has it that eight kings arrived at his cremation, and so the remains were divided eight ways to maintain the peace. When the important Mauryan emperor Ashoka (304–232 BCE) converted to Buddhism and sent missionaries across South Asia to teach Buddhism, the sacred remains of Buddha's body were accessed and further divided – enough, it was said, to build another 84,000 stupas.

The oldest surviving stupas go back to Ashoka's reign. These buildings anchored the Buddhist diaspora in memorial monuments that became focal points for pilgrimage and teaching. Sites known to contain relics of the originary Buddha (a single hair of the Buddha might be enough) were highly valued. When local variations of Buddhism created their own buddhas, celebrated figures who had achieved enlightenment, they too were memorialized in stupas or monastery complexes.

THE GREAT STUPA, SANCHI, MADHYA PRADESH, INDIA

The stupa commissioned by the emperor Ashoka at his wife's birthplace, Sanchi, in the third century BCE is one of the oldest stone buildings in India. It provided an architectural model for stupas in the centuries that followed. A brick hemisphere, built on a raised platform to contain relics of the Buddha, at its crown is a cube that makes a base for the *chatra*, a symbolic stone parasol rising above to protect the stupa from the sun, a sign of high status. Later additions doubled its size and added a stone railing and pathway around the base, to aid the ritual clockwise circumambulation of the stupa, which is an essential part of pilgrimage. Multiple circular pathways often lead pilgrims through an ascending set of paths to aid the contemplation of core Buddhist beliefs.

above: Sanchi Stupa is a Buddhist complex, famous for its Great Stupa, on a hilltop in the Raisen District of Madhya Pradesh, India.

Reliefs in stone may illustrate moments from the life of the Buddha for further inspiration. At Sanchi, later still, four grand stone portals decorated with stone reliefs were constructed around the stupa. Some of these tell the story of the War over the Buddha's Relics (fifth century BCE) and how Sanchi came to possess such significant sacred materials. Over time, Sanchi developed into a necropolis with additional stupas and temple sites.

It is possible to track the route of stupa reliquaries through the paths taken by Buddhist emissaries out of India, whether to Sri Lanka or to Java, where the complex at Borobudur – the largest Buddhist temple in the world – was built in around the ninth century BCE. Eventually abandoned and overgrown, it was brought to worldwide attention by Sir Thomas Stamford Raffles, a British colonial officer, Orientalist and then-governor-general of Java. Hermann Cornelius, the Dutch engineer Raffles sent to investigate local Javanese reports of a monument in the

below: Borobudur, the largest Buddhist temple in the world, near Magelang, Central Java, Indonesia. The central dome is surrounded by seventy-two Buddhist statues, each in its own stupa. Built in the ninth century, it astonished the world when rediscovered in 1814 by the British ruler of Java, Sir Stamford Raffles.

area, was astonished to discover the nine-stepped temple complex on an island that otherwise bore almost no surviving traces of Buddhist belief.

The path continues further, into East Asia and regions that are now Myanmar, Thailand, Laos and Cambodia, where Angkor Wat, a Hindu-Buddhist temple and mortuary complex, was built in the twelfth century and remains one of the largest religious structures in the world. There are distinct stupa designs associated with Tibet, built on an almost unvarying ritualistic and symbolic plan, and in China and Japan. Most notably, as Buddhism moves east, stupas become less like squat mounds and move into distinctive tower-shaped forms: the tiered pagodas.

BUDDHIST MUMMIES

Another element of Buddhist reliquaries, decidedly different from the preservation of cremated ashes in burial monuments, involves the mummification of the desiccated remains of monks. This is an ancient practice across many Buddhist cultures, and has continued in some places into the present day. Sometimes called 'whole-body relics', these are the bodies of exceptional adherents to the principles of Buddhism, who have committed fully to the path of awakening and whose bodies are preserved 'for the sake of living' – as inspirations for other seekers.

The ideal for strict devotees committed to the stringent path to enlightenment might be to die in the meditative lotus position, which is like a freeze-frame of the achieved state of spiritual attainment. The body becomes a memorial statue (some stone statues of monks are known to have been painted with a lacquer containing the ashes of the man they commemorate). The celebrated Chinese Buddhist ascetic Daoxiu was found dead but uncorrupted, sitting in the lotus position, in his hut in 627. His preserved condition became such a focus that his body was lacquered to preserve it further. Typically, such relics are moved into mausolea or temples for visitors to contemplate. Several such instances are outlined in the Chinese *Biography of Eminent Monks*, compiled by Hui Jiao in around 530.

The preserved body of Huineng (638–713) became an object of devotion in Chan Buddhism, which developed in China from the sixth century, because he was understood to have achieved *nirvana* through such disciplined control that he effectively chose his own moment of death-into-enlightenment. The most ascetic devotee may work through extreme dietary discipline to self-mummify even while they are still alive, eating 'drying' foods and

above: Shwedagon Pagoda, Yangon, Myanmar, built of brick covered with gold plates. It supposedly dates to the time of the living Buddha, although first records date from the fourteenth century.

below: The Mogao caves, a network carved between the fourth and fourteenth century near Dunhuang, China. Cave 17 houses the statue of the ninth-century monk, Hong Bian, as well as texts and artefacts that were sealed there in the eleventh century and rediscovered in 1900.

left: The mummified and gilded body of Ren Yi in the Tonghui female monastery in Jiuhuashan, China. Her body was placed in a terracotta jar at her death in 1995 and found naturally mummified two years later. Gilding is a way of venerating exemplars of enlightenment.

right: The mummified body of Buddhist monk Loung Pordaeng, displayed at Wat Khunaram on Samui Island, Thailand. He died in 1973 and was placed in an upright position within his casket, as he requested, to be preserved and encourage future generations to follow Buddhist teachings.

using fasting to strip the body of all excess fat so that the transition between life and death is almost imperceptible. In Japan between the eleventh and nineteenth centuries, particularly in Yamagata prefecture, 'self-mummification', or *sokushinbutsu*, ended in the removal of food entirely and eventual burial in a pine box packed with salt or charcoal. The monk would meditate, breathing through an air tube, until physical death. This practice was outlawed during the Meiji Restoration (nineteenth century), as part of the government's promotion of Shintō, Japan's oldest religion. Centuries earlier, in China, Huineng's body is said to have been prepared by processes of temporary burial for desiccation seated in a large jar, before his remains were lacquered by his fellow monks. The mummified Sixth Patriarch of the Chan tradition was preserved and displayed at the Nanhua Temple in Guangdong Province for centuries, even surviving the Cultural Revolution in the 1960s.

Mummies are often clustered in particular areas, which have become places of pilgrimage. Whole-body relics, preserved in charcoal after death, have been added to the temples of Mount Jiuhua in Anhui Province, one of Chinese Buddhism's four sacred mountains, long into the twentieth century. The British Sinologist Perceval Yetts wrote in his 1911 essay 'Notes on the Disposal of the Buddhist Dead in China' that such 'dried priests', as he bluntly called them, acted as 'relics that will not only attract the public to the temples but also inspire generous contributors.' As at Sanchi in India, there have been several tussles between rival monasteries over the ownership of these precious Buddhist relics.

THE NINE CEMETERY CONTEMPLATIONS

Disciplined contemplation of the fundamental impermanence of life is absolutely central to Buddhism. One early codified reflection, first written down in 20 BCE, invites the devotee to choose a body laid in charnel grounds and contemplate its nine stages of decay and deterioration. The *Navasivathika Pabba* recalls the practice of corpses being left in specified areas to decay naturally in the open, typical in the early Buddhist period and still echoed in practices such as Tibetan 'sky burial'. In Japanese Buddhist art, *Kusozu* is a watercolour sequence of the nine stages of bodily decay. *Kusozu* images nearly always depict the disintegration of a naked female body. These images were first made in the thirteenth century and remained popular aids to contemplation and instruction in Japan for over 500 years.

In the first stage, immediately after death, the body, laid out on the ground, discolours and begins to bloat. After a week, the body starts to smell and attract carrion animals that tear at the remains. In the third stage, the body is dismantled and strewn about. Soon, much of the flesh is gone, with only small traces of blood remaining. In the fifth stage, the body is only skeleton and sinews. In the sixth stage, that skeleton reduced to a jumble of bones. The bones begin to bleach in the sun by the seventh, and in the eighth stage, a few years after death, the bones have been broken up into small pieces. At the final stage the bones have been mixed into soil and dust, so that nothing remains to

contemplate. At each stage, the devotee repeats the mantra that 'The body on the charnel ground has undergone massive change in a short period of time' and 'This body, too, will not escape such a fate.' The dead, here, act as devotional objects to aid the living.

These graphic, unblinking contemplations of the post-mortem processes of decay find a perhaps unexpected echo in the Christian tradition of the *memento mori*, the skull that teaches the moral 'As I am, so will you be.' For all the different practices that different faiths have evolved to manage this rupture in life, placing death within the structures of the world's faiths can show chimes and echoes as much as unfamiliar customary divergences.

PART

THREE

†

THE

NUMBERLESS

DEAD

A PROBLEM OF MODERNITY

'THE GREAT MAJORITY'

In a few short, bewildering decades between 1780 and 1850, the industrial revolution transformed the economic and social order in Europe. The rapid shift of labour from agriculture to manufacture was driven by new kinds of economic accumulation, and it resulted in a profound disruption of traditional patterns of life – and death. In Britain, which went through this transformation early, one notable effect was the concentration of the growing population into new super-cities such as Manchester, Liverpool or London.

This sheer accumulation of people created all manner of interlocking social problems, not least of which was the number and concentration of the dead. In his 1721 play *The Revenge*, the Graveyard Poet Edward Young wrote the typically joyless lines 'Life is the desert, life the solitude:/Death joins us to the great majority.' This phrase, borrowed from the Latin tag *abiit ad plures*, 'he is gone to the majority', became very popular in the nineteenth century as a euphemism for the brute fact that the dead far outnumbered the living. In 1880, the poet Thomas Hardy wrote in 'The Levelled Churchyard':

> We late-lamented, resting here,
> Are mixed to human jam,
> And each to each exclaim in fear,
> 'I know not which I am!'

In this era, the Christian tradition of burying in churchyards began to come under intense pressure. The spiritual succour promised by sanctified ground was constantly undercut by the grim material reality of bodies stacked in soil that began to rise above street level. In the medical theory of the time, it was thought that decaying animal matter produced a miasma (literally 'bad air') that generated all kinds of fatal

opposite: The embalmed body of Jeremy Bentham on display, University College London. On his death in 1832 his body was publicly dissected and the remains preserved.

diseases. As piles of corpses were crammed into ever more saturated grounds, their pestilent presence seemed to threaten to speed the passage of the living into the decomposing arms of the great majority.

Any reform had to confront the conservative forces of ingrained Christian belief about burial in consecrated ground and the economic fact that many churches survived on the fees levied for burial. Part of the problem for the urban poor was the inability to pay relatively high Church of England burial fees, and consequently the proliferation of pauper burial grounds. These charged smaller fees, but were shrouded in shame and, in some notorious cases, became cash-cows for owners that had little respect for the bodies deposited there. In this strange interregnum, the city churchyard overflowed and gave birth to enduring terrors.

MODERN HORRORS:
FRANKENSTEIN AND THE BODY SNATCHERS

In Mary Shelley's Gothic shocker *Frankenstein* (1818), Doctor Victor Frankenstein uses ungodly modern knowledge of physiology, physics and chemistry to animate a body built from parts collected from anatomy laboratories and graveyards. Frankenstein passes over gruesome physiological details in a guilty rush: 'Who shall conceive the horrors of my secret toil, as I dabbled among the unhallowed damps of the grave?' Shelley was relying on her audience's awareness of how early nineteenth-century medicine was testing the boundaries of religious authority on questions of life and death. Medical men were seen as potential wreckers of Christian civilization. It did not help that they were also directly associated with the peculiar and horrifying consequences of rapid advances in the study of human anatomy: body snatching.

Body snatching emerged from a very specific situation in Britain. In 1540, Henry VIII had granted a Royal Charter to the Company of Barbers and Surgeons that provided them with just four human bodies a year for dissection and anatomical study, an essential component of medical training. Dissection was a sacrilegious act, imperilling the hope of bodily resurrection, and therefore bodies could be taken only from those executed by hanging, who by their crimes had forfeited the right to proper burial. Two hundred years later, this provision had increased to only six bodies, despite a great increase in the number of surgeons. In the more secular centres of study on the European continent and in Edinburgh there was greater latitude in the law – Edinburgh anatomy schools could also dissect the bodies of orphans, foundlings and those who had died by suicide – but there remained an association between dissection and punishment.

above: Thomas Hardy arranged tombstones around the base of an ash tree in the St Pancras Old Church, London, when part of the graveyard was cleared for the Midland Railway into St Pancras Station in the 1860s. Photograph *c.* 1960.

opposite: William Hogarth, 'The Reward of Cruelty', from *The Four Stages of Cruelty*, 1751. The image evokes the moral horror of the dissection table.

THE REWARD OF CRUELTY.

JAMES FIELD

Mac LEAN

Price 1ˢ.

Behold the Villain's dire disgrace!
Not Death itself can end.
He finds no peaceful Burial-Place,
His breathless Corse, no friend.

Torn from the Root, that wicked Tongue,
Which daily swore and curst!
Those Eyeballs, from their Sockets wrung,
That glow'd with lawless Lust!

Designd by W. Hogarth.

His Heart, expos'd to prying Eyes,
To Pity has no Claim:
But, dreadful! from his Bones shall rise,
His Monument of Shame.

Published according to Act of Parliament Feb.1.1751.

From about 1675, therefore, dead bodies became com-
modities. A shadow trade of so-called 'resurrection men' or
body snatchers rose to meet anatomy schools' demand by
robbing fresh graves. They exploited the legal anomaly that
since a corpse was neither property nor person it could not
be 'stolen' – hence prosecutions were often on the grounds
of offending public morals and carried lighter sentences than,
for example, poaching or theft.

In later years, most surgeons kept their suppliers at arm's
length to maintain plausible deniability. A fresh corpse could
fetch two guineas in the 1790s; an 1828 inquiry heard that it
could be as much as eight guineas. Rare 'anatomical specimens'
were worth considerably more. Teratology, the study of
congenital abnormalities, was a science that defined biological norms
via the study of deviations. The term was coined by Geoffroy Saint-
Hilaire in 1830 in a paper dedicated to creating a rational nomenclature
for 'Monsters'. The famous 'Irish Giant', Charles Byrne, who died
in 1783 after a life as a public sensation in London and Edinburgh,
went to great lengths to avoid his body ending up on display in an
anatomical museum. His will asked that he be buried at sea. The
leading London anatomist John Hunter is thought to have paid as
much as £500 to deny Byrne's wishes; he had the body snatched and
added it to his collection. Byrne's skeleton remained on display in
the Hunterian Museum at the Royal College of Surgeons until 2023,
despite a campaign to provide him his proper burial.

above: Body snatchers
engraving, press
illustration, 1888.

below: Edward Radclyffe,
interior of the Hunterian
Museum of medical
curiosities, Royal College
of Surgeons, Lincoln's
Inn Fields, London,
after Thomas Hosmer
Shepherd, c. 1800.

From the surviving testimony of resurrection men,
it is clear that pauper burial grounds, without guards
or mortuaries, were favoured terrain. Pauper grave-
pits were often left open until the deep holes were
filled with cheap, stacked coffins, sometimes up to
twelve deep. Many of the poor were only buried in
shrouds, further speeding exhumation. Meanwhile,
the fearful middle classes spent money on lead coffins,
iron grids and various 'mortsafe' devices – metal
cages cemented into stone around the coffin. Famous
examples of mortsafes survive in the Greyfriars kirk-
yard in Edinburgh, which was a known haunt of the
resurrection men.

There was strong community reverence for the
body in the burial rituals of the urban working class.
Revulsion at the desecration of graves is evident in
the repeated instances of public rioting when resurrection men were arrested, as in Great Yarmouth in
1827, and in 1832, in Aberdeen, where an anatomy

school was razed to the ground by an angry crowd. There were more disturbances in Cambridge, Greenwich and elsewhere in the same years.

These scenes intensified with the notorious case of William Burke and William Hare, who murdered an estimated sixteen people in Edinburgh over ten months in 1827 and 1828. They sold their first body for just over £7 to the eminent Edinburgh anatomist Robert Knox, and latterly cut out the risky process of exhumation by suffocating their victims after plying them with drink. Their last victim, Mary Paterson, was recognized by one of Knox's assistants when preparing the body for class. Although only initially suspected of murdering Paterson, Hare quickly turned king's evidence and revealed their deadly business model.

above: William Austin, 'The anatomist over-taken by the watch Carrying off Miss W--- in a hamper', 1773.

In January 1829, Burke was tried, found guilty of one murder, executed and – perhaps inevitably – dissected. It was said that over 40,000 people queued to see his ruined corpse. His skeleton is still on display in the Anatomical Museum of the Edinburgh Medical School. Surgeons often escaped any charge of complicity, but Robert Knox was forced to resign membership of the Royal College of Surgeons and soon left Edinburgh. The case of Burke and Hare poured into the popular imagination through a wave of popular broadsides, ballads and lurid sketches of the crimes.

In 1827, two years before Burke's trial, the medic and reformist Thomas Southwood Smith had published 'The Use of the Dead to the Living', an essay in favour of the benefits of dissection to aid the understanding of the body for the betterment of the living. Almost designed to enrage Christian believers and challenge social rituals of burial, the Anatomy Act was nonetheless passed in 1832, after another set of murders by a gang of London 'Burkers' became a sensation in 1831.

The expansion of the pool of bodies available to anatomy schools was made by allowing 'unclaimed' pauper bodies to be used for dissection – one of the earliest stringent results of the era of reform heralded by the new Poor Laws. If it ended the body-snatching trade, the Act hardly dispersed popular fear about the violation of bodies after death. Workhouse shame could now extend beyond burial in a pauper's grave to (legal) desecration by dismemberment.

Some who had argued for expanded access did, however, have the courage of their convictions. The influential Utilitarian philosopher Jeremy Bentham died in 1832, and Southwood Smith, a friend, undertook a public dissection of his body. Bentham's body remains dubiously 'in use' as an 'Auto-Icon' – 'a man preserved in his own image' – as stipulated in his will. His taxidermied remains spent many years sitting in a glass box in the passageways of University College London, gathering dust; he is

still there, having been plumped up a little, with a fresh view onto the Bloomsbury gardens of Gordon Square.

Popular disgust at body snatching seeped into the mass literature of the 'penny bloods' or 'penny dreadfuls', cheap magazines with open-ended serial melodramas that were often suffused with radical sentiment. George W. M. Reynolds's *Mysteries of London* serial (1844–56) had a recurrent monstrous Resurrection Man, a demonic emanation of the slums whose gang 'burks' their victims. Thomas Rymer's *Manuscripts from the Diary of a Physician* (started in 1844) opens with the melodramatic 'The Dead Restored; or, The Young Student', which recalls an incident in which the narrator is caught up in an act of grave-robbing.

above: Thomas Rowlandson, engraving, 1775. Two men place the shrouded corpse which they have just disinterred into a sack while Death leans in.

right: Hablot Knight Browne, 'Resurrectionists', 1847, illustration of gravediggers John Holmes and Peter Williams, who were jailed and publicly whipped for stealing a body from St George's Church in Bloomsbury in 1777.

Cultural memory of body snatching and the Burke and Hare case in particular was renewed in the late Victorian period, following Robert Louis Stevenson's use of the case as the basis of his 1884 Christmas shocker 'The Body Snatcher'. The volume was advertised in London with 'six pairs of coffin lids, painted dead black, with white skulls and cross-bones in the centre for relief' carried by men in 'long white surplices' purchased from a funeral establishment. The campaign was halted by the Metropolitan Police

on grounds of decency. The case cast such a deep shadow that the opening scenes of the 1932 film of *Frankenstein*, directed by James Whale, make Victor Frankenstein little more than a graveyard body snatcher, despite Mary Shelley's more metaphysical ambitions.

EMANATIONS FROM THE DEAD: GEORGE WALKER AND GRAVEYARD REFORM

Among a generation of Victorian reformers, one figure chose to focus on the scandalous state of city burial grounds: George Walker. Walker was a medical practitioner in Drury Lane, which bordered both the glitzy West End and some of the worst slums in inner London. Significantly, he – like many reformers – had been brought up a dissenter from Church

of England doctrine, with a willingness to challenge tradition and orthodoxy. His practice was in close proximity to a cluster of city-centre churchyards and burial grounds, which were in a parlous state when he began to explore them in the 1830s.

In 1839, Walker published *Gatherings from Grave Yards*, in which he surveyed 149 individual burial grounds close to his practice: a catalogue of a city slowly being poisoned, in his view, by ground saturated with its own dead. He denounced the condition of London burial grounds as menaces to public health and an outrage to Christian custom. Walker followed the predominant miasmatic theory of disease, recounting instances of gravediggers who had died suddenly from the inhalation of toxic fumes when working in the worst graveyards.

The poor laid out the deceased in their own rooms, often for days or even weeks at a time, partly to observe communal customs, but mainly because it took time for the family to raise fees for burial. The graveyards themselves were often patches in the same courtyards, unregulated grounds that had emerged to undercut higher Church of England fees. In these disregarded, unregulated grounds, the physical number of the dead was a constant problem. It was managed by burying paupers in communal pits and later removing their bodies illicitly, at night. Any remaining flesh and bone was surreptitiously burnt, in violation of common custom. That gravediggers often required large quantities of alcohol to blunt their senses was only the first of the moral outrages against Christian belief.

Church parishes, however, proved especially resistant to any change in the use of city churchyards and burial grounds, so heavily did they rely on burial and service fees. Walker's campaign eventually led to an 1842 Parliamentary Select Committee to investigate the 'effect of interment of bodies in towns.' Chaired by a sympathetic advocate for Walker's demand to put an end to interment in city graveyards, it received testimony about the places he had already made notorious in his many broadsides.

A short walk from Drury Lane stands St Clement Danes Church. In those days, its crypt was stuffed with the intramural dead, often expensively inhumed close to the holiest spaces of the church, in lead coffins known to burst with the gases built up from decomposition. Meanwhile, the churchyard outside St Clement Danes was overflowing, as was

above: Overflow burial ground for the parish of St Martin in the Field, Drury Lane, reported to be one of the worst graveyards in London. Engraving from *Illustrated London News*, 15 September 1849.

below: George Walker, *Gatherings from Grave Yards*, 1839.

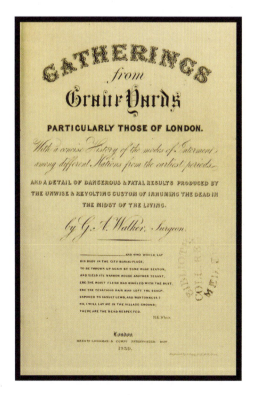

its overspill ground, just over the road in Clement's Lane. James Lane, a local resident, testified that he had seen grave-diggers at night digging up coffins, breaking down the wood for burning, removing bones and shovelling 'soft substance', or spreading quick lime to dissolve the bodies below (some of the poor in fact favoured quick lime, because it damaged bodies enough to save them from body snatchers). 'There is very little air attached to that quarter', Lane told the committee, and detailed his many health problems. John Eyles, a gravedigger, testified in clear terror of his tyrannical boss that he had been obliged to dig up coffins at night and break them up. He had even seen his own father's coffin dug up and broken down.

"LIVE AND LET LIVE."

Village Doctor (to the Grave-Digger, who is given to Whisky). "AH, JOHN! I'M SORRY TO SEE YOU IN THIS PITIABLE CONDITION AGAIN!" *Grave-Digger.* "TOOTS, SIR! CAN YE NO' LET A'E LITTLE FAU'T O' MINE GAE BY! IT'S MONY A MUCKLE ANE O' YOURS I HA'E HAPPIT OWRE, AN' SAID NAETHING ABOOT!"

PARISH OF Sᵗ CLEMENT DANES.

top right: Charles Keene, cartoon of a doctor reprimanding the drunkenness of the village gravedigger, who retorts that he does not criticise the doctor for his mistakes, only buries them, 1879.

above: Map from *Some Account of the Parish of Saint Clement Danes (Westminster), past and present*, London, 1868. The church and surrounding streets were saturated with graveyards, including the notorious Enon Chapel.

Enon Chapel was located in the same street. A Baptist dissenting chapel, opened in 1823 as a speculative venture, it had begun to offer cheap burial in its basement (there was no crypt as such). Soon enough, the congregation was contending with an 'abominable' stench and saprophagous corpse flies crawling sluggishly from the cracks in the wooden floor. Some fainted from the smell; many left services with insidious, miasmatic headaches. When another reformist venture – the building of drains – required entry to the basement of Enon Chapel, it was discovered that 12,000 corpses had been stuffed into a space measuring 50 × 30 feet (15.2 × 9.1 m). The 'master carman' William Burn testified that he had helped remove some of its contents when the sewer was built. Men repairing the road surface of Clement's Lane had asked for rubbish to fill potholes: 'they asked me to give them a few baskets of rubbish, which I did, and they picked up a human hand, and were looking at it, and there were crowds collected; it did not appear to have been buried probably a month; it was as perfect as my hand.' The bones got as far as Waterloo Bridge, where they were used as landfill to shore up the construction of Waterloo Road: infrastructure built on the bones of the city's impoverished dead. Long after the inquiry had concluded, Walker purchased the lease on the abandoned Enon Chapel and paid for an estimated 20,000 more bodies to be reinterred in a garden cemetery outside the city.

It is no surprise that the well-known penny dreadful *Sweeney Todd*, 'the demon barber of Fleet Street', was started in 1846. The serial's meat pies were baked just moments away from the real-life horrors of St Clement Danes and Enon Chapel.

right: Enon Chapel
Cemetery and Dancing
Saloon from the
Poor Man's Guardian,
4 December 1847.

ENON CHAPEL CEMETERY AND DANCING SALOON.

One of the principal modernizing reformers of this period, Edwin Chadwick, followed the inquiry with a *Supplementary Report … into the Practice of Interment in Towns* in 1843. Chadwick emphasized the detrimental effect of city burial on public morality, writing in the fashion of a 1790s terror novel: 'Neglected or mismanaged burial grounds superadd to the indefinite terrors of dissolution, the revolting image of festering heaps, disturbed and scattered bones, the prospect of the charnel house and its associations of desecration and insult.' Some historians have suggested that he was trying to break up the burial practices of the working classes, with their prolonged proximity to the corpse in the days after death. He sought instead to impose the norms of the middle classes, where death was politely mediated by the undertaking profession, which was becoming a major industry in the nineteenth century.

Walker, meanwhile, continued to pamphleteer through the 1840s. He had the perfect case when, in 1845, a serious fire started in the bone house of another private, unconsecrated burial ground. Spa Fields, near Exmouth Market in Clerkenwell, was in use for over fifty years. One estimate suggested that it had capacity for 1,361 adult burial plots, but Walker calculated that upwards of 80,000 bodies were crammed in, sometimes with as many as eight stacked in one grave.

The middle-class houses and businesses around Spa Fields had for years suffered from proximity to what Walker described as one of the worst 'reservoirs of pestilence' in the capital. The bone house was at its centre. Walker's inves-

above: The burying ground in Spa Fields, Clerkenwell, London, nineteenth century.

tigations turned up witnesses who noted that 'the custom … was to disinter the bodies after they had been three or four days buried, chop them up, and burn them in this bone house.' A gravedigger testified, 'I have been up to my knees in human flesh by jumping on the bodies so as to cram them in the least possible space at the bottom of the graves.' The agitation of the businesses in the area forced the situation to a local magistrate's court, and it turned out that the ultimate owner of Spa Fields, hidden behind a chain of managers, was the Marquis of Northampton. The scandal spilled into the national press.

The cholera outbreak of 1848–49 made another critical case for legislation, alongside a growing understanding of modes of disease transmission (John Snow's famous resolution of cholera as a water-borne, rather than airborne, disease arrived in 1854, after his investigation of an outbreak in the slums of Soho just a few minutes' walk from Walker's beat). The outbreaks prompted the Board of Health to push for the Metropolitan Interments Bill, but vested interests still stalled negotiations, despite substantial compensation offered to the Church of England.

In 1851, thinking back to the notion of 'the great majority', Walker began *On the Past and Present State of Intramural Burying Places* with the blunt maxim 'BULK MUST OCCUPY SPACE'. There is a powerful sense of a continuing, dangerous 'necrosociability' (as Thomas Laqueur calls it) in his writing. London is envisaged as a city stuffed with the dead, 'crowded into every inch of available space … Myriads of bodies, in every stage of decomposition, have been, and continue to be, stowed away in subterranean receptacles in the streets, lanes, and blind alleys in this metropolis.'

In 1852, the Burial Act finally passed, announcing that 'for the Protection of the Public Health Burials in any Part or Parts of the Metropolis, or in any Burial Grounds or Places of Burial in the Metropolis, should be wholly discontinued.' Local Burial Boards were established, fees fixed and inspection regimes formalized. Exceptions to the rule included the sites of national memorial, St Paul's Cathedral and Westminster Abbey, some family intramural vaults where resting places had long been purchased and judged healthy, the new Cemetery Companies and burial grounds for the Jewish and Quaker populations of the city.

Suburban garden cemeteries soon displaced the toxic churchyards. City grounds were abandoned, sometimes boarded up and left to rot or the land informally occupied and repurposed as goods and storage yards. The horrific complex of burial grounds so central to Walker's campaign for reform has now been almost entirely erased from the city. Even by the time Isabella Holmes set out to catalogue and save the remaining burial grounds for the Metropolitan Public Gardens Association in the 1880s, many had vanished. That swift erasure was in part a mark of how successful reform had been.

BURIAL REFORM AND THE RISE
OF THE GARDEN CEMETERY

PARIS: OLD BONES AND CIVIC MODERNITY

By the late 1700s, the central burial ground of Paris, the Holy Innocents' Cemetery, had received deposits of human remains from twenty-two parishes, the main city hospital and mass burials of plague and cholera victims for about a thousand years. The burial ground was several feet higher than the surrounding streets, flanked by charnel houses. Visitors described these ossuaries as a sea of bones, sometimes gently rippling as rats moved among the remains. 'Ten million cadavers at the very least have dissolved in that narrow space. What a crucible!' the historian Louis-Sébastien Mercier wrote.

The Parisian population was expanding rapidly, and the dead were multiplying. In 1765, the Parliament of Paris had issued a ban on further churchyard burials in the city and proposed clearing 200 churchyards of their remains. As in London, this edict was resisted by vested interests. And then, in 1780, after a long period of rain, the Holy Innocents' Cemetery burst with the sodden weight of the dead. It released into the neighbouring streets a tsunami of bones and corpse wax – adipocere, the fat from human bodies. Nearby houses were inundated; some collapsed.

In its very last years, the French Ancien Régime finally committed to closing Holy Innocents' and the central churchyards of St Roch, St Eustache and St Sulpice. The authorities came up with a modern solution that was a striking echo of the past. The city's bones would be moved to the disused underground quarries that had supplied limestone for its buildings for centuries. After first using those at Vaurigard and Monmartre, from 1786, in a section of the chiselled-out galleries of the Tombe-Issoire quarries, Paris developed its catacombs.

The entrance to the catacombs remains, ominously, at one of the surviving toll gates to the city, known as the Gate of Hell. A legend over the

opposite: *La Mort Saint Innocent (Death of Saint Innocent)*, Paris, 1520–30. The statue stood in the Holy Innocents' Cemetery from 1530 to 1786. The cemetery was closed after the dead burst its bounds and spilled into nearby streets.

door announces 'C'EST ICI L'EMPIRE DE LA MORT.' In December 1785
the first deposits from Holy Innocents' were taken in carts draped in black
cloth and accompanied by priests chanting the Office of the Dead through
the streets. The transfer continued even during the radical discontinuities
of the French Revolution, with each separate deposit marked by plaques,
the bones sometimes arranged in patterns made from skulls, tibias and
femurs. Mostly ancient, the bones also included some of those executed in
the last years of the Ancien Régime and the first years of the revolutionary
Republic. A deposit of executed Communards was added after the failed
uprising of 1870, eight years after they had been dumped in a mass pit.

Paris was one of the earliest dark tourism destinations: the catacombs
were first opened to tourists in 1810, although they closed in 1830 due to
damage and disrespect towards the remains. They reopened in 1867, and
are now one of the most visited sites in Paris, although the experience is
strictly guided and restricted to particular areas of the vast network. The
sheer number of skulls looming out of the dark conveys a radical sense
of equality in death, the republican ethos of the place backed up by its
largely secular quality, although there are crosses and an altar or two for

above: The catacombs of Paris.

below: The catacombs of Paris as tourist attraction, 1822.

services. 'So many dead bodies stacked up and pressed against the earth! Numbers are meaningless here,' one legend states in the Le Mierre Gallery. Meanwhile, Holy Innocents' itself was lost under that monument to commerce: the Forum des Halles.

From 1789, the French Revolution left no aspect of traditional society untouched – including death and burial. The guillotine had been invented as a rational, egalitarian device, designed to suppress mob reactions and eliminate class hierarchy in death. Joseph-Ignace Guillotin, a physician and member of the Chamber of Deputies, notoriously said that with his device, death was experienced only as 'a slight coolness on the back of the neck'. There was a concurrent, lively medical debate about how long consciousness might remain in a decapitated head. Could you be aware of your own death? Speak the impossible sentence 'I am dead' in your last seconds? Robespierre declared the guillotine 'nothing other than prompt, severe, inflexible justice; it is, therefore, an emanation of virtue.'

Yet its use as a tool of the Terror that consumed Paris from 1792 to 1794 instead rendered it the 'ensign of tyranny', and fostered a whole *genre noir* of grim tales of death and execution, including early sensational works by Victor Hugo and Honoré de Balzac. In 1818 the painter Théodore Géricault sketched images of severed heads as part of his opposition to the use of the death penalty. During the mass executions that took place in the summer of 1794, a ditch by the side of the Church of Sainte-Marguerite, near the Bastille, became a makeshift cemetery and a rallying place for counter-revolutionaries. This was heightened after the body of the young Louis XVII was placed there on his death in 1795, two years after his father's execution. A small, somewhat surreptitious stone now memorializes the king who never served.

In 1790, the Marquis de Villette proposed that the church of Sainte-Geneviève, not quite completed under the reign of Louis XV, be repurposed: 'Let it become the Pantheon of France! Let us install statues of our great men and lay their ashes to rest in its underground recesses.' When the great hero of the new Republic, Mirabeau, died

in 1791, it was again suggested that the empty church become 'a temple of the nation, that the tomb of a great man become the altar of liberty.' The Panthéon has since remained a mainly secular temple dedicated to the celebrated dead of the Republic. Sometimes they were quietly removed, as were the first remains once Mirabeau's reputation had collapsed. The first woman to be reinterred in the Panthéon for her own merits was Marie Curie, as late as 1995. Her remains were sealed in a lead-lined coffin, since she had died from leukaemia resulting from her constant exposure to radiation from her major chemical discoveries – radium and polonium.

above: Eugène Atget, *The Panthéon*, Paris, 1924.

Radical changes to burial practices were first discussed in 1794, as part of the secularization and modernization of Paris. But it took the newly installed First Consul, Napoleon Bonaparte, to realise these major changes from 1799. Further interment of bodies inside the city limits was ended, with some exceptions, and he instigated a competition to design three large-scale cemeteries on hills outside the city: one in the north at Montmartre, one in the south at Montparnasse and one in the east at Mont-Louis, which became Père Lachaise. When the city limits were expanded and redrawn by Baron Haussmann in 1860, all of these sites became urban burial grounds again. Haussmann created a fourth major ground, the Cimitière Parisien d'Ivry, in 1861, just beyond the new city boundary. Just as Napoleon had modelled himself on Rome's example by declaring himself Emperor, so Roman laws on extramural burial were to be repeatedly revived.

CIMITIÈRE PÈRE LACHAISE, 1804

Père Lachaise was to become the most important influence on cemetery design in Europe and America for over a hundred years. Nestled on a hill, in garden grounds already laid out under the former retreat for the Jesuit confessor of Louis XV, Père La Chaise, the site had commanding views over the city. It covered just over 100 acres.

Alexandre-Théodore Brongniart won the competition to redesign the gardens as a cemetery, and when it opened in 1804 (Year XII of the revolutionary calendar) it introduced the concept of the 'garden cemetery'. This was not a necropolis, a 'city' of the dead, but an integration of human culture with wild nature. The park cemetery emerged out of the landscape architecture of the mid-eighteenth century, democratized and turbo-charged by the emphasis on sublime emotional gestures typical of the writers and artists of the Romantic

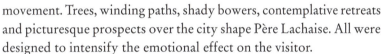

above: Pierre
Courvoisier, *View
of Père Lachaise
Cemetery from the
Entrance*, 1815.

below: Engraving of the
Abelard and Heloïse
tomb in the Père
Lachaise Cemetery,
Paris, 1845.

movement. Trees, winding paths, shady bowers, contemplative retreats and picturesque prospects over the city shape Père Lachaise. All were designed to intensify the emotional effect on the visitor.

In its first year it sold only about forty plots; it seemed alien, unanchored from consecrated church grounds. But its first director, Nicolas Frochot, was to prove a genius for promotion. He began transferring the remains of famous people there: the playwright Molière and the twelfth-century philosophers, theologians and lovers Heloïse and Abelard were among those moved into the grounds. By 1830, over 30,000 plots had been bought and it was wildly fashionable, and by the 1860s the tradition of visiting family graves or promenading there brought hundreds of thousands to Père Lachaise and its counterparts on the central Christian day of remembrance, All Saints' Day.

Frochot sold individual plots on a sliding scale, in different sizes, rented for ten or twenty years or in perpetuity. The class hierarchy of the cemetery reflected that of the living city, a fact sardonically emphasized by the meagre burial of the protagonist at the end of Balzac's 1834 novel *Père Goriot*. There were only minimal restrictions on the style of monument. The steep path leading to the Greek Doric chapel on the brow of the hill is festooned with small headstones, ledger stones, sarcophagi and large family vaults or mausolea in styles that range from neo-classical, Gothic, Romanesque, Egyptian, Byzantine and art nouveau to striking individual funerary sculpture. Its role

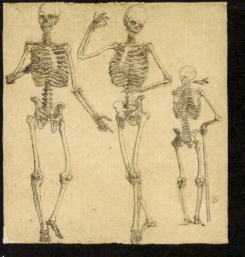

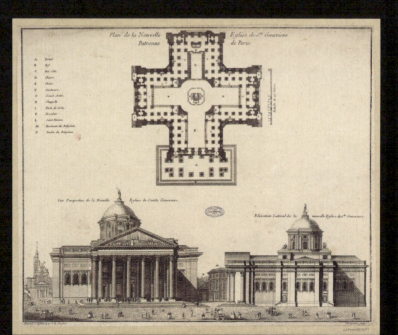

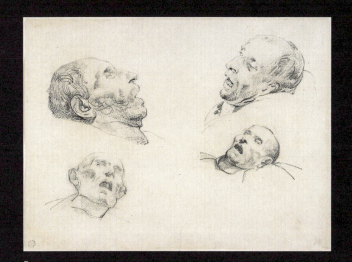

5

6

7

8

as a multi-faith burial site is evident in monuments to those of all faiths and none. There is a memorial to the radical Communards, who staged their last stand among the tombs and were executed along the interior wall of the cemetery in 1870. The Mur des Fédérés has been a site for protest ever since, and a locus for burials of prominent radicals, resistance heroes and communists. Close by are the memorials to the Jews deported to Nazi concentration camps from Paris.

Saints had long attracted proximate burials, and by the 1860s there was a new kind of sanctification: celebrity. Tourists still seek out writers, painters or film stars in the cemetery, using maps to navigate the sectored grid of burials. Graffiti and damage are associated with the graves of American rock singer and poet Jim Morrison and the English writer Oscar Wilde. Wilde had died in 1900 in relative poverty and was initially buried modestly in Bagneaux Cemetery outside Paris. In 1909, his friends and admirers decided to move his remains to Père Lachaise, and commissioned the sculptor Jacob Epstein to create a suitable monument. The remarkable angelic creature emerging out of the stone was praised when shown in London, but covered by tarpaulin on its unveiling in situ because its prominent genitals were declared obscene. That problem was solved by a fig-leaf (long gone),

but the stone currently stands behind ugly Plexiglas in an attempt to stop the thousands of lipstick kisses planted on the stone causing further damage. Wilde's grave is the most popular plot in the most visited cemetery in the world.

top: Funerary monument in Père Lachaise Cemetery, Paris. A classical revival of the figure of the mourning woman.

above: Jacob Epstein, Oscar Wilde's memorial in Père Lachaise Cemetery. The memorial was initially considered obscene and covered up by the cemetery authorities; today it is one of the most visited graves in the cemetery.

Parisian modernization did not end with Napoleon's grand plans. The man who transformed Paris from a medieval into a modern city was Baron Georges Haussmann, Prefect of the Seine from 1853 to 1870 under Louis-Napoleon III. Haussmann punched wide, straight boulevards through the old city, to eliminate the tangles of streets where revolution was fomented and barricades had been easily erected in the uprisings of 1789, 1830 and 1848. The new Paris was to be a city of circulation: of people and money, but also of troops and police. In Haussmann's grand vision, the dead needed clearing further out of the city. He commissioned a report that suggested all future burials in the city should take place thirteen miles outside Paris, at Méry-sur-Oise, a giant burial place to be served by a special necropolitan railway. This would depart from terminals located in the three main cemeteries, which had been swallowed up by his redrawn city boundaries. There was wide public protest at this idea in 1870, denounced by Victor Fournel in one screed as the vision of 'a vast and glacial funereal Siberia.'

Haussmann's reign over Paris planning came to an end that year, along with the fall of the Second Empire. His funeral railway was never realized in Paris – but it was in London, where the dead had a special terminal at Waterloo that took mourning parties out to Brookwood Cemetery in Surrey. In Australia, another necropolitan railway served Rockwood Cemetery outside Sydney, where from 1913 a twice daily service ferried the dead (no ticket required) to their last resting place in the loving arms of mechanical modernity.

THE GARDEN CEMETERY, EXPORTED

Detached from churchyards, the garden cemetery started to transcend the exclusionary logic of many denominational burial grounds. In Britain, the first experiments – Rosary Cemetery in Norwich in 1819, Chorlton Row Cemetery in Manchester in 1820 – were driven by Dissenters, commited to non-denominational burial after their long exclusion from Christian burial by the Church of England. Crucially, for these grounds to work, a law was passed allowing joint-stock private companies to be established to raise money for the land and to make a profit from burial. Burial was big business.

The Glasgow Necropolis was opened in 1833, on a hill rising out of the city known as Fir Park, already considered an important health benefit for a city of heavy industry. From the beginning it was intended as much as a botanical and sculpture garden as a place of burial. By 1836, a grand entrance

below: Grave markers at Forest Lawn Memorial Park, Glendale, California.

had been designed, taking funeral processions over the Molendinar Ravine by bridge – a symbolic passage over the Styx into the land of the dead. It became known as 'the Bridge of Sighs' for the mourning parties that followed the hearses. The Necropolis was non-denominational, including very early on a separate plot for Jewish burials. Just before it had become a cemetery, the hill had been chosen for the location of a tall monument to the Presbyterian church leader John Knox, and this attracted many of his followers to be buried close by. Many of the prominent buildings and funerary monuments were in the Greek Revival style; one Victorian visitor admired the 'dreamlike vision of Attic splendour on the hill by the cathedral.' But there was also a miniature imitation of the Knights Templar Church of the Holy Sepulchre at Jerusalem (for Major Monteath, of the East India Company) and a Moorish design for the travel writer William Rae Wilson. A vault near the entrance was built in the new Egyptian Revival style, with pylons and a prominent cavetto curving over the entrance. Perambulation in the garden cemetery could become a way of travelling the world.

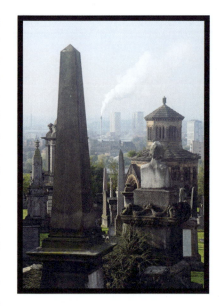

above: The Glasgow Necropolis, one of the earliest garden cemeteries in Britain, opened in 1833.

below: Thomas Chambers, *Mount Auburn Cemetery*, c. 1850. America's first garden cemetery, Cambridge, Massachusetts.

The garden cemetery ethos also found purchase in America, in particular with writers and intellectuals of the Transcendentalist movement such as Ralph Waldo Emerson, who found it echoed their spiritual theories of Nature. The first garden cemetery in the United States was built on the land of Stone's Farm in Cambridge, Massachusetts, and opened in 1831 as the non-denominational Mount Auburn Cemetery. The founder, Dr Jacob Bigelow, was inspired by Père Lachaise, but designed the site as an experimental botanical garden and arboretum as much as a working cemetery, aiming to welcome and instruct its visitors in the glory and variety of the natural world. Emphasizing nature meant restricting the sizes of tombs and monuments to ensure they remained integrated with the landscape rather than seeking to dominate it. Seeds and saplings arrived from around the world to populate the rolling glades and hills of the cemetery, turning it into a park retreat over the river from Boston. In his address at the cemetery dedication, Joseph Story argued that it was time to move beyond 'loathsome vaults' and embrace the 'rural Cemetery', where Nature could work 'to tranquillize human fears, to secure the

best religious influences, [and] to cast a cheerful light over the darkness of the grave.' This combination of 'natural and artificial scenery, which is fitted to awaken emotions of the highest and most affecting character' was soon seeded across America: at Lauren Hill in Philadelphia (1836), Greenwood in Brooklyn (1838) and many other cities.

In Barcelona, modernity was marked by Antonio Ginesi's design for the Cementiri de Poblenou, which opened in 1819 on the site of a cemetery destroyed by Napoleon's troops. More austere than the garden cemeteries, the squares of wall tombs built in grids behind rectangular high walls reflect southern European traditions of burial above ground. Most areas of the cemetery are in a regular pattern of six niches high down long avenues, with small shelves on each 'door' for tokens of remembrance. These niches are rented rather than held in perpetuity, meaning that it remains a living and working cemetery. Ginesi's plan emphasized equality in death, asserted for the majority buried there in the lack of ornamentation. In later divisions, individual expression has returned; the Poblenou Cemetery is particularly famous for Jaume Barba's

above: The sphinx monument in Mount Auburn Cemetery, commissioned to commemorate the American Civil War, 1872.

below: John Bachmann, 'Bird's Eye View of Greenwood Cemetery, New York', 1852.

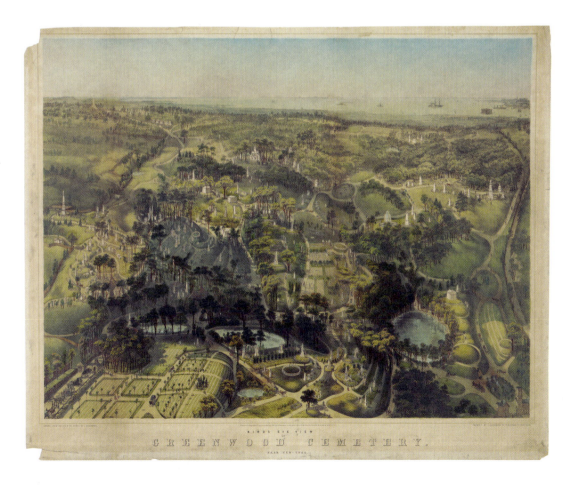

GREENWOOD CEMETERY.

dramatic funerary sculpture *The Kiss of Death*, in which skeletal Death, with folded wings, stoops to embrace the corpse held limp in his arms. Romanticism, perhaps, wins out over classical Formalism.

LONDON'S 'MAGNIFICENT SEVEN'

In London, cemetery reform led to the rapid creation of seven new private cemeteries in a ring around the inner city: Kensal Green (1833), West Norwood (1836), Highgate (1839), Nunhead (1840), Abney Park (1840), Brompton (1840) and Tower Hamlets (1841). They are justly famous as snapshots of Victorian attitudes to death, picturesquely overtaken by inner-city flora and fauna, each of them rescued from ruination and neglect by dedicated societies and each with a distinct ethos and atmosphere.

Tower Hamlets, the last of the seven to open, served poor, East End communities and by 1889 held some 270,000 bodies, mostly in common graves without monuments. It was bombed in the Second World War, and the post-war decision to clear the buildings and larger monuments to create a park gives its remnants a very different atmosphere – smashed about, yet clinging on. Memorials such as the striking cluster of pointed headstones to the 'Poor Brothers' who died in the almshouse of Sutton's Hospital, or the memorial to the drowned of the *Princess Alice* disaster on the Thames in 1871, are all the more affecting for their survival of this second ruination.

above: *The Kiss of Death* monument, Poblenou Cemetery, Barcelona, erected 1930.

below: The Egyptian Avenue, Highgate Cemetery, London. The garden cemetery opened in 1839.

The most similar of the seven to Père Lachaise is Highgate Cemetery, located on a steep hill in North London. The garden cemetery model emphasizes the stimulus of constant variety, and while Highgate is quite small – the hilly West Cemetery is seventeen acres, the later East side nineteen acres – it somehow folds several distinct zones into its trim dimensions. Graves ascend the hill from the Tudor-Gothic chapels by the gate; the steep main path later opens out to the famous Egyptian Avenue, its gloomy entrance flanked by lotus columns and tall obelisks.

This solemn corridor in turn opens onto the base of a gigantic cedar tree that pre-dates the cemetery, around which was built a circular continuation of the Avenue. This 'Circle of Lebanon' was the *pièce de résistance* of the entrepreneurial founder and designer of the West Cemetery, Stephen Geary.

Victorians were not initially keen to abandon all Christian orthodoxies, and this part of the cemetery took a while to fill. It seems appropriate that the dissident lesbian author Radclyffe Hall, whose novel *The Well of Loneliness* was banned as an obscene publication, is housed there with her lover, the singer Mabel Batten, in the Batten family chamber. A columbarium to hold cremated ashes was also built – another modern innovation that disturbed traditional Christian burial practices. It did not take off.

These cemeteries have become places where folktales circulate and evolve. Highgate's Gothic atmosphere is heightened by the story of a heartbroken Dante Gabriel Rossetti burying a notebook of poems with his dead muse, the artist and model Elizabeth Siddal, there. She had overdosed on laudanum in February 1862, a possible suicide that left Rossetti consumed with guilt. Seven years later, he rather wanted the poems back and had to apply to the Home Secretary for permission to exhume the coffin and retrieve his works.

Permission was granted, the notebook disinfected. The story goes that Siddal's hair – that archetypal red mane beloved by the Pre-Raphaelite Brotherhood – had continued to grow wildly as she lay in her grave.

Much later, at a low point of neglect for these Victorian cemeteries in the late 1960s and early 1970s, Highgate's very own vampire caused a minor sensation in the tabloid press. The place became entangled in the Hammer House of Horror's run of Dracula sequels, appearing in a couple of late additions to the genre in the early 1970s. Over the road, in the East Cemetery, the giant bust of Karl Marx glowers his rigorously materialist disapproval of these shenanigans. The bust was installed at the height of the Cold War, and the grave became a location for demonstrations of socialist and communist political groups and visitors from the Soviet bloc. Marx's own grave marker had been modest, his funeral attended by only eleven people.

THE METROPOLITAN GARDEN MOVEMENT

Inner-city churchyards and burial grounds, no longer active, were increasingly neglected spaces. Some were recorded by Charles Dickens in his strange account of night-time journeys through London, *The Uncommercial Traveller*. In the 1870s, the Kyrle Society, founded by the English sisters and social reformers Octavia and Miranda Hill, began to argue that these graveyards could be cleared of their deadly associations and turned into parks. There were successes in turning Bunhill Fields – called 'a desolate wilderness' by *The Times* in 1866 – into a picturesque park (pilgrims still leave flowers on the grave of William Blake almost every day), and the once gloomy retreat of Mary Shelley, Old Pancras church, was cleared up and remodelled as a formal public garden in 1877; Thomas Hardy arrayed old headstones around

1

VIEW IN HIGHGATE CEMETERY.

2

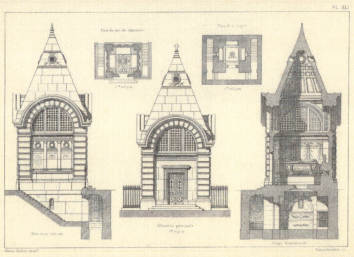

LES TOMBEAUX MODERNES

PL. XLI

Plan du rez-de-chaussée

Plan de la crypte

Élévation latérale

Direction principale

Coupe transversale

TOMBEAU DE LA FAMILLE JULES BEER
A LONDRES
Mr ROTHWENG VAN DER BOVEN ARCHITECTE

3

a tree when working as an architect in the area. Campaigners like the Hill sisters and, later, Isabella Holmes secured many spaces from London's indifferent or unscrupulous developers. In the 1880s, Holmes was active in setting up the Metropolitan Public Gardens Association. After a law protecting disused burial grounds was passed in 1884, she used ancient maps of London to collect a list of 362 burial grounds in the County and City of London and set about trying to find every one of them, writing that 'An appearance of utter insignificance and an air of knowing where you are going is what you want, is the passport for all parts of London'. The product of these researches was *London Burial Grounds* (1896), which included sections on grounds for different denominations, faiths and nationalities.

Just a year after Holmes published her record, Bram Stoker's *Dracula* was saturated with ideas of grave mould, pollution and disease emanating from the grave. The Count's daily need to marinade in the grave dust of his ancestral lands marks a limit to his ability to adapt to spaces more typical of fin-de-siècle modernity. Dracula represents a fearful reversion to the insidious proximity of the living to the dead, a pollution that had been caught so luridly in the mid-century campaigns of George Alfred Walker. The Gothic imagination still owns many of these spaces, remnants and reversions that ground shiny, amnesiac modernity in the ashes and dust of those that have lived before.

TOMBS FOR THE RULERS

Given the vast accumulation of the dead, those whose traces survive beyond chance or accident are often those singled out for special treatment. The rhetoric of Death the Leveller is everywhere contradicted by the hierarchies marked out in funerary rites and memorial practices. Grave goods often seem to speak as eloquently as a jumble of human bones, and the quality and quantity of grave goods often (if not always) increase with social and political status.

Religious belief has long elevated certain bodies as deserving of special treatment, their burial sites focal points for pilgrimage or proximate burial. Many states have attempted to elide this divine aura with the everyday grind of retaining political power among the living. Whether in Mesopotamia, Egypt or Rome, political power invested in the individual can be legitimated by the claim of divine sanction, and this is reinforced by a funerary monument designed to survive for all the ages. At Sutton Hoo in Suffolk an undisturbed treasure trove was discovered in a funerary complex that contained an unusual Saxon ship burial of a powerful man. Yet the site spoke to archaeologists only through the grave goods, the soil having entirely dissolved the body of the man they were meant to accompany.

The construction of a tomb might become one of the consuming works of a living ruler. Funerary monuments can be read as an attempt to defy the supremely dangerous moment of rupture that is physical death, and to mark out an undying continuity of power invested in a ruling dynasty. *The king is dead, long live the king.*

If a ruler can appeal to their ancestral dead for legitimacy, then the divine transfer of power to the rightful heir might be made more secure. The tomb of the ruler slots them into a dynastic succession – although of course, all dynasties fall in the end. Humans claiming the protective

opposite: Jade burial suit bound with gold thread, Han Dynasty, China, 202 BCE–9 CE.

cloak of immortality often find themselves falling back to Earth as mere historical dust.

Legitimating power is one aspect of the political work that the dead undertake for the living. This chapter considers a series of burial sites of rulers and the ways in which such tombs help to shape the social and political world of the living, from the rulers of ancient China and the two bodies of medieval European kings, to the peculiar afterlife of Vladimir Lenin, leader of the Russian Revolution in 1917.

ANCIENT CHINA:
JADE SUITS AND TERRACOTTA ARMIES

China was unified as a territory under its first emperor in the third century BCE, and since the 1960s archaeological research has transformed understandings of the diverse burial practices that emerged across its thousands of miles of terrain. As Jessica Rawson observes in *Life and Afterlife in Ancient China*, for all the diversity of cultural practices in this vast region, a constant is the preservation of ancestral memory, a deep familial duty later codified in the Confucian *Book of Rites* in the Zhou period (1046–256 BCE). The core Confucian idea of filial piety used the tomb as a concrete instantiation of this principle.

As early as Xinglongwa culture (6200–5400 BCE), burial practices particularly focused on the power ascribed to jade. Jade is a hard, translucent stone with a cloudy, magical glow. It is very difficult to work with tools, and its durability became associated with survival or immortality. It was first placed in the mouth – a polished 'sucking jade' stone 'to constrain the body,' as Li Schuicheng says, 'with the hope of eternally preserving the souls of the deceased.' Later, jade was placed over the mouth, nose and eyes – the risky portals of the body – to protect the dead in their passage to a new state of being.

Jade is also a way of marking out social and political status. One of the most notable ancient burial sites was discovered in the 1980s at Fanshan in the Yangtze River Delta, part of the extensive city of the Liangzhu culture (3300–2200 BCE). The eleven tombs that survive there were grouped together for important city officials or leaders, and made extensive and elaborate use of jade grave goods. One grave contained over 600 pieces of jade, placed around the body in a possibly protective array. Jade workers had learned to manipulate and shape jade: the eyes of fantastical creatures swim up from the cloudy interiors of the stone. The circular disks and enigmatic square *cong*, drilled and covered with markings and divisions, have had various symbolic significances ascribed to them (disc of the sun? square of

the earth?) and are found at many grave sites, but their purpose remains enigmatic despite being folded into later structures of religious meaning.

The later Han Dynasty (202 BCE–9 CE) is responsible for the most remarkable jade burial finds, which further develop the protective function of placing jade over the body's orifices. *Yù yī*, or full-body jade burial suits, are stitched from many thousands of tiles of jade that cover the whole body to keep its spirit protected and intact. Jade was understood to protect from malign influences the part of the soul that remained with the body and had to be propitiated if it was to reunite with the spirit-soul that had gone on ahead.

The first undisturbed suits were found in 1968, in the graves of Liu Sheng (who died in 113 BCE) and his wife Dou Wan at a site in Mancheng. Subsequent finds, such as the suit of Prince Huai and the kings Zhao Mo and Liu Wa, reveal the strict hierarchy also recorded in the fifth-century *Hòu Hànshū* (Book of the Later Han). Kings or emperors had these jade elements stitched together with gold thread, princes or princesses with silver and their children's suits with copper. Lesser aristocrats had silk thread, and those lower in the social structure did not receive such grave goods. This strict hierarchy signals the concentration of power and labour that made the Han Dynasty pivotal to the creation of modern China. It is also a mark of the belief in Confucian principles of observing proper social order. The jade suits assert the eternal continuity of imperial might.

1

2

3

4

5

6

below: The Terracotta Army that protected the tomb of the Chinese emperor, Qin Shi Huang, *c.* 210 BCE, uncovered in 1974.

There are many texts from this period of early China that debate the propriety of such ostentatious burials. Followers of more severe Taoist doctrines tended to be contemptuous of the costly funerals of the social elite, Yang Wang-Sun writing 'A lavish burial is of absolutely no benefit to the dead man, and yet foolish people strive to outdo each other in extravagance, wasting their money, exhausting their resources, putting it all in the ground to rot.' Yet the ruling class in Han found themselves on a familiar escalator of spiralling funeral expenses, the Eastern Han dynastic emperors diverting increasing amounts of tax revenue to the vast construction of their own burial plots as soon as they came to power. This spiral came to an end in around 220.

The most lavish ancient tomb complex yet to be rediscovered in China is the tomb of the first emperor of unified China, Qin Shi Huang, created in about 210 BCE. Building started almost as soon as Quin Shi Huang inherited the throne from his father at the age of thirteen, and hundreds of thousands of indentured labourers and prisoners worked on it for decades (they left their more ephemeral messages, scratched on terracotta tiles, in their own graveyard nearby). Resting in the afterlife, the emperor is protected by rows of ever-vigilant terracotta soldiers, ranks carefully marked on their armour, their eight facial types perhaps meant to represent the different ethnicities of the soldiers from across the Qin empire. Only a small portion of this army has been uncovered: thousands of soldiers still stand guard in the earth.

First excavated in 1974, the scale of the tomb is breathtaking. It was sunk 24 metres below ground, and around the central tomb of the emperor is effectively a wholesale recreation of his living imperial territory, complete with chariots and horses to travel to every far-flung district of the state. Continuity of power across the boundary between life and death is central to this exercise. Elsewhere on the site, many of the emperor's retinue were sacrificed and buried in the tomb complex alongside him, to continue to serve without interruption. This sends a message to the surviving populace about the reach of imperial political power in death. The tomb of Qin Shi Huang was the culmination of hundreds of years of consolidation of power into a single dynasty that moved steadily to defeat and incorporate its rivals and create a vast empire.

above: Members of the Terracotta Army even reflect different ethnicities, perhaps to indicate the vast reach of the Qin empire.

Historians after Foucault have talked about a modern 'biopolitics of power': the increasing manipulation and control of living bodies from cradle to grave, particularly by the apparatuses of the state – police, prison, hospital. The tomb complexes of ancient rulers reveal a *necropolitics* of power, the sovereign's absolute control over the life and death of their subjects, even while attempting to raise their own power above this mortal divide.

THE KING'S TWO BODIES

The death of the ruler is a moment of immense danger to sovereign power. In medieval Europe, scholars of ecclesiastical canon law, political theorists and jurists came up with a somewhat convoluted solution to this inevitable problem: the king's two bodies. The jurist Edmund Plowden, writing in sixteenth-century England under Elizabeth I, the Crown still newly divorced from the Catholic Church and in a febrile time of contested succession, explains it like this:

> The King has in him two Bodies, *viz.*, a Body natural, and a Body politic. His Body natural (if it be considered in itself) is a Body mortal, subject to all Infirmities that come by Nature or Accident, to the Imbecility of Infancy or old Age, and to the like Defects that happen to the natural Bodies of other People. But his Body politic is a Body that cannot be seen or handled, consisting of Policy and Government ... and this Body is utterly void of Infancy, and old Age, and other natural Defects and Imbecilities, which the Body natural is subject to.

The kingship that inhabits the Body politic is 'not subject to death', another jurist confirmed in 1608. This second, metaphysical body was sometimes called the Dignity, and jurists began to use the phrase *Dignitas*

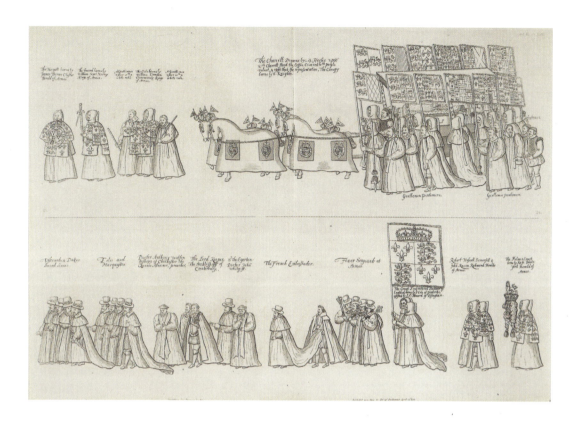

above: Engraving of the funeral procession of Queen Elizabeth I in 1603, from *Ancient Monuments*, London, 1791.

below: The state funeral of Queen Elizabeth II at Westminster Abbey, London, 19 September 2022.

non moritus: the Dignity cannot die. The famous phrase 'The king is dead, long live the king' also emerged at this time.

This explains some of the peculiar rituals around the death and funerals of English and French kings in the early modern period. One witness to the burial in 1498 of Charles VIII of France at the Basilica of Saint-Denis in Paris recorded that once the king was laid in the tomb his staffs of office were broken and placed with the body, but the banner of France was merely dipped for a moment before being raised again to the cry '*Vive le roi*!' Elements of this ritual tradition were witnessed again at the funeral of Elizabeth II in 2022, when among the last acts before the committal of the body at St George's Chapel at Windsor Castle were the removal of the Crown, Orb and Sceptre from the coffin, to be placed on the altar for the transfer of power, and the Lord Chamberlain snapping his Wand of Office in half for it to be buried with the monarch.

A practice that has *not* survived from early modern royal funerals is the strange literalization of the two bodies, in which a small effigy of the king made from wood, leather and plaster, dressed in coronation garments with the crown, orb and sceptre of office, was placed on the coffin for the funeral procession. This rite was first recorded in England in 1327 at the funeral of Edward II – possibly just a practical matter, because Edward's

body had to be embalmed and was buried at Gloucester Cathedral some three months after his actual death. The ritual seems to have been transposed to France in the difficult dynastic moment around the deaths in 1422 of Henry V of England and, only three weeks later, Charles VI of France.

In France, the division between the treatment of corpse and effigy had become even more marked by the death of Francis I in 1547. The king's body was exhibited, lying in state, for ten days, but then removed and replaced with an effigy wearing the imperial crown and carrying the sceptre of justice, at which point the décor was changed from sombre mourning to bright colours. Clergy were posted around the effigy, food and wine were served to it and visitors could sprinkle holy water on it 'as though,' Kantorowicz says, 'the dummy were the living king himself.' Funerary processions began to distinguish between the triumph of death over the Body natural, which was mourned with appropriate solemnity, and the triumph over death represented by the effigy of the Body politic, either carried by representatives of the state who were not dressed in mourning clothes (because this king was not dead), or pulled on a triumphal chariot. This double burial can be read into the double monuments, or *transi* tombs, that became briefly fashionable in the sixteenth century. Louis XII's tomb in the Basilica of Saint Denis presents a typical divide of the devout living king above and the dead king below, gaunt and wretched. The split of the Body politic and Body natural had made its way into funerary sculpture.

above: Illustration of a *transi* tomb from *Disputacion Betwyx the Body and Wormes*, 1435–40.

The worst disruption of this delicate doctrinal split is the act of regicide. To remove the head, as happened to Charles I in the English Civil War in 1649 and Louis XVI during the French Revolution in 1793, was in each case meant to strike directly at both the Body natural of the mortal king and the divine right of the Body politic of kingship. The notion of the ruler as head, their people figured as the lowlier members of the body, had been a political metaphor for hierarchical government for centuries.

opposite: The funeral effigies of kings and queens, Westminster Abbey. Left to right, top row: Charles II; Anne of Bohemia, wife of Richard II; Henry VII. Middle row: Elizabeth I; Elizabeth of York; Mary I. Bottom row: Mary II; Anne of Denmark, wife of James I; William III.

Oliver Cromwell was declared Lord Protector of England for life in 1653. He died in 1658, and on the Restoration of King Charles II in 1660 his crimes against kingship were not forgotten. Punishment was focused on destroying whatever 'kingly' power might have remained in the Lord Protector's abject Body natural. His corpse was exhumed from Westminster Abbey on the twelfth anniversary of Charles I's execution and dragged through the streets of London, before being hanged at Tyburn gallows like a common criminal (the execution of a corpse in this way had many precedents). After being killed again, Cromwell was decapitated, his body thrown into a pit and head impaled on a spike at Westminster Hall, where it remained at the heart of the restored establishment for forty years before it was blown down in

187

a storm. It was allegedly paraded as a curiosity in travelling shows before being bought by John Wilkinson in 1814 (although by now some doubted its authenticity). Frances Larson's history of Cromwell's severed head ends with its final burial in the antechapel of Sidney Sussex College in Cambridge, where Cromwell had studied. Finally, his exhausting posthumous career had come to an end.

The metaphysical or magical power ascribed to rulers has often meant that their corpses have extremely lively afterlives. One of the most famous cases of this involves the remains of Eva Perón, known as Evita, the young, glamorous wife of the Argentine president Juan Domingo Perón, who died of cancer in 1952 at the age of only thirty-three. 'In Argentina,' Edwin Murphy notes, 'political corpses are political capital'. Her husband aimed to retain her populist following, first by a carefully staged lying-in-state in a glass coffin, at which over two million Argentinians paid their respects, and second by placing her in perpetuity at the centre of a national memorial. Over the course of a year, the body was treated in secret by the embalmer Dr Pedro Ara, who is thought to have constructed several wax and vinyl doubles as potential decoys to foil enemy designs on the corpse.

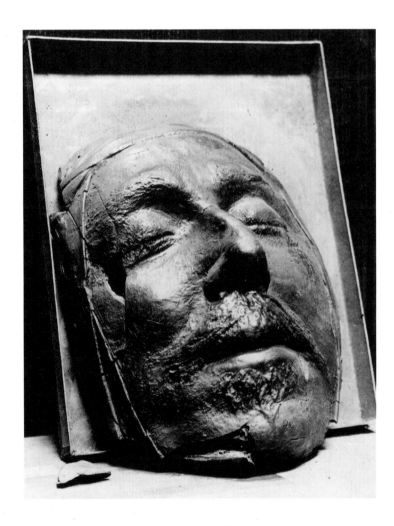

Perón was overthrown and forced into exile in 1955, leaving his wife's body behind. The military junta at first thought that the uncannily preserved corpse was a statue; they cut off a finger to check. The Catholic Church refused permission to cremate the body and thus dissolve its political potency. After several failed attempts to bury it in secret to avoid creating a rallying point for Perónists, eventually the body was smuggled out of the country through Germany and, in 1957, buried in Italy. Evita lay hidden in a grave under a different name until 1971, when the leader of Argentina's military junta was himself kidnapped, executed and his body withheld until it could be exchanged for hers. The transfer of power was sealed with a corpse exchange: Evita was delivered to the house of her still-exiled husband and his third wife, Isabel Martínez de Perón, in Madrid. Her open coffin stayed there for two years, a companion for the Peróns and their guests, it was said, in the dining room. After Juan died in 1974, Evita's body was finally returned to Argentina and laid to rest in the Duarte family vault in the Cementerio de le Recoleta, alongside many of the presidents of Argentina. The cemetery, a product of the era of reform in 1822, is regularly voted one of the most beautiful in the world. Tourists still stream to visit the final resting place of Evita – egged on by an eponymous global smash-hit musical and by Tomás Eloy Martínez's novel *Santa*

above: Torchlit parade in memory of Eva Perón, a year after her death in 1952, Buenos Aires, Argentina.

below: The coffin of president Juan Domingo Perón and the displayed body of his second wife Eva Perón before burial in Buenos Aires, from *Life* Magazine, 1974.

Evita (1995), adapted for TV in 2022, about her posthumous perambulations. In 1987, an addendum was made to the story: Juan Péron's tomb was broken into, the hands of the corpse sawn off and held to ransom for eight million US dollars. The state refused to pay.

The model for the preservation of Eva Perón's corpse was, of course, the body of the miraculous, incorruptible saint. Grubby politics sought to be doused in the odour of sanctity, and Juan Perón longed for something of the eternal in his hold on power. The embalmer, Ara, meanwhile, was driven by a desire to outdo one of the most famous and unlikely acts of embalming in the twentieth century: the preservation of the leader of the Russian Revolution, Vladimir Lenin, after his death in January 1924.

LENIN'S TOMB, RED SQUARE, MOSCOW

below: Carl Hassmann, 'The Russian Crown', *Puck* magazine, 27 December 1905.

Vladimir Lenin had returned from exile to join the Russian Revolution in 1917, his Bolshevik faction driving pitilessly for the violent overthrow of the remains of the Tsarist state. In 1918, at the start of the Russian Civil War, he was severely wounded in an assassination attempt. He was eventually forced to retire from frontline politics after a series of strokes, and died away from Moscow in January 1924.

Both his widow and Leon Trotsky's faction in the ruling group were steadfast in their materialist and atheist principles, arguing that Lenin himself had wanted no monuments or grandiose memorials. But Joseph Stalin, already pushing Trotsky out of government, wanted to build his own bid to succeed Lenin. He would recycle the place of the saint in the Russian Orthodox Church in the service of Communist state power. In the first week after his death, Lenin's body was placed

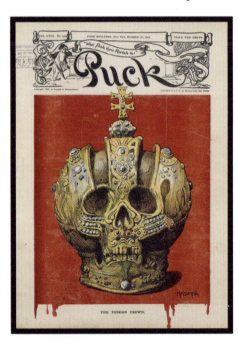

in a temporary mausoleum near the centre of power in the Kremlin, alongside which revolutionaries had once been executed, in what would become Red Square. Millions queued to file past the body of the dead Soviet hero, confirming Stalin's instinct that there was a reservoir of mass sentiment to be tapped.

But Lenin's body was already starting to decay. The brain had been removed to be studied by Party-approved scientists for what it might reveal about the ideal Soviet Man. After a month, the eyes were also removed. Party apparatchiks favoured freezing the body; chemical experts, including leading Bolshevik sympathizer Boris Zbarsky, suggested embalming. Zbarsky's son, Ilya, records in his memoir how his family business became not only permanent attendants to the preserved body of Lenin, but also the preferred embalmers of Communist leaders around the world.

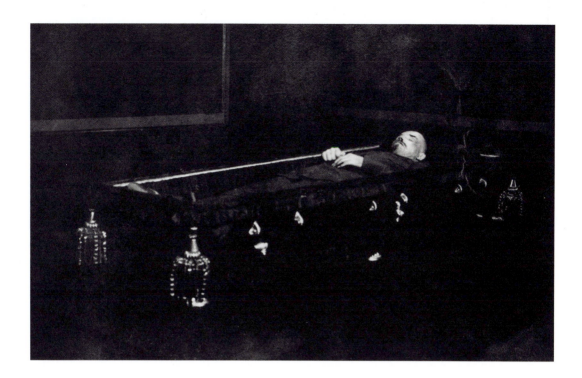

In May 1924, a more permanent mausoleum was constructed in Red Square – a cube, half-buried in the ground, where Lenin's body, face and hands exposed, could be viewed in a hushed hall under dimmed lights. The radical Constructivist artist and architect Konstantin Melnikov designed a futuristic diamond-shaped crystal sarcophagus. The cube was topped with a six-stepped pyramidal structure and incorporated a rostrum on which Communist leaders would stand and salute Red Army parades and revolutionary anniversaries for the next seventy years. This structure reached its final form in 1929, in blocky red and black granite, 'LENIN' etched on its side. Its shape was meant to echo the design of a Mesopotamian ziggurat, but there was also an obvious echo of the Egyptian pyramids. There is no doubt that the discovery of the preserved body of Tutankhamun less than a year before Lenin's death fed into the Soviet design.

Bolshevik ideology was *supposed* to be strictly materialist, but in fact, many Bolsheviks were influenced by the mystical writings of the eccentric Russian philosopher Nikolai Fedorovich Fydorov. His ideas led to the philosophy of 'cosmism' – a strand of Bolshevism directed at expanding Russia into space – but he also believed that the rapid advances

above: The hero of the Bolshevik Revolution, Lenin, lying in state in a temporary mausoleum. Moscow, January 1924.

below: Konstantin Melnikov, designs for the sarcophagus of Lenin, 1924.

of science in the nineteenth century would shortly lead to the ability to resurrect the dead. In a chapter titled 'Parents and Resurrectors', the philosopher explained, somewhat opaquely, that scientists would soon:

> become capable of transforming the ashes of their forefathers ... by gathering them together into the bodies in which they originally belonged. The reverberation and quivering (vibration) of which molecules and the ashes of the dead are capable ... will ... unite the particles and turn them into the live bodies to which the particles used to belong.

above: Lenin's mausoleum, a granite ziggurat, Red Square, Moscow.

below: Laboratory where the body of the Communist president of Czechoslovakia, Klement Gottwald, was embalmed, inside the National Memorial on the Vitkov Hill, Prague, now in Czechia.

Fyodorov had died in 1903, but many Bolsheviks seemed to imbibe the idea that immortality might be achieved by the new chemical and physical sciences. In 1921, Leonid Krasin, one of Lenin's inner circle, said that science would soon 'be capable of restoring life to the great figures of history, fighting for the freedom of humanity.' After Lenin's death, it was obvious where such efforts should be directed. In 1929 a permanent laboratory was constructed under Lenin's tomb for Boris Zbarsky and his growing team. For decades, they attended to the body at least twice a week with injections and chemical baths. When Mayakovsky proclaimed 'Lenin lived, Lenin lives, Lenin shall live,' this may have had a much more literal interpretation than the usual funerary rhetoric. Lenin became the embodiment of eternal Communist rule.

This cult of sainthood and immortal power was soon transposed to other authoritarian Communist leaders. In 1949 Zbarsky embalmed the leader of Bulgaria, Georgi Dimitriov.

The chemist had escaped Stalin's purges by keeping his recipe for embalming fluid secret – Stalin had to keep him alive to benefit from this immortalization himself. When Stalin died in 1953, he was indeed embalmed and placed next to Lenin, but the exposure of his crimes against the people in the years after his death led to his removal from the tomb in 1961.

At Stalin's funeral, the leader of the Czechoslovak Communist Party caught a

above: The Ho Chi
Minh Mausoleum,
Hanoi, Vietnam.

cold that would lead to deadly pneumonia: he too was embalmed by Zbarsky. In 1969, amid the Vietnam War, the team helped preserve the body of Ho Chi Minh, whose body had a peripatetic afterlife, only coming to rest in the mausoleum designed for him in Ba Dinh Square in Hanoi in 1976. This mausoleum also has a step-pyramid roof – an echo of Lenin, of the International Soviet Style, of Ancient Egypt, of the immortal transfer of power. In 1976, they also preserved the body of the Angolan leader Agostinho Neto, who had died on a trip to Moscow.

Gwendolyn Leick visited many of these memorial complexes for her book *Tombs of the Great Leaders*, which also includes fascist leaders and the heroes of national struggles for independence, mainly on the African continent. Many such monuments situate the un-dead ruler at the heart of national memorials. Bodies imbued with power remain disturbingly lively: in Spain, 'The Valley of the Fallen' memorial complex was a rallying point for Franco's fascist regime, which ruled from 1936 to 1975. Franco invested inordinate amounts of time in designing and planning the complex, and inevitably planned for his own corpse to be the centrepiece. The transition to democracy soon after his death rendered the site a problematic locus of fascist resistance, and it was frequently closed for unspecified maintenance. After a number of court cases, judgments and appeals, Franco's body was removed from the memorial space in 2019 and reburied in a municipal cemetery next to his wife: a clear attempt to recategorize the body as no longer one of the special dead.

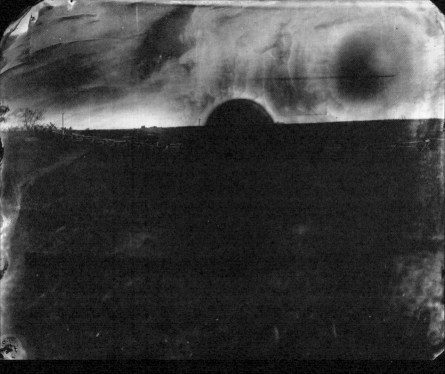

RECRUITING THE DEAD

THE NATION'S SACRIFICIAL DEAD

In 1882, Ernest Renan, the French historian of Christian civilizations, delivered an influential lecture at the Sorbonne in Paris titled 'What is a Nation?' 'Where national memories are concerned,' Renan wrote, 'griefs are of more value than triumphs, for they impose duties, require a common effort.' At the core of many nation states are sites of ritual remembrance; in the modern era, these often take the form of national cemeteries. Nations are modern constructions built around cults of the sacrificial dead; their political leaders have used this elevated memory of sacrifice to ask their populations to repeat the gesture in turn.

Many radical eighteenth-century European thinkers conceived the modern nation state as a secular entity. The new French Republic took over the last king's church, Sainte-Geneviève, and turned it into the Panthéon, a grand monument to the nation's heroes. Arlington National Cemetery, the burial ground at the centre of the American Republic, came in 1864, amid civil war. Conservative advocates insisted on a solemn moral debt to the dead, but the dead of these new republics did not exactly weigh them down; instead, they could be recruited to the new nationalist story.

William Godwin wrote his *Essay on Sepulchres* (1809) in an England at war with post-revolutionary France under Napoleon. He argued that monuments to the notable national dead could 'paralyse the hand of oblivion', creating stability in times of crisis that threatened full, revolutionary erasure. 'Let us erect a shrine to their memory,' Godwin proposed, 'let us visit their tombs; let us indulge all the reality we can now have, of a sort of conference with these men, by repairing to the scene which, as far as they are at all on earth, they still inhabit.'

opposite: Sally Mann, *Battlefield, Antietam (Black Sun)*, 2001. Photograph, using nineteenth-century techniques, of one of the key battles of the American Civil War.

above: Arlington National Cemetery, Virginia. The central memorial burial site of the United States of America, opened in 1864.

The Battle of Waterloo in Belgium in 1815, fought against Napoleon by allied forces opposed to his expansionism, accelerated the shift from the understanding of a professional army as a small force almost entirely separate from ordinary life, to an army and its sacrifices being bound into core national narratives. But the treatment of the dead was cavalier, to say the least: on a later visit to the site, the English travel writer Charlotte Eaton recalled bones still poking from the ground. The absence of any mass graves for the estimated 17,000 British, 7,000 Prussian and 24,000 French troops has suggested to the conflict archaeologist Tony Pollard that bones from the battlefield might have been ground down and used for fertilizer in the fields.

On battlefields dominated by new weaponry, what to do with the sheer number of dead began to present a problem. During the American Civil War (1861–65), even the briefest of engagements – a day, a morning – generated large numbers of dead and wounded. Thousands of rapid burials in shallow graves followed engagements at places like Antietam, or were conducted under flags of temporary truce, as at Petersburg in 1864. The photographer Sally Mann has made haunting images of a number of these sites using the laborious nineteenth-century wet-plate collodion process. Soldiers saw the rapid processing of bodies and fallen comrades in fields and wrote home, as one did from the front in Virginia, that 'I have a horror of being thrown out in a neglected place or be trampled on as I have seen a number of graves here.' As Jeremiah Gage lay dying at Gettysburg, he wrote to his mother of his wish for his body 'to be buried like my comrades,' rather than repatriated. His last words, Drew Gilpin Faust reports, added the caveat, 'But deep, boys, deep, so the beasts won't get me.' Particularly in the South, among the states that formed the Confederacy, battlefield sites are still invested with an idealized doomed heroism, crucial rallying points for identarian politics.

The fates of soldiers killed on foreign battlefields in territory that remained hostile were the most difficult of all. Of the 22,000 British soldiers killed in the Crimean War (1853–56), many died in notorious engagements such as the Charge of the Light Brigade and many more through cold, negligence and disease. The Haydarpaşa Cemetery still holds thousands of British soldiers who died of wounds and disease there. The Crimea also produced a new discourse of memorializing the war dead.

Initially, troops had been buried near where they fell, the rank and file in communal pits, officers given grave markers or memorials where possible. When reports emerged of neglect and even grave-robbing, popular sentiment in Britain was outraged. Some tombs were found 'smashed to fragments' in 1869, prompting an official government investigation that recommended consolidating eleven memorial sites – significantly, only moving and protecting the markers, leaving the dead safely buried. But further attacks on monuments resulted in the officers' graveyard known as Cathcart's Hill becoming the sole, crowded but defensible cemetery. At first, as Brigadier General Sir James Edmonds recorded in 1908, it was 'a sorry sight, looking like a derelict stonemason's yard.' In the aftermath of the war, the graves were so inaccessible to mourning British families that images of Cathcart's Hill in lithographs, books and even, in one case, 3D model, circulated widely. Crimea became a major battleground during the Nazi occupation of Ukraine in the 1940s, and the cemetery was smashed up again in the battle around Sevastopol. The politics of the Cold War ground it down further: parts were reduced to rubble in 1956, and other parts seized and redeveloped. Another attempt to preserve it, started in 2011 by the writer Louise Berridge, came to a halt with the Russian annexation of Crimea in 2014. Sevastopol was a renewed battlefield in the Russian invasion of Ukraine in 2023. No rest for the dead in Crimea.

The one era in which the cemetery at Cathcart's Hill was relatively stable was after 1924, when it was folded into the responsibilities of an institution key to placing the war dead at the centre of British and imperial narratives of sacrificial nationhood: the Imperial War Graves Commission.

below: Headstones designed by the Imperial War Graves Commission, established in 1917.

bottom: Tyne Cot Cemetery, Flanders, where over 3,000 fallen soldiers are commemorated.

The first autumn of the First World War basically eliminated the standing armies of Europe's powers, and conscription sent each nation's young men to be killed in waves. The problems of recording mass death along 400 miles of front were immense. The poet Edmund Blunden wrote of visiting a trench that was 'cancerous with bodies … The whole zone was a corpse, and the mud itself mortified.'

Fabian Ware, a former colonial administrator and newspaper editor who was too old to fight by 1914, volunteered for the Red Cross ambulance service and soon began documenting lists of the dead and their places of burial. By March 1915, in recognition of the emotional and moral force of such records, Ware was appointed head of a formalized Graves Registration Committee. Two years later, after a particularly deadly Autumn, the British government agreed to form the Imperial War Graves Commission (IWGC). Ware's vision recruited the dead of the British Empire to help bind it into a unified whole, just as war risked pulling its white settler dominions apart. The IWGC was headed by the Prince of Wales, and centrally involved were those two laureates of the British Empire, Rudyard Kipling (who lost his only son at the Battle of Loos in 1915) and Winston Churchill.

In the first months of the formation of the IWGC, Sir Frederic Kenyon of the British Museum helped establish rules for the cemeteries. Repatriation of bodies had been excluded early on; instead, all graves, without overt hierarchy, were to be marked by an identical Portland stone headstone of fixed size, with name, rank, regiment, date of death and age marked. Regimental badges and a simple marker of religious and denominational affiliation were etched into the stone. In the initial phase after Armistice in November 1918, some 580,000 individual graves and headstones were made, a feat that Kipling compared to the labour of the Egyptian pyramids. The architect Edwin Lutyens was responsible for much of the sparse symbolism and tone of the cemeteries, serried ranks of headstones framed by simple walls or low planting. To visit them is, still, to step into an odd pocket of timelessness.

But for the vast numbers who could never hope to visit cemeteries abroad, the question of how to commemorate the absent dead remained agonizing. On Peace Day in July 1919, a march through London was arranged and Lutyens was given just eleven days to design and build a monument to those laid forever in some corner of a foreign field.

At first, the Cenotaph in Whitehall was a temporary structure. It was actually a *catafalque*: a pylon designed to lift up the tomb of a great hero, which in this case was empty to symbolize the war dead overseas. The authorities were surprised by the crowds that flocked to the monument, laying flowers and wreaths in their millions, and after attempts to move it out of Whitehall failed, Lutyens designed a

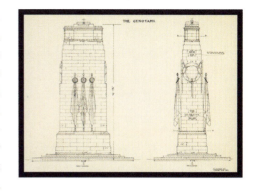

version in Portland stone to be unveiled by the king on Armistice Day in 1920 – the same day that the Grave of the Unknown Soldier was dedicated in Westminster Abbey. War memorials had rapidly become part of a core national narrative of sacrifice, sited at the heart of government.

A mark of the overwhelming grief focalized by the Cenotaph is evident in the famous photographs made by the Spiritualist medium Ada Deane on Armistice Day in 1922 and 1923. Above the gathered crowds, Deane's images showed a second hovering crowd: the spectral war dead, summoned by the act of remembrance. The image comforted some and outraged many.

Elsewhere, the Western Front Association website carries an evocative photographic record by Mike St Maur Sheil of isolated German memorials and the stone gateways built to now-vanished battlefield cemeteries during months and years of stalemate at the front. There is no centralized record of these lone monuments – why would a defeated nation want to remember them? Erich Maria Remarque testified to the horrific German experience in *All Quiet on the Western Front* (1928), but in the 1920s and 1930s Nazi ideology also exploited the sense of defeat, humiliation and class betrayal of German soldiers in the myth of the *Dolchstosslegende*: the Stab in the Back.

Defeated nations have a complicated relationship with memorialization, even if, as the German historian Wolfgang Schivelbusch has noted, there is often 'a strange kind of euphoria' associated with defeat. Germany did not centralize records of its dead, regiments buried their own and after the war, no government organization was really allowed to care for the burial sites. A private, resolutely non-political charity called the VDK, or 'Care for German War Graves', was set up in 1919 by a former officer to memorialize and preserve the German dead on French soil. There has been a

above: Sir Edwin Lutyens, design for the Cenotaph, London, c. 1920.

left: Ada Deane, photograph taken near the Cenotaph on the Armistice Day, November 1923.

below: German Military Cemetery in Bouconville, France, 1935 postcard.

slow consolidation of these burial grounds over the decades: Langemark has a memorial sculpture of mourning soldiers by Emil Krieger, and at Vladslo cemetery there is Käthe Kollwitz's *Grieving Parents* monument, created after the death of her son in 1914. Langemark also holds the 'Comrades Grave', which initially consolidated over 25,000 unknown dead, although many have since been identified, their names inscribed on plaques in a continuing process. This feels decidedly more provisional and belated than the government-sanctioned work of the IWGC.

These displacements are heightened in the history of Russian commemorative monuments. The cult of the war dead had grown in nineteenth-century Tsarist Russia, and in 1916 major memorials were planned by the Russian Society for Remembrance of Soldiers of the Russian Army Who Fell in the War. Revolution swept many of these plans aside. The First World War was dismissed by the Bolsheviks as the grubby conflict of imperialist rulers and their bourgeois enablers. Instead, exiles and émigrés recruited the war dead to their cause against the Soviet Union by building monuments elsewhere. The USSR, meanwhile, commemorated its revolutionary heroes in the Kremlin Wall Necropolis.

Memory of the First World War dead has been doubly eclipsed in Russia. The deaths of millions during the Nazi invasion of Russia became the focal point of narratives of sacrifice for the Communist regime, with the Siege of Stalingrad, in which two million people died, at the centre of that history. This has only been intensified in the nationalist and imperialist rhetoric of Vladimir Putin since his rise to power in 2003. In 2020, Putin dedicated the Main Cathedral of the Russian Armed Forces in Moscow on Victory Day in the Great Patriotic War, the principal date in the Russian memorial calendar. The vast cathedral opened on 22 June, the Day of Remembrance and Sorrow, which marks the first day of the Nazi invasion of Soviet territory in 1941. The floor of the Orthodox cathedral is constructed of melted-down metal from Nazi tanks and weaponry. The Russian state has continually justified the war against Ukraine, started in 2014 and renewed in 2023, by the claim that it represents a renewal of the fight against fascism, disregarding atrocities committed against the Ukrainian population by the Nazi army after its invasion in 1941. As Benedict Anderson emphasizes, narratives

above: Emil Krieger's statues of soldiers at the Langemark Military Cemetery, West Flanders, Belgium.

below: Monument to the heroes of the First World War in the memorial complex, Victory Park, Moscow.

right: António
Agostinho Neto
Memorial, Luanda,
which holds Angola's
first president.

of nationalism are strictly limited imaginings, which can end up caught in compulsive, melancholic repetitions.

In the decades after the Second World War, many newly independent nations, having overthrown their colonial occupiers, recruited the dead of their anti-colonial struggles to new national narratives. The tombs of independence leaders have formed the focal point for national cemeteries, as in Agostinho Neto's extraordinary, unfinished space-rocket monument in Luanda in Angola, which sits between the presidential palace and national assembly, at the centre of the national narrative.

One of the most striking designs is Zimbabwe's National Heroes' Acre, begun in 1981, a year after the overthrow of the vicious British colonial regime of Southern Rhodesia. On a hill outside Harare, the cemetery embraces ideas of revolutionary struggle in its layout, which is the shape of two AK-47s laid back-to-back. The iconic Soviet gun was designed in the 1940s and exported across the globe, often to the USSR's Cold War allies. The monument's design echoes that of the Taesongsan Revolutionary Martyrs' Cemetery in Pyongyang, North Korea – the same firm, Mansudae, designed both cemeteries. The black marble graves of the heroes are meant to represent a magazine of bullets, and the memorial to the Unknown Solider takes the form of a trio holding a rocket launcher, gun and flag. It is unapologetic in claiming the necessity of violence and martyrdom to the revolutionary cause. The socialist realism of Mansudae Overseas Projects characterizes a number of memorial sites on the African continent, including Namibia's Heroes' Acre cemetery, south of Windhoek, and the Tiglachin Monument, Addis Ababa, Ethiopia, which commemorates the Ethiopian and Cuban soldiers of the Ethio-Somali War.

above: National Heroes' Acre monument in Harare, Zimbabwe. A monument to those who died in the struggle for independence, designed after the gun of the freedom fighter, the AK-47.

below: The Pylon Monument, built at the gate of the Majdanek concentration camp outside Lublin, Poland.

The central political leader of the independence struggle for Zimbabwe, Robert Mugabe, is not buried in the National Heroes' Acre. Mugabe fell from favour after decades of repressive and tyrannical leadership and was finally deposed in 2017, when an attempt to install Grace Mugabe, his wife, as his successor failed. When he died in 2019 at the age of ninety-five, the family refused to release his body to be inserted into the national monument. He was buried instead in a steel coffin under concrete at the family compound in his home village. A court order in 2021 to exhume the body and relocate it in the national cemetery suggests that this 'Body natural' will suffer the kind of disturbances typical of corpses that have been invested with the power of the 'Body politic'.

The United Nations Convention on the Prevention and Punishment of the Crime of Genocide was adopted in 1948, in the wake of growing understanding of the Nazi 'Final Solution': the systematic extermination of over six million Jewish people and an equivalent number of Roma and Sinti people, prisoners of war, political opponents, disabled people and others considered 'undesirable'. The majority had been murdered in the large network of concentration camps built across Europe between 1933 and 1945. Allied troops reached Bergen-Belsen in April 1945; the images from that camp, wrote Susan Sontag, formed an 'inventory of horror'. Yet Belsen was only a satellite. Soviet troops had already encountered the major extermination camps in Poland from mid-1944. The decision of the USSR to preserve the camps – at Majdanek, at Auschwitz – has made them centres of Holocaust memorial.

The camps were places of mass murder and might now be regarded as *anti*-cemeteries: places built precisely to erase culture and memory. The deliberate targeting and destruction of Jewish burial grounds and cemeteries by the Nazis in their rise to power was intrinsic to the logic of genocide, which must also kill the already dead as the holders of cultural and religious continuity. In the camps solely constructed for extermination, such as Sobibor,

above: Memorial space at the almost completely destroyed Sobibor concentration camp, Poland. Opened in 2022.

around 178,000 people were murdered between 1942 and 1943, although some estimates have been considerably higher. People were gassed, their bodies hurled in pits. Later, they were removed, incinerated, ground to dust, mixed with soil and dispersed through woodlands, among trees planted by the prisoners. Cremation better covered up the Nazis' crimes, but it was also a calculated insult to the murdered Jews, in opposition to Jewish burial traditions. Sobibor closed after a prisoner uprising in 1943, and there was a concerted attempt to erase all trace of the site. The attempt to destroy all records was another part of the genocidal erasure of the name, a final offence to Jewish belief.

How to memorialize the dead at this site where so very few survived to testify? In 1965 a low mound was built in the clearing where the burial pits had been, suggestive of an ancient round barrow. The Holocaust scholar James Young's *Texture of Memory*, written on the cusp of the collapse of the Soviet bloc in the early 1990s, detailed how Polish memorials were often dedicated at that time either to victims of fascism or to heroes of the anti-fascist struggle, recruiting the dead to a political narrative that sidestepped the question of any Polish complicity in the destruction of Jewish communities. The European history of anti-Semitism was eclipsed. At the end of the Cold War, fifty years after the end of the Second World War, the framing of many camps was being reconfigured. Memorial complexes could not and should not fix things in stone, Young suggested, but instead were always places of active and contested memory.

In 2022, the new memorial and museum at Sobibor opened. The designers tried to address the issue that to walk to the woodland clearing to visit the memorial mound was effectively to tramp through the human remains scattered in the woods, inadvertently deepening the offence. After almost ten years of intensive debate with communities impacted by the decisions, the clearing is now sealed by a bed of white crushed marble stones, and only glimpsed through a boundary wall that suggests the absolute division of the worlds of life and death. This is a design intended to be more sensitive to the customs of Jewish burial sites and modes of memory.

The memorial at Sobibor was also designed to counter a trend for what the architect and architectural psychologist Krzysztof Lenartowicz termed 'the architecture of dread': the tendency of some Holocaust memorial sites to immerse the visitor in an experiential repetition of the path of those deported to the camp from arrival, to death chamber, to ash-pit. The example the design team offer is the 'Crevasse Road' memorial at the Belzec extermination camp, where the visitor is plunged into the ground through a narrow concrete gouge in the earth that passes through the field of stones that covers the ash-pits: an experience of engulfment.

Since the Genocide Convention was affirmed in international law in 1951, use of the term has continued to be fraught with political risk. Memorialization is always contested, particularly when perpetrators remain involved in contemporary politics. In Cambodia, the extent of the genocide inflicted by the Khmer Rouge regime between 1975 and 1979 remains uncertain, with a Documentation Centre and a Mass Grave Project only established in 1995. The Communist purges of the population killed between 1.5 and 2 million people, and over 20,000 mass graves have been detected, usually close to the security centres where perceived enemies of the state were tortured and killed. The Tuol Sleng Genocide Museum, a former school used as Security Prison 21, has served as a locus for memorializing the victims of torture; the

Choeung Ek extermination centre outside Phnom Penh contains 9,000 bodies in mass graves, the shape of which are still visible, overlooked by a Buddhist stupa memorial that displays 5,000 human skulls behind glass.

Ossuary-type accumulations of bones are also one of the principal means of memorialization in Rwanda, where an estimated one million predominantly Tutsi people were massacred by Hutu militias in 1994 during the civil war, underpinned by a violent colonial history that had amplified and exploited the divide between Hutu and Tutsi people. Rwanda has six national memorial sites, including the mass grave of the Kigali Genocide Memorial outside the capital, where 250,000 people are buried. An ongoing Wall of Names project documents them. At Murambi, a former technical school where 50,000 people seeking shelter were murdered, the memorial includes ossuary displays and corpses preserved in their last agonies.

above: Photographs of victims of the 1994 genocide, Kigali Genocide Memorial, Rwanda.

below: Clothes belonging to the victims at Murambi Genocide Memorial Centre outside Gikongoro, Rwanda.

There is an ongoing programme of exhuming bodies from provisional mass graves, relocating them to official sites and removing earlier memorials. As Laura Major has observed, this process is controversial, since it is overseen by a government that came into power in the course of these murderous months and now recruits the murdered to a familiar sacrificial nationalist story. Individuals entangled in local acts of murder and dismemberment are transposed

into the simplified narrative of collective memorials, the ossuaries themselves a form foreign to local burial practices.

The Rwandan genocide accelerated the formation of the International Criminal Court in 2002. The court's combination of forensic anthropology, archaeology and crime scene investigation was formulated largely in the aftermath of the Srebrenica genocide in July 1995. The mass graves of over 8,000 Bosniak

Muslim men and boys murdered by Bosnian Serb forces had been deliberately disturbed, churned and reburied several times by the perpetrators in order to frustrate discovery and identification. The development of DNA identification techniques was accelerated by the investigation, which provided evidential basis for the prosecution of the military commanders of the Army of Republika Srpska.

above: Srebrenica–
Potočari Memorial
Centre and Cemetery for
the victims of the 1995
genocide, Bosnia and
Herzegovina.

below: Women search
for traces in the Atacama
Desert of those killed by
the Chilean military junta.
Nostalgia for the Light, a
documentary by Patricio
Guzmán, 2010.

Many of the investigators had been trained by the American forensic anthropologist Clyde Snow, who had identified the remains of the Nazi doctor Josef Mengele, Auschwitz's 'Angel of Death', after his death under an assumed name in Brazil. Snow had been politicized in his specialism by a request to explore the graves of those who had been 'disappeared' – systematically tortured and murdered – in Argentina in the 1980s, following the end of eight years of rule by the military junta. Forensic teams went into Argentina, Chile and Guatemala as juntas fell, and despite conservative political resistance to proper investigation or prosecution of the perpetrators, were able to document sites of mass killing. There are now memorials to Disappeared Detainees across South America, including the Parque de la Memoria in Buenos Aires in Argentina and a monument in Santiago General Cemetery in Chile. A trilogy of documentaries by the Chilean film-maker Patricio Guzmán, beginning with *Nostalgia for the Light* (2010), has focused

The women who search for their dead

on attempts to recover the memories of those erased by military and political conservative forces in Chile.

The Missing are a particular order of the political dead, 'occupants', Jenny Edkins writes, 'of a zone of indistinction between life and death.' Their memorialization or reburial insists on a counternarrative to their vanishment, a move to a different kind of political trajectory.

opposite: Paolo Pellegrin, seventeenth anniversary of the Srebrenica massacre, 2012. The bodies of those newly identified by DNA are buried in the cemetery each anniversary.

above: The Al-Faluja Cemetery near Jabaliya, Gaza, destroyed by advancing Israeli Defence Forces, December 2023.

At Srebrenica, Eric Stover and other forensic anthropologists worked patiently to document the mass burials, a process documented in the book *The Graves*, made by Stover and the photographer Gilles Peress. Since 2003, the bodies of those identified have been buried in the Srebrenica-Potočari Memorial Centre and Cemetery in the town. The site remains intensely contested: local Bosnian Serbs resent the presence of the memorial in their town, while on the anniversary of the massacre in July, the newly identified dead are buried by Bosniak mourners; at the twenty-second such collective burial, in July 2017, seventy-one people were interred. Here, the dead remain very active participants in the politics of the region.

In January 2024, a team of lawyers representing South Africa filed a case against the government of Israel in the International Criminal Court, accusing its military, the Israeli Defence Force, of committing genocide against Palestinians in its invasion of the Gaza Strip. The ICC ruled that the case was deserving of further investigation. The systematic destruction of the infrastructure of the Gaza Strip by the IDF included the clearance by bombs and bulldozers of at least six Palestinian graveyards, as documented by satellite footage analysed by the *New York Times* from the first weeks of the invasion.

The already dead remain a persistent target in war, never more lively than when recruited to shore up the narratives of people and nations.

GRAVES AFTER
GRAVEYARDS?

Is it inevitable that concluding remarks in histories of funerary practices and burial rites are written in a mood of pessimism about the present and future state of cemeteries? Philippe Ariès set the tone in *The Hour of Our Death*, with a sense that medicalization had bracketed death from cultural life where once it was central. Death has been locked away from us in hospital wards or the waiting rooms of hospices. Julian Litten believes that increasing secularization in Europe and America has 'diminished the pomp and panoply' of ritual and left us with a sad falling-away from solemnity. Ken Worpole's thoughtful *Last Landscapes* ends with a chapter on 'The Disappearing Body', in which he considers fundamental changes in the practice of memory: 'It should always be remembered that the last landscapes of human culture were also among the very first. For it is when people began to mark the passage and place of death that they discovered their humanity.'

Do all afterwords come to bury graveyards, not to praise them?

There have certainly been a number of trends towards the etherealization or dispersal of the material presence of the dead body in burial practices since the 1960s, and I want to sketch some of these out in my last words. Many new avenues seem to eschew the static memorialization of the monument or cemetery, but I do not necessarily want to read these as instances of decline or diminishment. Rather, we need to see these as part of a history of constant mutation and transformation of practices that bridge the space between the two deaths outlined by Robert Hertz; an unending renewal of human ingenuity in seeking comfort from the unbearable rupture that separates the living and the dead.

opposite: Hugo Simberg, *The Garden of Death*, 1896.

The sense of unnerving change in Europe and America no doubt comes in part from a relatively rapid shift in attitudes to cremation, which in the nineteenth century began to find advocates among reforming medics and public health officials in the more Protestant areas of northern Europe. In 1873, a crematorium device was displayed at the Vienna World Exposition. The furnace, patented by Ludovico Brunetti, was shown with a small, neat pile of human ashes alongside it.

This exhibit was seen by the surgeon to the British Queen Victoria, Sir Henry Thompson, who wrote an essay on the virtues of this hygienic method of disposal in the *Contemporary Review* in 1874. That year Thompson became president of the newly formed Cremation Society of England. An experimental crematorium was built in Woking, although the Home Secretary intervened to prevent its first use on a human body in the name of public order and decency. It was not technically illegal to cremate human beings, but even so, the eccentric Welsh doctor William Price, who believed he was descended from Druids, was unsuccessfully prosecuted for cremating his son in 1884. The case clarified the legal standing of the practice somewhat, and legal cremation began at the Woking site in 1885.

Slowly but steadily, crematoria began to be built across Britain. Thompson was on hand to open the notable Golders Green Crematorium and Mausoleum in 1902, with an arcaded columbarium and memorial gardens. The 1902 Cremation Act further clarified the status of the practice, although its provisions about locating crematoria away from human settlements and highways perhaps contributed to the sense that rituals of death have been compelled to hide away in garden retreats in outlying suburbs. 'No amount of architectural sanitisation,' Edwin Heathcote writes in *Monument Builders: Modern Architecture and Death*, 'can hope to succeed in gloss-

ing over the elementality of the function of the crematoria. It is only surprising that so many try.' Heathcote favoured the functionalism of some of the most daring Modernist crematoria, such as the remarkable Vienna Crematorium designed by Clemens Holzmeister in 1921, a glowering, squat mass, the ominous crushed arch of the Gothic entrance topped by two chimney stacks that refuse to hide their purpose. Form follows function, even unto death.

Cremation took several decades to shake off the sense of being either a practice of self-conscious secular modernity, or a deliberate, even ideological, refusal of Christian traditions, though the practice can be aligned with Christian beliefs if a vaguer sense of spiritual transcendence of the earthly plane is envisaged, the soul soaring above the complex logistics of bodily resurrection. Père Lachaise, that product of anticlerical revolution, pointedly included a crematorium from the late 1880s. Advocates for cremation used the language of decay and corruption deployed so effectively in the campaign against the horrors of urban burial, but residual resistance continued until after the Second World War. Since the 1960s, cremation has overtaken burial as the favoured method of handling bodies, although it is still less favoured in communities where burial is tied more firmly to doctrine.

Another trend away from the cemetery as a distinct and bounded city of the dead has been the rise in natural burial. In the UK, the Natural Burial Movement was founded in 1993 and is associated with Ken Webb, who worked in many local governments managing crematoria and memorial gardens. In 1983, he was given permission to develop twenty acres of a wildflower conservation area outside Carlisle in north-west England as a burial ground. The popularity of such spaces has developed alongside a growth in ideas of ecology and conservation. They position death less as a traumatic interruption than an integrated element of natural biological cycles of decay and renewal. The purest forms of this approach eschew the use of anything other than biodegradable materials and refuse artificial headstones, monuments or other markers. Trees may be used as natural markers, their roots directly fed by the nutrients of the body below, but for the most part the human tendency to want to mark death's interruption by intervening in the landscape is explicitly rejected in this conception, which may indeed register a very profound change – a reinvention of the idea of the grave after the epoch of the graveyard has passed.

The seeds of this eco-burial movement go back to the garden cemetery idea of the early nineteenth century, implemented in sites across Europe and America and inspired by Romantic and Transcendental ideas about natural sublimity of landscape. Even so, most historians agree that the Woodland Cemetery in Stockholm, Sweden, provided an influential new paradigm for these settings in the twentieth century. Erik Gunnar Asplund and Sigurd Lewerentz won a competition for the new design in 1915, and over the following twenty years, Asplund in particular created a new kind of austere style that bridged classicism and functional Modernism in cemetery architecture, but also crucially developed the passage through the natural landscape as a kind of spiritual journey. The woodland site was left largely untouched, and paths wend their way through dappled glades of light and dark. The Woodland Chapel, finished by Asplund in 1920, is a modest, low-lying building with a pyramidal roof resting on squat Doric columns. It opens into a surprising circular space, lit from above and centred on a catafalque for the coffin. The funeral procession moves through patterns of dark and light, restriction and release, the natural landscape integrated into a pathway that becomes a processional deathway. There is a separate crematorium and columbarium that works with this same logic. Edwin Heathcote has pointed out that this sequence integrates ancient barrows, sacred groves, Greek and Roman classicism, Nordic mythology, Christian and secular Modernism: the landscape is a kind of recapitulation of many forms of burial history. One of the first people to be cremated and memorialized here was Asplund himself, who died in 1940.

Just as there is an International Style in post-war Modernism, Stockholm's Woodland Cemetery has produced an International Cemetery Style. In many major post-1945 examples there is a familiar kind of minimalism, processional spaces hugging landscapes in austere concrete or hardwoods, the interiors mostly stripped of any inbuilt religious iconography. These are spaces where

below: The Skogskyrkogården (Woodland Cemetery), Stockholm, Sweden. Opened in 1920 with an influential design integrating the cemetery within the natural landscape.

opposite: The Kaze-no-Oka crematorium, Nakatsu, Japan, designed by Fumihiko Maki, 1997.

ritual meanings are open to construction. Fumihiko Maki's Kaze-no-Oka crematorium in Nakatsu City in Japan has long, concrete pathways open to a garden landscape of grass and trees, leading to asymmetric ceremonial spaces lit using lightwells. The design language is clearly indebted both to Asplund's Scandinavian Modernism and the local Japanese vernacular. It is built in a landscape that includes an older cemetery and ancient burial mounds stretching back millennia. Once more, it has a sense of being the culmination of a whole history of burial. But does this mean that a history of graveyards is coming to an end in citational spaces of postmodern pastiche?

In *The Work of the Dead*, Thomas Laqueur places the acceptance of cremation as part of a process of the disenchantment of death by modern science, medicine displacing the metaphysics of religion. The scientific disenchantment of the world was the thesis of the German sociologist Max Weber in his famous lecture 'Science as a Vocation' in 1919. In death studies, it was picked up by Edward Gorer, Philippe Ariès and others.

We might consider that one of the most humanistic or rational desacralizations of death is the gesture of those who leave their bodies to science – to training the next generation of doctors or furthering medical research. Once something that evoked the horror of grave-robbing, this act of donation can be a resolutely practical and materialist gesture. It was certainly how Jeremy Bentham considered the donation of his body to a public dissection on his death in 1832: it was to make his death *useful*, an acting-out of his Utilitarian philosophy.

opposite: Sally Mann, *Untitled (Tunnel)*, 2000.

This act of donation is met in the same spirit in the work of the photographer Sally Mann, whose series *What Remains* (2003) includes photographs of the bodies donated to the 'Body Farm' at the University of Tennessee in Knoxville, where corpses are left to decay in different environments to aid forensic scientists in pursuit of more accurate data about the decomposition rates of cadavers. In her memoir *Hold Still* (2015), Mann remembers being out in the fields of the Body Farm and coming across rotting bodies: 'I could hear the maggots noisily eating, a sound sometimes like the crackling of Rice Krispies in milk and other times like raw hamburger being formed by hand into patties. The bulging skin roiled with their movements beneath it.' She slips on corpse fat and scrapes it off her shoes, and later finds clumps of human hair on the pedals of her car. Mann relishes the abject physicality of the body, refusing to look away, in the spirit of strict observation. Her images are a secular mode of memorial. *What Remains* has a similar kind of austere materialism to *The Act of Seeing with One's Own Eyes* (1971) by the experimental filmmaker Stan Brakhage, the title a literal translation of the word 'autopsy'. Brakhage's camera holds its unblinking gaze as a corpse is progressively dismantled in the course of a routine hospital autopsy.

These works suggest a level of secular accommodation to the facticity of death, no longer shrouded in holy dread. Yet many have questioned this Weberian narrative of the steady, inevitable progress of secularization. They look at the many ways spiritual or religious thinking continues to enchant or re-enchant the world. Death's fundamental enigma still sparks all kinds of unexpected forms of magical

thinking, to borrow from the title of Joan Didion's memoir *The Year of Magical Thinking*. Written about a year of mourning following the deaths of her husband and her daughter, it became a bestseller in part because we do, in fact, still need scripts to chart the intense and bewildering terrain of grief.

Institutional forms of religion may have ceded some of their authority to science, but they have hardly been entirely displaced. One of the fastest growing religions in the twenty-first century is the cult of Santa Muerte, a folk religion begun in Mexico and based around a female deity of the same name. In her many shrines, Santa Muerte is depicted as skeletal and robed, often carrying a scythe and a globe; the largest is a twenty-two-metre tall figure at Tultitlán, on the outskirts of Mexico City. She has become the patron saint of the marginalized and dispossessed, associated with people living precarious or dangerous lives, including many travelling to cross the border from Mexico into America. Shrines follow the contours of the border, at which transactional offerings are left in exchange for the saint's protection. Condemned by both Catholic and Protestant churches as Satanic, Santa Muerte has nevertheless acquired millions of followers. Perhaps this is unsurprising in a society where, between 2006 and 2016, over 2,000 mass graves have been uncovered, holding tens of thousands of those disappeared and murdered either by drug cartels or through acts of 'suppression' by paramilitary

above: Santa Muerte shrine, Tepito, Mexico City, 2023.

below: *Cempasúchil* (Mexican marigold) flowers in the cemetery of San Miguel Canoa during Day of the Dead celebrations, 2013.

security forces. 'Mexico increasingly looks like one enormous grave,' the journalists Alejandro Guillén, Mago Torres and Marcela Turati concluded in a 2019 investigation. Where state systems or formal religious institutions fail to protect the population, systems of folk belief have stepped in.

Santa Muerte has provoked a fascination in some quarters that once again risks exoticizing particular beliefs about death and dying. Claudio Lomnitz has observed that Mexico is often intrinsically linked to death in the collective imagination, and dark tourism has bloomed around the distinct rituals associated with the Mexican Day of the Dead (All Souls' Day, on 2 November). These have spilled out of local graveyard ceremonies in Mexico and, in the US in particular, been appropriated and commercialized, sometimes blended with the Hallowe'en celebrations that have their own roots in Christian remembrance of the dead and the Pagan festival of Samhain.

DEATH SUSPENDED?
FROM CRYONICS TO THE DIGITAL DEAD

In 1964, Robert C. W. Ettinger published *The Prospect of Immortality*, a book which opened with the grand claim: 'Most of us now breathing have a good chance of physical life after death – a sober, scientific probability of revival and rejuvenation.' If medical science hadn't quite yet solved the problem of biological death, the technology was available to entirely arrest any further decay by deep-freezing the body in liquid nitrogen. Suspended in this way, the frozen could wait until such time as medical advances in the future could cure death. The term 'cryonics' was coined by Karl Werner, another advocate, the following year.

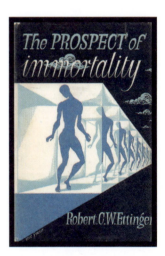

above: Robert C. W. Ettinger, *The Prospect of Immortality*, 1965 edition.

Ettinger, directly inspired by the science fiction of his youth, set up the Cryonics Institute in 1976. The company continues to freeze people and pets. A rival company, the Alcor Life Extension Foundation, preserves bodies in a facility outside Scottsdale, Arizona. You can visit the vessels that store your loved ones: a new kind of high-tech graveyard. After Ettinger died in 2011, he was preserved at the Alcor facility alongside his mother and two wives. There is a persistent folktale, always denied by the family, that Walt Disney's head was cryopreserved in 1966.

Cryonics no doubt rode the wave of post-1945 technological optimism and innovation, particularly in medicine, but life extension continues to obsess Silicon Valley billionaires in the twenty-first century. Calico (the California Life Company), set up in 2013 by the parent company of Google, researches methods to overcome ageing (and death, ultimately) at a cellular level. Leading entrepreneurs such as Jeff Bezos, Peter Thiel and Elon Musk have backed exploratory life-extension companies and

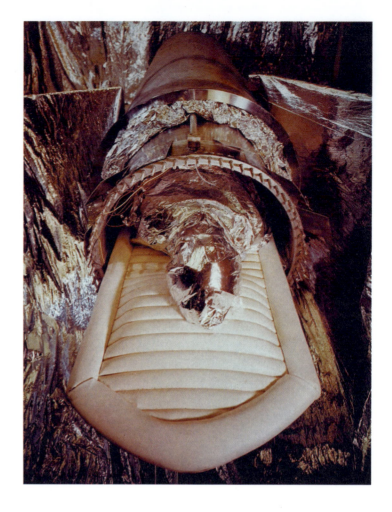

right: Cryonics freezing
capsule, 1967.

opposite top: Professor
Leslie's Vacuum
Cooling Device,
nineteenth century.

opposite bottom:
Trans Time Inc.,
a company offering
the freezing of bodies,
Oakland, California.

research. The European Biostasis Foundation in Switzerland, meanwhile, offers a process of vitrification, storing bodies turned into a kind of glass at a temperature near absolute zero so that 'all metabolic processes in the body are suspended.' In an interview, the founder of the United Therapeutics med-tech company Martine Rothblatt casually tells Tad Friend: 'Clearly, it is possible, through technology, to make death optional.' This is the subject of Don DeLillo's novel *Zero K* (2016), in which a billionaire builds a facility where the transition between life and death is smoothed to a blurry vanishing point and essentially erased for the super-rich.

Ideas about states of suspension in the early 1960s ran parallel with the invention of a new medical ensemble that radically extended the chance of surviving extreme medical conditions: the intensive care unit. ICUs could soon measure and regulate multiple systems of the body simultaneously: they sustain respiration, organ function and blood circulation, and record brain activity. But the ICU created a new issue. There were patients who seemed to suffer a complete absence of brain activity – who were 'brain dead', in twentieth-century parlance – yet whose bodily survival could be ensured by machines, because their pulmonary system could be kept working artificially.

What to do with people caught in this newly opened space between life and death?

At the same time, organ transplant techniques were improving. It was in this climate that in 1968, a group of medics redefined the criteria for death. In a short, four-page report, the 'Ad Hoc Committee of the Harvard Medical School' proposed to relocate death from the cessation of a heartbeat and shift it to the complete absence of brain activity. This became a medical and legal standard. Now an ICU keeping a patient artificially alive could be switched off. Death would follow, but transplant teams had legal room to work quickly.

As medical technology has continued to improve, so the boundary between life and death has again wavered. Electroencephalogram (EEG) results could show disturbingly lively activity in those apparently brain dead. The famous legal case of Karen Ann Quinlan in 1976 resulted in permission to turn off her respirator to allow biological death, but she lived on, unaided by machines, without ever leaving her coma, for another ten years. Since 1968, a number of specific states in this 'grey zone' (as brain imaging pioneer Adrian Owen calls it) have been named and refined by medics: persistent vegetative state; permanent vegetative state; whole brain death; minimally conscious state. As the population has aged in certain parts of the world, various forms of advanced dementia have become problematically adjacent to some of these definitions. Margaret Lock has written that 'In late modernity … the numbers of people recognized as candidates for social death have increased exponentially.' We have been living through a biomedical revolution from the late 1960s, and breakthroughs in this area constantly feed the prospect of extending life, or even cheating death – for some. Outside that charmed circle, Death's scythe is still kept quite busy.

The redefinition of death in culture has privileged genres that work through anxieties about the potential unravelling of the borders between life and death. It seems telling that in the same year that death was redefined by the Ad Hoc Committee, George A. Romero released *Night of the Living Dead*, the first modern zombie film. The film starts, of course, in a graveyard. And how do we learn to kill a zombie in the course of the

film? Not by old-fashioned stake to the heart, but by a bullet to the head. Robin Cook's thriller *Coma* (1977) capitalized on the new fears that unscrupulous medical corporations might harvest organs if they could induce brain death on the operating table. The novel (and later film, directed by Michael Crichton) introduces a new vision of the mass storage of bodies caught in this state between brain death and biological death: ranks of corpses in suspended states, hidden in corporate facilities, awaiting the immensely profitable harvesting of their organs. Another modern anti-graveyard.

Science fiction visions of transcending death have spilled over not only in cryogenics, but other postmortem memorial services. Since 1994, Celestis Memorial Spaceflights has offered to send a portion of the cremated remains of loved ones into space as part of commercial payloads on space launches. These can be sent into orbit, landed on the moon (so one only needs to look up to visit the grave) or, at another price point, board the Infinity Flight tumbling out into deep space. This service unabashedly appropriates the language of the technological sublime used in *Star Trek* and other expansive space operas. Other companies will extract the carbon from cremated remains to be compressed and placed in a crystal matrix to produce diamonds.

The internet has produced the phenomenon of the digital undead, data trails that remain in cyberspace long after our physical death. Social media platforms have rapidly had to develop policies about what to do with the 'digital estate' and profiles of the dead; Facebook and Instagram will both 'memorialize' accounts. The development of large language-model Artificial Intelligences, meanwhile, promises to create avatars of the dead from their digital traces and effectively reanimate them for us. In 2024, the pioneering digital artist Laurie Anderson confessed that she had been chatting to an AI version of her dead partner Lou Reed for many years. The company Replika created an app that customizes 'AI companions', including those of dead friends and loved ones. It was conceived by Eugenia Kuyda, its CEO, in a state of grief at the sudden loss of a friend. Replika avatars actualize what the science fiction TV episode of *Black Mirror* 'Be Right Back' could only queasily imagine in 2013 – a woman in mourning who orders up an AI double in her crippling grief, only to become progressively more irritated and bored with his insistent presence.

Many of these developments seem to conform to the idea that we are turning away from traditional burial practices in a will to transcend the inconvenient fact of death. Might technology, if it cannot end death, alleviate the rawness of grief and traumatic loss? Will we shortly never need to visit a cemetery or memorial garden again?

Yet the possibilities I've just outlined remain vanishingly rare. They exist, I think, in a dialectic with humanity's unending and very grounded struggle with how to best face death and mourning, and how best to memorialize those who pass out of our lives. Our fascination with graveyards and graveyard history, our curiosity at the endless cultural diversity in the ways humans send their loved ones on the path between two deaths, show that these are still vital rituals and places of transition for us. The earliest *Homo sapiens* seem to have buried their dead at thresholds and limits, perhaps staring out from shore to sea, in the twilight of dawn or dusk. We will always need these ritual spaces, these cemeteries, these heterotopic mirror-worlds of the living, to manage our endless dance with death.

overleaf: Bodies awaiting organ-harvesting in *Coma*, directed by Michael Crichton, 1977.

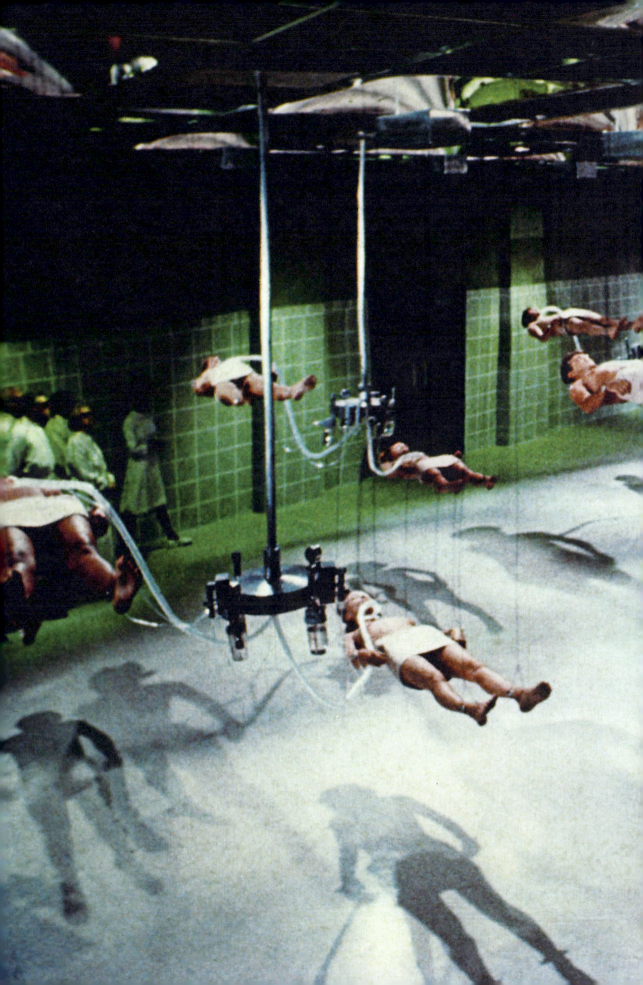

BIBLIOGRAPHY

Geraldine Kendall Adams, 'American Museum of Natural History Removes All Human Remains from Display', *Museum Association* (17 October 2023).

Benedict Anderson, *Imagined Communities: Reflections on the Origin and Spread of Nationalism* (London: Verso, 1983; rev. edn 2016).

Daniel Arasse, *The Guillotine and the Terror*, trans. C. Miller (London: Penguin, 1989).

B. Arensburg and I. Hershkovitz, 'Artificial Skull "Treatment" in the PPN B Period: Nahal Hemar', in *People and Culture Change*, ed. I. Hershkovitz (1989), 115–31.

Philippe Ariès, *The Hour of Our Death* (New York: Knopf, 1981).

Catharine Arnold, *Necropolis: London and its Dead* (London: Simon & Schuster, 2006).

Bernardo T. Arriaza, *Beyond Death: The Chinchorro Mummies of Ancient Chile* (Washington, D. C.: Smithsonian Books, 1995).

Robert Bard, *Graveyard London: Lost and Forgotten Burial Grounds* (London: Historical Publications Ltd, 2008).

Louis Berk, *East End Jewish Cemeteries: Brady Street and Alderney Road* (Stroud: Amberley Publishing, 2017).

Jan Bondeson, *Buried Alive: The Terrifying History of Our Most Primal Fear* (New York: W. W. Norton, 2002).

Mark Bowden et. al., *The Stonehenge Landscape: Analysing the Stonehenge World Heritage Site* (London: Historic England, 2015).

Elisabeth Bronfen, *Over Her Dead Body: Death, Femininity and the Aesthetic* (Manchester: Manchester University Press, 1992).

Elisabeth Bronfen and Carol Davison (eds), *Gothic and Death* (Manchester: Manchester University Press, 2017).

Peter Brown, *The Cult of the Saints: Its Rise and Function in Latin Christianity* (Chicago: University of Chicago Press, 2015).

Sir Thomas Browne, *Hydriotaphia, or Urne-Buriall* (1658), in *Religio Medici and Urne-Buriall*, ed. S. Greenblatt et al (New York: New York Review Books, 2012).

Frederick Burgess, *English Churchyard Memorials* (Cambridge: The Lutterworth Press, 1963).

Carolyn Campbell, *City of Immortals:*

Père Lachaise Cemetery, Paris (San Francisco: ORO Editions, 2019).

Edwin Chadwick, *A Supplementary Report on the Results of a Special Inquiry into the Practice of Interment in Towns* (1843).

R. Andrew Chesnut, *Devoted to Death: Santa Muerte, the Skeleton Saint* (Oxford: Oxford University Press, 2012).

Marcus Tullius Cicero ('inspired by', as original lost), *How to Grieve: An Ancient Guide to the Lost Art of Consolation*, trans. M. Fontaine (Princeton: Princeton University Press, 2022).

Aaron Cohen, 'Commemoration, Cult of the Fallen (Russian Empire)', *International Encyclopedia of the First World War*.

Charles L. Cohen, *The Abrahamic Religions* (Oxford: Oxford University Press, 2020).

Brian Connell and Adrian Miles, *The City Bunhill Burial Ground, Golden Lane, London* (London: Museum of London, 2010).

David Crane, *Empires of the Dead: How One Man's Vision Led to the Creation of WWI's War Graves* (London: William Collins, 2013).

David Cressy, 'Lamentable, Strange and Wonderful: Headless Monsters in the English Revolution', in *Monstrous Bodies/Political Monstrosities*, ed. L. Knoppers and J. Landes (Ithaca: Cornell University Press, 2004), 40–63.

Zoe Crossland, 'The Archaeology of Contemporary Conflict', in T. Insoll (ed.), *The Oxford Handbook of the Archaeology of Ritual and Religion* (Oxford: Oxford University Press, 2011), 285–306.

Joan Carroll Cruz, *The Incorruptibles: A Study of the Incorruption of the Bodies of Various Saints and Beati* (Charlotte: TAN Books, 1974).

Joe Cummings, *Buddhist Stupas in Asia: The Shape of Perfection* (Melbourne: Lonely Planet, 2001).

James Stevens Curl, *The Victorian Celebration of Death* (Stroud: Sutton Publishing, 2000).

Glyn Daniel, *The Megalithic Builders of Western Europe* (London: Hutchinson, 1958).

Edwin P. de Jong, *Making a Living Between Crisis and Ceremonies in Tana Toraja* (Berlin: Brill, 2013).

Charles Dickens, *The Uncommercial Traveller*, ed. Daniel Tyler (Oxford: Oxford University Press, 2015).

Jenny Edkins, *Missing: Persons and Politics* (Oxford: Oxford University Press, 2011).

Amelia Edwards, *Pharaohs, Fellahs and Explorers* (New York: Harper & Brothers, 1891).

Michel Eltchaninoff, *Lenin Walked on the Moon: The Mad History of Russian Cosmism* (Rome: Europa Editions, 2023).

Robert C. W. Ettinger, *The Prospect of Immortality* (New York: Doubleday, 1964).

Wael Salah Fahmi and Keith Sutton, 'Living with the Dead: Contested Spaces and the Right to Cairo's Inner City Cemeteries', *The Fourth World Sustainability Forum* (2014).

Drew Gilpin Faust, *This Republic of Suffering: Death and the American Civil War* (New York: Knopf, 2008).

Mary Favret, 'A Feeling for Numbers: Representing the Scale of the War Dead', *Essays and Studies* (2014), 185–204.

Gavin Flood, *An Introduction to Hinduism* (Cambridge: Cambridge University Press, 1996).

Tad Friend, 'The God Pill: Silicon Valley's Quest for Eternal Life', *New Yorker* (3 April 2017), 54–67.

Robert Garland, *The Greek Way of Death* (Ithaca: Cornell University Press, 1985).

Arnold van Gennep, *The Rites of Passage*, trans. M. Vizedom and G. Caffee (Chicago: University of Chicago Press, 1960).

Mitch Ginsburg, 'On Mount Herzl, with the Keepers of the Graves', *Times of Israel* (5 May 2014).

William Godwin, *Essays on Sepulchres; or, A Proposal for Erecting Some Memorial of the Illustrious Dead in all Ages on the Spot where their Remains have been Interred* (London: W. Miller, 1809).

Geoffrey Gorer, *Death, Grief, and Mourning in Contemporary Britain* (London: Doubleday, 1965).

Alejandro Guillén, Mago Torres and Marcela Turati, 'Mexico, Country of 2000 Clandestine Graves', *Vision Carto* (2 July 2019).

Edwin Heathcote, *Monument Builders: Modern Architecture and Death* (Winterbourne: Academy Editions, 1999).

Robert Hertz, *Death and The Right Hand*, trans. R. and C. Needham (Abingdon: Routledge, 1960).

Harold Hickerson, 'The Feast of the Dead Among the Seventeenth Century

Algonkians', *American Anthropologist* 62: 1 (1960), 81–107.

Rosemary Hill, *Stonehenge* (London: Profile Books, 2008).

Isabella Holmes, *The London Burial Grounds: Notes on their History from the Earliest Times to the Present Day* (London: T. F. Unwin, 1896).

Valerie Hope, *Roman Death: The Dying and the Dead in Ancient Rome* (London: Bloomsbury, 2009).

Mary Elizabeth Hotz, *Literary Remains: Representations of Death and Burial in Victorian England* (Albany: State University of New York Press, 2008).

Ronald Hutton, *Pagan Britain* (New Haven: Yale University Press, 2013).

Donald Johnson, 'The Palaeoanthropology of Hadar, Ethiopia', *Comptes Rendus Palevol* 16: 2 (2017), 140–54.

Christopher Joyce and Eric Stover, *Witnesses from the Grave: The Stories Bones Tell* (New York: Ballantine Books, 1991).

Peter C. Jupp and Clare Gittings (eds), *Death in England: An Illustrated History* (Manchester: Manchester University Press, 1999).

Ernst H. Kantorowicz, *The King's Two Bodies: A Study in Medieval Political Authority* (Princeton: Princeton University Press, 1957).

Thomas Keenan and Eyal Weizman, *Mengele's Skull: The Advent of Forensic Aesthetics* (London: Sternberg Press, 2012).

Christoph Koetti and Christiaan Triebert, 'Satellite Imagery and Video Shows Some Gazan Cemeteries Razed by Israeli Forces', *New York Times* (14 December 2023).

Paul Koudounaris, *The Empire of Death: A Cultural History of Ossuaries and Charnel Houses* (London: Thames & Hudson, 2011).

Paul Koudounaris, *Heavenly Bodies: Cult Treasures and Spectacular Saints from the Catacombs* (London: Thames & Hudson, 2013).

Lara Kriegel, *The Crimean War and its Aftermath* (Cambridge: Cambridge University Press, 2022).

Peter Kyslan, 'Transhumanism and the Issue of Death', *Ethics and Bioethics* 9: 1–2 (2019), 71–80.

Thomas W. Laqueur, *The Work of the Dead* (Princeton: Princeton University Press, 2015).

Frances Larsen, *Severed: A History of Heads Lost and Found* (London: Granta, 2014).

Gwendolyn Leick, *Tombs of the Great Leaders: A Contemporary Guide* (London: Reaktion, 2013).

Denise Patry Leidy, 'Lacquer, Relics and Self-Mummification', *Smithsonian National Museum of Asian Art*, https://asia-archive.si.edu/essays/lacquer-relics-and-self-mummification/

J. John Lennon and Malcolm Foley, *Dark Tourism: The Attraction of Death and Disaster* (London: Continuum, 2002).

Julian Litten, *The English Way of Death: The Common Funeral Since 1450* (London: Robert Hale, 1991).

Margaret Lock, *Twice Dead: Organ Transplants and the Reinvention of Death* (Berkeley: University of California Press, 2002).

Claudio Lomnitz, *Death and the Idea of Mexico* (Princeton: Princeton University Press, 2005).

Roger Luckhurst, *The Mummy's Curse: The True History of a Dark Fantasy* (Oxford: Oxford University Press, 2012).

Roger Luckhurst, 'Why Have the Dead Come Back? The Instance of Photography', *New Formations* 89–90 (2017), 101–15.

Roger Luckhurst, 'The Death of Death: Zero K, Don DeLillo', in S. Bacon, *The Undead in the 21st Century* (2022), 273–9.

Laura Major, 'Spectres of Death: Exhuming the Remains of the 1994 Genocide in Rwanda', *Humanity Journal* (2018), https://humanityjournal.org.

Sally Mann, *Hold Still* (New York: Little, Brown, 2015).

C. F. A. Marmoy 'The "Auto-Icon" of Jeremy Bentham at University College, London', *Medical History* 2 (1958), 177–86.

Marcel Mauss, *The Gift: Forms and Functions of Exchange in Archaic Societies*, trans. Ian Gunnison (1925; London: Cohen & Lane, 1966).

Achille Mbembe, 'Necropolitics', *Public Culture* 15: 1 (2003), 11–40.

David McAllister, *Imagining the Dead in British Literature and Culture, 1790–1848* (London: Palgrave Macmillan, 2018).

Chris McCabe, *The East Edge: Nightwalks with the Dead Poets of Tower Hamlets* (London: Penned in the Margins, 2019).

Allison C. Meier, *Grave* (London: Bloomsbury, 2023).

Catherine Merridale, *Night of Stone: Death and Memory in Russia* (London: Granta, 2001).

Magdalena Midgley, *The Monumental Cemeteries of Prehistoric Europe* (Cheltenham: Tempus, 2005).

Lukacsz Mieszkowski, 'At Bay: Beyond the Architecture of Dread (Notes on the New Sobibor Memorial)', *K: Jewish People, Europe and the XXIst Century* (16 June 2022).

Jessica Mitford, *The American Way of Death Revisited* (New York: Simon & Schuster, 1963; rev. edn, 1998).

Raymond A. Moody, *Life after Life* (1975; London: Ebury, 2001).

Ian Morris, *Burial and Ancient Society: The Rise of the Greek City-State* (Cambridge: Cambridge University Press, 1987).

Projit Bihari Mukharji, 'The "Cholera Cloud" in the Nineteenth-Century "British World"', *Bulletin of the History of Medicine* 86: 3 (2012), 303–32.

Edwin Murphy, *After the Funeral: The Posthumous Adventures of Famous Corpses* (New York: Barnes & Noble, 1995).

Harold Mytum, *Mortuary Monuments and Burial Grounds of the Historic Period* (London: Springer, 2004).

Ronald Niezen, *Spirit Wars: Native North American Religions in the Age of Nation Building* (Berkeley: University of California Press, 2000).

Hiroshi Obayashi, *Death and Afterlife: Perspectives of World Religions* (New York: Bloomsbury, 1992).

Erwin Panofsky, *Tomb Sculpture: Four Lectures on its Changing Aspects from Ancient Egypt to Bernini* (1964; New York: H. N. Abrams, 1992).

Jonathan Parry, *Death in Banaras* (Cambridge: Cambridge University Press, 1994).

Stephen Perkinson (ed.), *The Ivory Mirror: The Art of Mortality in Renaissance Europe* (New Haven: Yale University Press, 2017).

Paul Pettitt, *The Palaeolithic Origins of Human Burial* (Abingdon: Routledge, 2011).

Paul Pettitt, 'When Burial Begins', *British Archaeology* 66 (2002).

Abu Ameenah Bilal Philips, *Funeral Rites in Islam* (Riyadh: International Islamic Publishing House, 2005).

Tony Pollard, 'These Spots of Excavation Tell: Using Early Visitor Accounts to Map the Missing Graves of Waterloo', *Journal of Conflict Archaeology* 16: 2 (2021), 75–113.

Susan Pollock, *Ancient Mesopotamia: The Eden that Never Was* (Cambridge: Cambridge University Press, 1999).

Trent Portigal, 'Grave Contamination in Second Empire Paris', *Medium* (16 June 2021).

Jessica Rawson, *Life and Afterlife in Ancient China* (London: Allen Lane, 2023).

Ernest Renan, 'What is a Nation?', in H. Bhabha (ed.), *Nation and Narration* (Abingdon: Routledge, 1990).

Colin Renfrew, Michael J. Boyd, Iain Morley (eds), *Death Rituals, Social Order, and the Archaeology of Immortality in the Ancient World* (Cambridge: Cambridge University Press, 2016).

'Report of the Ad Hoc Committee of the Harvard Medical School: A Definition of Irreversible Coma', *Journal of the American Medical Association* 205: 5 (1968), 85–88.

Report from the Select Committee on Improvement of the Health of Towns (Effect of Interment of Bodies in Towns) (1842).

Ruth Richardson, *Death, Dissection and the Destitute* (Chicago: University of Chicago Press, 1988).

Justin Ritzifer and Marcus Bingenheimer, 'Whole-Body Relics in Chinese Buddhism: Previous Research and Historical Overview', *Indian Journal of Buddhist Studies* (2006).

Mary Roach, *Stiff: The Curious Lives of Human Cadavers* (London: Penguin, 2003).

Alice Roberts, *Buried: An Alternative History of the First Millennium in Britain* (London: Simon & Schuster, 2022).

John Romer, *Valley of the Kings* (New York: Henry Holt & Company, 1981).

Adam Rosenblatt, 'International Forensic Investigations and the Human Rights of the Dead', *Human Rights Quarterly* 32: 4 (2010), 921–50.

Peter Ross, *A Tomb with a View: The Stories and Glories of Graveyards* (London: Headline, 2020).

Fiona Sampson, *In Search of Mary Shelley: The Girl Who Wrote* Frankenstein (London: Profile Books, 2018).

Chris Scarre (ed.), *Monuments and Landscape in Atlantic Europe: Perception and Society During the Neolithic and Early Bronze Age* (Abingdon: Routledge, 2002).

Wolfgang Schivelbusch, *Cultures of Defeat: On National Trauma, Mourning and Recovery* (London: Picador, 2003).

Arnold Schwartzman, *Graven Images: Graphic Motifs of the Jewish Gravestone* (New York: H. N. Abrams, 1993).

Yael Shapira, *Inventing the Gothic Corpse: The Thrill of Human Remains in the Eighteenth-Century Novel* (London: Palgrave Macmillan, 2018).

Robert H. Sharf, 'On the Allure of Buddhist Relics', *Representations* 66 (1999), 75–99.

Mary Shelley, *Frankenstein; Or, The Modern Prometheus* [The 1818 Text], ed. Marilyn Butler (Oxford: Oxford University Press, 2008).

Mike St Maur Shiel, 'German Memorials on the Western Front', Western Front Association.

Ralph Solecki, *Shanidar: The Humanity of Neanderthal Man* (London: Allen Lane, 1972).

Susan Sontag, *On Photography* (New York: Farrar, Straus and Giroux, 1977).

Jean Sprackland, *These Silent Mansions: A Life in Graveyards* (London: Jonathan Cape, 2020).

Susan Merrill Squier, *Liminal Lives: Imagining the Human at the Frontier of Biomedicine* (Durham: Duke University Press, 2004).

Peter Stanford, *How to Read a Graveyard: Journeys in the Company of the Dead* (London: Bloomsbury, 2013).

Philip Stone et al. (eds), *The Palgrave Handbook of Dark Tourism* (London: Palgrave Macmillan, 2018).

Eric Stover, *The Graves: Srebrenica and Vukovar* (Zurich: Scalo Verlag, 1998).

William Stukeley, *Stonehenge, A Temple Restor'd to the British Druids* (1740).

Debadrita Sur, 'Dark Tourism: Varanasi, the Indian City where People Seek Death', *Far Out Magazine* (April 2022).

Charles Taylor, *A Secular Age* (Cambridge: Harvard University Press, 2007).

Mark C. Taylor and Dietrich Christian Lammerts, *Grave Matters* (London: Reaktion, 2002).

Dick Teresi, *The Undead* (New York: Pantheon Books, 2012).

Gilles Thomas with Diane Laglumé, *The Catacombs of Paris* (Paris: Parigramme, 2020).

Peter Thorsheim, 'The Corpse in the Garden: Burial, Health and the Environment in Nineteenth-Century London', *Environmental History* 16: 1 (2011), 38–68.

Elisabeth Tooker, *An Ethnography of the Huron Indians, 1615–49* (Washington, D. C.: Smithsonian Institute, 1964).

J. M. C. Toynbee, *Death and Burial in the Roman World* (Baltimore: Johns Hopkins University Press, 1971).

John Turpin and Derrick Knight, *The Magnificent Seven: London's First Landscaped Cemeteries* (Stroud: Amberley Publishing, 2016).

Katherine Verdery, *The Political Lives of Dead Bodies: Reburial and Postsocialist Change* (New York: Columbia University Press, 1999).

Helga Vogel, 'Death and Burial', in *The Sumerian World*, ed. H. Crawford (Abingdon: Routledge, 2013).

Toby Alice Volkman, 'Visions and Revisions: Toraja Culture and the Tourist Gaze', *American Ethnologist* 127: 1 (1990), 91–110.

Jack G. Voller (ed.), *The Graveyard School: An Anthology* (Richmond: Valancourt Books, 2015).

Sarah E. Wagner, *To Know Where He Lies: DNA Technology and the Search for Srebrenica's Missing* (Berkeley: University of California Press, 2008).

George Walker, *Gatherings from Graveyards, Particularly Those of London, with a Concise History of the Modes of Interment Among Different Nations* (1839).

George Walker, *On the Past and Present State of Intramural Burying Places, with Practical Suggestions for the Establishment of National Extramural Cemeteries* (1851).

Paul Westover, *Necromanticism: Travelling to Meet the Dead, 1750–1860* (London: Palgrave Macmillan, 2012).

Walter Perceval Yetts, 'Notes on the Disposal of the Buddhist Dead in China', *Journal of the Royal Asiatic Society* 43: 3 (1911), 699–725.

James E. Young, *The Texture of Memory: Holocaust Memorials and Meaning* (New Haven: Yale University Press, 1993).

Ilya Zbarsky and Samuel Hutchinson, *Lenin's Embalmers* (London: The Harvill Press, 1998).

Richard Zettler and Lee Horne (eds), *Treasures from the Royal Tombs of Ur* (Philadelphia: University of Pennsylvania Museum of Archaeology and Anthropology, 1998).

Fritz Zimmerman, *The Native American Book of the Dead* (independently published, 2020).

ILLUSTRATION CREDITS

a=above
c=centre
b=below
l=left
r=right

2–3 Library of Congress Prints and Photographs Division, Washington, D.C. (2003679939)

4 Wellcome Collection, London (567830i)

6–7 Photo SuperStock/Michael Runkel/ Robert Harding Picture Library

10 Published by J. Nichols, London, 1786

11 Published by Pardon and Son, London, 1869

12a The Miriam and Ira D. Wallach Division of Art, Prints and Photographs: Photography Collection. The New York Public Library (85260)

12b Photo Valentina/Adobe Stock

13 Photo Timothy A. Clary/AFP/ Getty Images

14–15 Photo Moviestore Collection Ltd/ Alamy

16 Photo Red Bank Films/Collection Christophel/ArenaPAL

17a Gallerie dell'Accademia, Venice (671)

17b Museu Nacional de Arte Antiga, Lisbon (Inv. 828 Pint)

18 Published by J. Nichols, London, 1786

19a Photo SuperStock/TWO CITIES/ RANK/Album/Album Archivo

19b Loan from the Trustees of the Arthur Stone Dewing Greek Numismatic Foundation. Harvard Art Museums/Arthur M. Sackler Museum, Cambridge, MA (1.1965.1505)

20 Musée du Louvre, Paris (INV 7300)

21 Photo Staatliche Museen zu Berlin, 1936

24 Photo Associated Press/Alamy

27a Photo Pablo Blazquez Dominguez/ Getty Images

27b Photo Svarshik/Adobe Stock

28a Photo Oz Rittner. From *On holes and strings: Earliest displays of human adornment in the Middle Palaeolithic.* © 2020 Bar-Yosef Mayer et al.

28b Published by Pocket Books, New York, 1972

29 Photo Marla Sela/Shutterstock

30 Photo Lisa Maree Williams/Getty Images

31 Photo Creative Touch Imaging Ltd/ NurPhoto/Shutterstock

32 Photo Martin Bernetti/AFP/Getty Images

34 Photo dimamoroz/Adobe Stock

35 Photo Steven Mithen. From S. Mithen, B. Finlayson, D. Maricevic, S. Smith, E. L. Jenkins and M. Najjar, *Excavation of an Early Neolithic Settlement in Southern Jordan*, CBRL Research Monograph, 2018

36a Photo Dostbulut/Adobe Stock

36b Photo Sailingstone Travel/Adobe Stock

37a From C. L. Woolley, *Ur Excavations, Volume II: The Royal Cemetery*, Trustees of the British Museum and The Museum of the University of Pennsylvania, Oxford and Philadelphia, 1934

37b Photo akg-images/Erich Lessing

38 The British Museum, London (121201)

39a Photo Illustrated London News Ltd/Mary Evans

39b Penn Museum, Philadelphia. Photo courtesy Penn Museum, Philadelphia (8704)

40 (1) Rogers Fund, 1932. The Metropolitan Museum of Art, New York (32.1.124a)

40 (2) Purchase, Edward S. Harkness Gift, 1926. The Metropolitan Museum of Art, New York (26.7.919)

40 (3) Rogers Fund and Edward S. Harkness Gift, 1914. The Metropolitan Museum of Art, New York (14.3.69–.70-related)

40 (4) Penn Museum, Philadelphia. Photo courtesy Penn Museum, Philadelphia (B17711A)

40 (5) The British Museum, London (2003,0718.1)

41 (6) Dodge Fund, 1933. The Metropolitan Museum of Art, New York (33.35.3)

41 (7) Photo DEA/G. Dagli Orti/De Agostini/Getty Images

41 (8) Rogers Fund, 1925. The Metropolitan Museum of Art, New York (25.3.183a, b)

41 (9) Rogers Fund, 1915. The Metropolitan Museum of Art, New York (15.2.9a, b)

41 (10) Bequest of Theodore M. Davis, 1915. The Metropolitan Museum of Art, New York (30.8.54)

41 (11) Gift of J. Pierpont Morgan, 1912. The Metropolitan Museum of Art, New York (12.183.1b.1, .2)

42a Photo Svetlaili/Adobe Stock

42b Photo Mike P Shepherd/Alamy

43a Photo DEA/G. Sioen/De Agostini/ Getty Images

43b The Elisha Whittlesey Collection, The Elisha Whittlesey Fund, 1973. The Metropolitan Museum of Art, New York (1973.608.2.3)

44a Library of Congress Prints and Photographs Division, Washington D.C. (2019637458)

44c Griffith Institute, University of Oxford (0643)

44b Rogers Fund, 1930. The Metropolitan Museum of Art, New York (30.4.108)

45 Rogers Fund, 1911. The Metropolitan Museum of Art, New York (11.139)

46a Rogers Fund, 1911. The Metropolitan Museum of Art, New York (11.154.1a, b)

46b Rogers Fund, 1930. The Metropolitan Museum of Art, New York (30.3.31)

47a Harvard Art Museums/Straus Center for Conservation and Technical Studies, Forbes Pigment Collection, Cambridge, MA (Straus.17)

47b Photo SuperStock/UNIVERSAL PICTURES/Album/Album Archivo

48 From Inigo Jones's The Most Notable Antiquity of Great Britain, vulgarly called Stone-Heng on Salisbury Plain, London, 1655

49 The British Museum, London (1859,0625.4)

50 Photo Geography Photos/Universal Images Group/Getty Images

51a Photo Tim Graham/Alamy

51b Photo Look and Learn/Illustrated Papers Collection/Bridgeman Images

52a © Ken Williams/ Shadowsandstone.com

52b Published by J. Murray, London, 1872

53a Photo Emmanuel Lattes/Alamy

53b J. Paul Getty Museum, Los Angeles (84.XC.873.300)

54 Private Collection

55 From James Mackay, *Derek Jarman Super 8*, published by Thames & Hudson, London, 2011. Courtesy and © LUMA Foundation

56 Funds from various donors, 1927. The Metropolitan Museum of Art, New York (27.228)

58 Rogers Fund, 1954. The Metropolitan Museum of Art, New York (54.11.5)

59a Bequest of Grenville L. Winthrop. Harvard Art Museums/Fogg Museum, Cambridge, MA (1943.445)

59b From Julio Gailhabaud, *Monumentos Antigos and modernos*, I. Roix, Madrid, 1845

60a, b Gilman Collection, Museum Purchase, 2005. The Metropolitan Museum of Art, New York (2005.100.1312 & 2005.100.1313)

61a Rijksmuseum, Amsterdam (RP-P-1938-938)

61b The Miriam and Ira D. Wallach Division of Art, Prints and Photographs: Picture Collection. The New York Public Library (836635)

62 (1) Gift of Henry L. Moses in memory of Mr. and Mrs. Henry P. Goldschmidt. The Jewish Museum, New York (JM 5-50)

62 (2) Museum of Fine Arts, Boston. Photo Museum of Fine Arts, Boston. All rights reserved/William Amory Gardner Fund/Bridgeman Images

62 (3) Photo Gianni Dagli Orti/Shutterstock

62 (4) Museum purchase with funds provided by the S. & A. P. Fund, 1964. The Walters Art Museum, Baltimore (VO.106)

62 (5) Gift of Lenore Barozzi. J. Paul Getty Museum, Los Angeles (75.AM.19)

62 (6) Museo Nazionale Etrusco di Villa Giulia, Roma (6646). Photo SuperStock/DeAgostini

63 (7) J. Paul Getty Museum, Los Angeles (85.AD.76)

63 (8) Photo Sepia Times/Universal Images Group/Getty Images

63 (9) Funds from various donors, 1900. The Metropolitan Museum of Art, New York (00.2.19)

63 (10) J. Paul Getty Museum, Los Angeles (84.AE.745)

63 (11) Gift of Dr. Harry G. Friedman. The Jewish Museum, New York (F 4714)

63 (12) Rogers Fund, 1906. The Metropolitan Museum of Art, New York (06.1021.230)

64 Photo Adriano/Adobe Stock

65 Photo SuperStock/DeAgostini

66a, l, r Birmingham Museums Trust (1952P19.9.2)

66b The Miriam and Ira D. Wallach Division of Art, Prints and Photographs: Picture Collection. The New York Public Library (1619927)

67 Funds from various donors, 1900. The Metropolitan Museum of Art, New York (00.2.5)

68a Photo Realy Easy Star/Alamy

68b Library of Congress Prints and Photographs Division Washington, D.C. (2001700923)

69 Gift of Mrs. Henry Osborn Taylor in memory of her father William Bradley Isham. Harvard Art Museums/Fogg Museum, Cambridge, MA (M2869.2.2)

72 Private Collection. © Succession Picasso/DACS, London 2025

74 Bibliothèque nationale de France, Paris (btv1b86029431)

75 Photo Courtesy Martyrs' Shrine, Ontario

76 © Library and Archives Canada, Ottawa. Reproduced with the permission of Library and Archives Canada, Ottawa

77 Photo Michal Sikorski/Alamy

78 Photo Craig Lovell/Eagle Visions Photography/Alamy

79 Photo ccgocke/Adobe Stock

80 Photo Hariandi Hafid/SOPA Images/LightRocket/Getty Images

82–83 Photo Royal Collection Trust, London

87 Photo Duby Tal/Albatross/Alamy

88 Photo mychadre77/Adobe Stock

89a Photo Simon Balson/Alamy

89b Photo Lois GoBe/Adobe Stock

90 Gift of Mr. and Mrs. Stuart Blank in Memory of Barbara and Meyer Perlberg. The Jewish Museum, New York (2004–55). © Bette Blank

91 Photo Janericloebe

92 Photo SuperStock/Eye Ubiquitous

93 Photo pwmotion/Adobe Stock

94a Photo babble/Adobe Stock

94b Photo Menahem Kahana/AFP/Getty Images

95 Photo SuperStock/Jason Langley/Cavan Images

96 Rogers Fund, 1919. The Metropolitan Museum of Art, New York (19.57.15)

98 Photo SuperStock/Album/Prisma/Album Archivo

99 Photo akg-images/Paul Koudounaris

100 The J. Paul Getty Museum, Los Angeles (83.ML.103.131v)

101a Gift of Leonard C. Hanna Jr. The Cleveland Museum of Art (1923.266)

101b Photo DavidE

102–3 Library of Congress Prints and Photographs Division Washington, D.C. (2006675723, 2020683312, 2020683308, 2020683305, 2020683310 & 2020683317)

104a Photo Hermes Images/AGF Srl/Alamy

104b © Tommy Weir

105 Photo The Canadian Press/Jonathan Hayward/Alamy

106 Wellcome Collection, London (45066i)

107a Library of Congress Prints and Photographs Division Washington, D.C. (2020683105)

107b l, r Rogers Fund, 1919. The Metropolitan Museum of Art, New York (19.57.34 & 19.57.36)

108 (1) Wellcome Collection, London

108 (2) The State Historical Society of Missouri, Columbia, MO (1953-123-0001)

108 (3) The State Historical Society of Missouri, Columbia, MO (1983-097-0001)

108 (4) Wellcome Collection, London

108 (5) Gift of Mrs. J. Amory Haskell, 1941. The Metropolitan Museum of Art, New York (41.42.1)

108 (6) Wellcome Collection, London

108 (7) Wellcome Collection, London

108 (8) The State Historical Society of Missouri, Columbia, MO (1965-109-0003)

109a DeGolyer Library, Southern Methodist University, Dallas

109b Photo dbrnjhrj/Adobe Stock

110a, b The British Museum, London (16186001 & 1929,0713.89)

112 The Khalili Collections, London (MXD 276)

114–15 Sadberk Hanım Museum, Istanbul

117 Purchase, Francis M. Weld Gift, 1950. The Metropolitan Museum of Art, New York (50.23.2)

118 Photo Анастасия Смирнова/Adobe Stock

119a Photo Qassem al-Kaabi/AFP/Getty Images

119b Photo Rania/Adobe Stock

120 (1) Library of Congress Prints and Photographs Division Washington, D.C. (2019636463)

120 (2) Edward L. Whittemore Fund. Cleveland Museum of Art (1950.9)

120 (3) The Khalili Collections, London (ARC.ct 10)

120 (4) Gift of J. Pierpont Morgan, 1917. The Metropolitan Museum of Art, New York (17.190.991)

121 (5) Rogers Fund, 1948. The Metropolitan Museum of Art, New York (48.101.3)

121 (6) Photo godongphoto/Shutterstock

121 (7) From Pascal Coste, *Monuments Modernes de la Perse*, A. Morel, Paris, 1867

121 (8) Bibliothèque de France, Paris (btv1b8422965p)

121 (9) Gift of Terence McInerney, 2012. The Metropolitan Museum of Art, New York (2012.207.2a, b)

122a, l Rare Book Division, The New York Public Library (1268776)

122a, r Photo DEA/A. VERGANI/ Universal Images Group North America LLC/DeAgostini/Alamy

122b Library of Congress Prints and Photographs Division Washington, D.C. (2018681276)

123 From Robert Byron, *The Road to Oxiana*, Macmillan and Co., London, 1937

124 Gift of Charles K. and Irma B. Wilkinson, 1977. The Metropolitan Museum of Art, New York (1977.683.28)

125 Photo borisb17/Adobe Stock

126 Photo Melvyn Longhurst/Getty Images

127a Photo kpphotography/Adobe Stock

127b Photo Herotozero/Adobe Stock

128 Wellcome Collection, London (574866i)

130 Cynthia Hazen Polsky and Leon B. Polsky Fund, 2002. The Metropolitan Museum of Art, New York (2002.506)

131 Photo Azim Khan Ronnie/Alamy

132 Photo The British Library Archive (P761)/Bridgeman Images

133a Photo Lala Deen Dayal. Private Collection

133b Photo Valentina Pasquali/Alamy

134 Cynthia Hazen Polsky and Leon B. Polsky Fund, 2004. The Metropolitan Museum of Art, New York (2004.367)

135 Purchased with the John T. Morris Fund, 1955. Philadelphia Museum of Art (1955-11-2)

136 Acquired by Henry Walters. The Walters Art Museum, Baltimore (W.649.19B)

138 Tokyo National Museum. Photo Daderot

139 The British Library Archive, London (WD 698)

140a J. Paul Getty Museum, Los Angeles (84.XA.755.7.247)

140b Photo Frederic Reglain/Alamy

141a Photo Chetan Soni/Adobe Stock

141b Photo martinscphoto/Adobe Stock

142a Photo Kalyakan/Adobe Stock

142b Photo Heiko Junge/NTB/Alamy

143l Photo akg-images/Henri Bancaud

143r Photo Pornchai Kittiwongsakul/ AFP/Getty Images

144–45 Wellcome Collection, London (766666i)

146–47 © FuyukoMATSUI

150 Photo akg-images

152 Photo Frederick Wilfred/Hulton Archive/Getty Images

153 Harris Brisbane Dick Fund, 1932. The Metropolitan Museum of Art, New York (32.35(121))

154a Private Collection

154b Wellcome Collection, London (38390i)

155 Carl H. Pforzheimer Collection of Shelley and His Circle, The New York Public Library (57263687)

156a Wellcome Collection, London (25772i)

156b From Camden Pelham, *The Chronicles of Crime; or, The New Newgate Calendar*, T. Miles & Co., London, 1887

157a From *Illustrated London News*, 15 September 1849

157b Wellcome Collection, London

158a Wellcome Collection, London (13821i)

158b The British Library, London (10349.g.8)

159 The British Library Archive, London (P.P.1103)

160 Private Collection. Photo Look and Learn/Peter Jackson Collection/ Bridgeman Images

162 Musée du Louvre, Paris (RF 2625)

164 Musée Carnavalet, Paris (P620)

165a Photo Joe de Sousa

165b Wellcome Collection, London (44452i)

166 J. Paul Getty Museum, Los Angeles (90.XM.64.34)

167a Bibliotheque des Arts Decoratifs, Paris, France

167b Wellcome Collection, London (555088i)

168–69 (1) Musée Carnavalet, Paris (D.14133)

168–69 (2) Gift of Alden Scott Boyer. George Eastman Museum, Rochester, NY (1974.0193.0096)

168–69 (3) Bibliotheque nationale de France, Paris (cb412477759)

168–69 (4) Musée Carnavalet, Paris

168–69 (5) Bequest of Richard B. Sisson and through the generosity of Anthony and Celeste Meier. Harvard Art Museums/Fogg Museum, Cambridge, MA (2005.137)

168–69 (6) Musée Carnavalet, Paris (D.13606)

168–69 (7) Rijksmuseum, Amsterdam (RP-F-F111990)

168–69 (8) Bibliotheque nationale de France, Paris (btv1b84244482)

168–69 (9) Musée Carnavalet, Paris (PH80556)

170a Photo Amaury Laporte

170b Photo Philipp/Adobe Stock

171 Photo David McNew/Getty Images

172a Photo SuperStock/Flowerphotos/ Eye Ubiquitous

172b Gift of Edgar William and Bernice Chrysler Garbisch. National Gallery of Art, Washington D.C. (1958.5.1)

173a Library of Congress Prints and Photographs Division Washington, D.C. (ma1378)

173b Library of Congress Prints and Photographs Division Washington, D.C. (2003679939)

174a © Roger Luckhurst

174b Photo Eggy/Adobe Stock

175 Photo John Gay/English Heritage/Heritage Images/Getty Images

176 (1) Houghton Library, Harvard University, Cambridge, MA (MS Eng 769)

176 (2) The British Library, London (HMNTS 010349.l.1.)

176 (3) From Pierre Chabat, *Les Tombeaux modernes*, Librairies-imprimeries réunies, Paris, 1890

177 Photo SuperStock/Hammer/Warner Brothers/Album/Album Archivo

178 Collection of the Xuzhou Museum. Image courtesy of China Institute Gallery, New York. 'Dreams of the Kings: A Jade Suit for Eternity', 2017

180 Photo ANL/Shutterstock

181 Photo akg-images/Erich Lessing

182(1) Photo Xinhua/Shutterstock

182 (2) Photo Xinhua/Shutterstock

182 (3) Worcester R. Warner Collection. Cleveland Museum of Art (1917.974)

182 (4) Lucy Maud Buckingham Collection. The Art Institute of Chicago (1926.2029)

182 (5) Photo Imaginechina Limited/Alamy

182 (6) Edward and Louise B. Sonnenschein Collection. The Art Institute of Chicago (1950.526)

183 Photo MediaProduction/iStock

184 Photo SuperStock/Guenter Lenz/imageBROKER

185a The British Library, London (Add MS 5408)

185b Photo Ben Stansall/WPA Pool/Getty Images

186 Photo Eric de Maré/English Heritage/Getty Images

187 The British Library, London (Add MS 37049)

188 Photo Hulton Archive/Getty Images

189a Photo Bettmann/Getty Images

189b Photo Keystone/Getty Images

190 Library of Congress Prints and Photographs Division Washington, D.C. (2011645766)

191a Photo API/Gamma-Rapho/Getty Images

191b © the artist

192a Photo bbsferrari/Adobe Stock

192b Photo Martin Sterba, Josef Horazny/CTK/Alamy

193 Photo Marek/Adobe Stock

194 Courtesy the artist and Gagosian. © Sally Mann

195 Photo Westend61 GmbH/Alamy

196 Library of Congress Prints and Photographs Division Washington, D.C. (2001698869)

197 J. Paul Getty Museum, Los Angeles (84.XA.755.7.78)

198a Photo Kartouchken/Adobe Stock

198b Photo SL-Photography/Adobe Stock

199a Imperial War Museums, London (Art.IWM ART 3991 a)

199c Photo Ada Deane/Fortean/Topfoto

199b Private Collection

200a Photo Arterra/imageBROKER/Shutterstock

200b Photo KAL'VAN/Adobe Stock

201 Photo David Stanley

202a Photo Gérard Sioen/Gamma-Rapho/Getty Images

202b Photo Olena Buyskykh/Alamy

203 Photo Józek Gruszczyk/Dreamstime

204 Photo Jolanta Wojcicka/Dreamstime

205 Photo Andrew Holbrooke/Corbis/Getty Images

206a Photo J. Countess/Getty Images

206b Photo Per-Anders Pettersson/Getty Images

207a Photo Ajdin Kamber/Adobe Stock

207b Courtesy Patricio Guzmán, Icarus Films

208a, b Photo Paolo Pellegrin/Magnum Photos

209 Photo Reuters/Abed Sabah

210 Ateneum Art Museum, Helsinki (A II 968:16). Photo Finnish National Gallery/Jenni Nurminen

212 Photo Look and Learn/Bridgeman Images

213 Wien Museum (235426)

214 Photo Torbjrn/Adobe Stock

215a, b Photo Toshiharu Kitajima. Courtesy Maki and Associates, Tokyo

217 Courtesy the artist and Gagosian. © Sally Mann

218a Photo Gerardo Vieyra/NurPhoto/Getty Images

218b Photo Miguel Tovar/LatinContent/Getty Images

219 Chris Beetles Gallery, St. James's, London on behalf of the Estate of Eric Fraser

220 Photo Henry Groskinsky/The LIFE Picture Collection/Shutterstock

221a Photo Sheila Terry/Science Photo Library

221b Photo Peter Menzel/Science Photo Library

224–25 Photo Mgm/Kobal/Shutterstock

ROGER LUCKHURST is Professor of Nineteenth-Century Studies at Birkbeck College, University of London and has written for the *Financial Times*, *Guardian* and *London Review of Books*, as well as being a regular contributor for the BBC. His books include *Gothic: An Illustrated History* (2021), *Zombies: A Cultural History* (2015) and various editions of novels by Bram Stoker, Robert Louis Stevenson and H. P. Lovecraft.

Published in the United States and Canada in 2025 by
Princeton University Press
41 William Street
Princeton, New Jersey 08540
press.princeton.edu

First published in the United Kingdom in 2025 by
Thames & Hudson Ltd
6–24 Britannia Street,
London, WC1X 9JD

Published by arrangement with Thames & Hudson Ltd., London

Graveyards: A History of Living with the Dead
Copyright © 2025 by Thames & Hudson Ltd, London

Text copyright © 2025 by Roger Luckhurst

Designed by Tom Etherington

Library of Congress Control Number 2025933344

ISBN 978-0-691-27837-7

Printed in Malaysia by Papercraft

FRONT COVER: Richard Gough, 'A body found in the S. aisle of Lincoln minster...1781', from Gough's *Sepulchral Monuments in Great Britain*, J. Nichols, London, 1786.

BACK COVER: Michael Wolgemut, the Dance of Death, from Hartmann Schedel's Nuremberg Chronicle, Anton Koberger, Nuremberg, 1493.

10 9 8 7 6 5 4 3 2 1